Investing in Fixer-Uppers

A Complete Guide to Buying Low, Fixing Smart, Adding Value, and Selling (or Renting) High

Investing in Fixer-Uppers

A Complete Guide to Buying Low, Fixing Smart, Adding Value, and Selling (or Renting) High

Jay P. DeCima

McGraw-Hill

New York Chicago San Francisco Lisbon London
Madrid Mexico City Milan New Delhi San Juan
Seoul Singapore Sydney Toronto

The *McGraw·Hill* Companies

4 5 6 7 8 9 0 DOC/DOC 0 9 8 7 6 5 4 3

ISBN 0-07-141433-9

Editorial and production services provided by CWL Publishing Enterprises, Inc., Madison, WI, www.cwlpub.com.

This publication is designed to provide accurate and authoritative information in regard to the subject matter covered. It is sold with the understanding that neither the author nor the publisher is engaged in rendering legal, accounting, or other professional service. If legal advice or other expert assistance is required, the services of a competent professional person should be sought.

> —*From a Declaration of Principles jointly adopted by a Committee of the American Bar Association and a Committee of Publishers*

McGraw-Hill books are available at special quantity discounts to use as premiums and sales promotions, or for use in corporate training programs. For more information, please write to the Director of Special Sales, McGraw-Hill, 2 Penn Plaza, New York, NY 10128. Or contact your local bookstore.

 This book is printed on recycled, acid-free paper containing a minimum of 50% recycled de-inked fiber.

Contents

Introduction   **xiii**

Part One. Getting Started in Fixer-Uppers   **1**

  1. How to Make $1,000,000 Working Smarter   **3**
      White Picket Fences Provide Big Payback   4
      Fix-up Profits vs. Wages at the Sawmill   5
      Making Serious Money Requires Extra Helpers:
         Compounding and Leveraging   6
      Where Does All the Money Come From?   6
      It Doesn't Cost a Ton of Money to Begin   9
      Why Fixers Are the Perfect Place to Start   10
      The "Adding Value" Strategy and Why Properties
         Must Have Potential   10
      Less Competition Always Equals Better Bargains   12

  2. The Haywood Houses: A Textbook Fixer-Upper   **16**
      Classified Ads Can Sometimes Lead to the Gold Mine   16
      Find What You're Looking For and Act Quickly   17
      Fixing People Problems Is Worth Big Bucks   18
      Flexible Sellers Provide High-Profit Opportunities   20
      Good Financing Sets the Stage for Big Profits   21
      Looking for Loans in All the Wrong Places   22
      Fixer Skills Turn Ugly Duckling Into Beautiful Swan   23
      To Make Big Money You Need a Profit Plan   25
      The End of a Very Profitable Season   25
      Waiting for "Mr. Good Buyer"   25

Contents

3. The Profit Advantage Using Fix-up Skills   **27**
   Learn to See the Money-Making Potential in Ugly Houses   27
   Only Two Methods to Make Money in Real Estate   28
   Selecting the Right Strategy Is Key to Success   28
   Fixing Up Looks and Management Earns Profits   29
   Fixing Houses Is Equal Opportunity for All   30
   Save 70% Doing Your Own Fix-Up   31
   Fix-up Skills Earn Average Wages but Knowledge
      Builds Fortunes   32
   Sizzle Fix-Ups Provide High Investment Returns   32
   Biggest Payday Comes from Knowing Where to Kick   33
   Size Yourself Up—What Are You Capable of?   34

4. How to Get Started Investing in Fixer-Uppers   **36**
   Getting Started Ranks First   36
   Continuing Education—A Must   37
   Specialization Is the Quickest Way to Learn This Job   37
   Real Estate Investors Must Think Like Business Folks   37
   Jay's Formula for Making Money in Real Estate   39
   Investing My Way—Four Basic Ingredients   39
   It's Important to Position Yourself to Make Money   43
   If You're Short on Knowledge or Money, "Adding Value"
      Strategy Is a Perfect Opportunity   44
   Looking for Mr. Right, Not Mr. Perfect   45
   Selecting a Property That's Right   46
   Finding Sellers Who Truly Want to Sell   46
   Don't Be Stopped by Lack of Cash   47
   Don't Buy Until You Know How Much to Pay   48
   Spreading the Risk   48
   Diversification Later Is the Best Strategy   49
   The Best Odds for Your Success   50
   10 Must-Do's That Will Speed Up Your Success   51

5. Finding the Right Properties and a Motivated Seller   **53**
   The House Detective Approach   53
   Before You Invest, Do Your Homework—Obtain
      a Property Profile   54
   The Four Basic Methods of Finding and Buying Fixers   56
   Finding Sellers Who Truly Need to Sell   64
   Most Common Reasons That Motivate Sellers   66
   Key Factors for Making a Bargain Purchase   68

Contents

Beware of Over-Financed Property   69
Look for Owners with Equity   69
Avoid Deals Like HUD, FHA, and VA Foreclosures   70
It Pays to Be Snoopy   70
What to Do When You Find the Right Property   73
Equity and Profits Are Greater with Larger Properties   75
The Courage to Look Where Others Don't:
    Nontraditional Properties   75
Break Ranks with the Typical Buyer   75

**6. My Yellow Court Houses: The Right Property
    and Seller Make for a Profitable Deal   77**
Why Banks Want to Unload REOs   78
Timing Is Everything, from Wine-Making to Real Estate   78
Determining How Much to Pay   79
Making an Offer   79
Affording the Fix-Up   82
Success!   82
The Goal Is Finding Profitable Deals   84

**7. Good Realty Agents Don't Cost You Money—They
    Help You Make It   85**
How to Find an Agent Who's Right for You   86
Five Important Benefits an Agent Provides   88
No-No's to Avoid If You Expect Loyalty   90
Your Real Estate Agent Can Help You Build Wealth   91

8. The Price Is Determined by Income and Location   92
Complex Formulas Are Not Necessary   92
What Are Gross Rent Multipliers and Why
    Are They Important?   93
Selecting the Right Location   94
Five Common Locations and Their Investment Potential   97
How to Calculate What You Should Pay   100
Jay's Super Simple Profit Strategy: Up the Rents
    and Improve the GRM   102
There's a Time to Sell and a Time to Buy   103
Real Estate Prices Go Up and Down   104
Rely on Cash Flow, Not Speculation About the Future   104
Overpaying—The Deadliest Investor Sin   105
Investing Long Term for Future Growth   106

Contents

9. Thoroughly Analyze the Deal Before Making an Offer   **108**
Study the Numbers and Keep It Simple   108
Unit Cost and Rent-to-Value Ratios: How to Determine
    if a Property Will Be Profitable   109
Jay's Income Property Analysis Form   110
The Basis for Negotiating a Purchase   116
The Most Controversial Expenses   116
Always Get a Second Opinion   117

10. Negotiating Deals That Earn Big Profits   **118**
Real Profits Don't Come from Playing Games   118
Develop the Right Approach   118
Winning Over the Seller Leads to Winning Negotiations   120
Don't Play Games if You Want Real Benefits   121
The Three Most Important Buyer Objectives   121
Your Chief Negotiating Tool   122
It's Always Best to Let the Seller Participate   122
Verify the Actual Expenses   123
Favorite Concessions for Buyers to Ask For   124
Typical Negotiations Work Like This   125
Successful Negotiations Put Money in Your Pocket   127

11. Jay's Moneymaker Foo-Foo Fix-Up Strategy:
What to Fix and What to Leave Alone   **129**
Don't Fix Things That Don't Pay You Back   129
Most Buyers and Renters Lack Vision   130
What You See Counts for Everything   130
My Two-Part Fix-Up Strategy   131
What You See Is the Foo-Foo   132
The Foo-Foo Cover-Up Strategy Exposed   132
Sizzle Fix-Up Offers the Biggest Profits   133
Houses with All the Right Things Wrong   135
The Fix-Up Revolution—Made to Fit and Ready to Use   139
How to Estimate What the Job Will Cost   143
Knowing What to Fix   144
Recovering Fix-Up Costs   144
Keep Your Eye on the Ball   147

12. Where Do All the Profits Come From?   **148**
Playing the Appreciation Game   148
The Magic of Compounding   151
Four Ingredients That Produce Profits   153

Contents

Leverage Lets You Soar with the Eagles   155
Not Everything Can Be Measured in Dollars   155
Brain Compounding Can Increase Your Wealth   156
Don't Walk Away from Your Gold Mine   157
Adding New Profit Bulbs on My Money Trees   157
My First Profit Bulb and Best Source of Continuous Income   158
Fixer Jay's Favorite Profit Bulbs   158

13. **The Ingredients of a Super Deal:**
    The Hillcrest Cottages   **162**
    Creating Equity with Very Little Cash   162
    Hillcrest Cottages—A Million-Dollar Problem   163
    Knowing the Real Reason for Selling Is a Big Advantage   163
    Hillcrest Purchase: Zero Cash Down   165
    The Hillcrest Cottages Transaction   165
    Fixing up Hillcrest Cottages   166
    Selling the Fixed-up Hillcrest Cottages   167
    Removing the Risk from a "No-Down" Sale   167

Part Two. Creative Financing   169

14. **The Value of Seller Refinancing**   **171**
    Borrowing from the Bank Is Good for the Bank   171
    New Bank Loans Should Be an Investor's Last Choice   172
    Buyers of Ugly Properties Get the Best Terms   173
    Seller Financing Is the Cadillac of All Financing   174
    Financing That Fits the Needs of Both Parties   174
    Buying Back Your Own Debt Is Worth Big Bucks   175

15. **Investing with Others: Small Partnerships**   **176**
    Why Would Anyone Want a Partnership?   176
    Partnerships Must Be Based on Mutual Needs   177
    Looking for Partners: The Selection Process   178
    How to Find a Money Partner   179
    Jay's 60/40 Rule for Investing with a Money Partner   180
    A Simple A-B Partnership Plan   181
    Alternate Partnership Plan: Option to Purchase   185
    A Tenants-in-Common Partnership   186
    A Partnership Design Is Negotiable   187
    The Partnership Promise: A Co-Ownership Agreement   188
    Never Invest Without a Written Agreement   189
    Finding Money When You Don't Have Any   190

Contents

A Sample Co-Ownership Agreement   191

16. Sell Half the Property to Increase Your Income   195
The Best Computer in the World Doesn't Help Broke Investors   196
50% Sales Can Greatly Improve Cash Flow   196
The Task Is to Quickly Fix Up the Property and Add Value   198
Rents and Gross Multipliers Go up Together   198
How to Market a Fixed-Up, Fixer Property   198
Converting Negative Cash Flow into Positive   200

17. Jay's 90/10 Money Partner Plan for Cash-Poor Investors   202
How the 90/10 Plan Works   203
For Just 10% Cash, I Receive 50% Profit   203
High Returns and Buying Power Are Keys to Plan   204
Contributions Are Equal for Both Investors   205
The Main Street Apartments: An Ideal 90/10 Partnership   206
Give More of Yourself Than You Expect in Return   210

18. 100% Financing with Seller Subordination   212
Seller Subordination: A No-Money Technique That Works   213
Loan Terms Are More Important Than Interest Cost   213
The Attraction of the Southside Property   214
An Ideal Candidate for My 30-30 Seller Subordination Plan   214
Where Does All the Money End Up?   215
How Does a Seller Benefit?   216
Advantages to the Buyer   217
Lenders Want Clean, Sweet-Smelling Properties   217
Paying Back the Sellers' Note   219
No Limit to Creativity in Real Estate   220
Variable Rate Mortgages Offer Another Option   221
Investor's Success Requires Borrowed Money   222
Making Yourself a Better Borrower   222
Bankers Like Homeowners with Steady Jobs   222
Banker Enemy Number One: An Unemployed Loan Applicant   223
Jay's Five Basic Financial Documents for Borrowing   224

19. Free Fix-Up Money from Uncle HUD   227
More Than One Way to Profit   227
Uncle Sam Provides Money for Fixing Affordable Houses   228
Fix Up Your Rental Properties for Half the Normal Price   228
How to Get Started from Scratch   231
Dealing with the Local Housing Authority   232

Contents

No-Money-Down Deals Are Very Possible   233
Selecting the Right Property   234
Multi-Units Earn You More Profit for Each Dollar Spent   235
Watch Out for the Hidden Costs   235
HUD Assistance with My Viola Cottages   236
City Loans Work in Tandem with Grant Funds   237
The Flip Side: Other Requirements by the City   237
The City Is a Flexible Lender   238
The Easiest Loan in Town   238
The Application Process: Steps to Take with
    Properties You Own   239
It Pays to Learn What Makes City Housing Tick   240
You Help Yourself Most When You're Helping Others   241

20. Buying Back Mortgage Debt for Bonus Profits   **243**
Setting the Stage for Discount Profits   244
Look for Property with Private Mortgages   244
Most Sellers Would Rather Have Cash   246
When and How to Talk about Discounting the Mortgage   247
Jay's Red Mustang Strategy   247
Where Your Negotiating Skills Will Earn the Biggest Profit   249
Timing Is Critical: Buy Back the Mortgage *After*
    Purchasing the Property   250
Factors That Motivate Sellers to Give Discounts   251
The Top Reasons Why Mortgage Holders Sell for Discounts   252
Finding the Right Mortgages Is Well Worth the Search   253
Note-Buying Strategy Requires Detective Work   254
Jay's Christmas Letter Generates Profits Year-Round   255
Value, Like Beauty, Is in the Eye of the Note Holder   256
Investors Need a Healthy Financial Diet   256

21. Landlording Skills Can Make You Very Wealthy   **257**
We Do It for the Money   257
The Dream: Working for Yourself   258
Total Control over Money Decisions Is Key   258
Proprietorship—A Must   259
Success Means Wearing Many Hats   259
The First Rule of Business Is to Define Your Customer   260
Reasons Behind My Renting Strategy   261
Increasing My Odds for Success   261
The Value of Tenant Cycling   262

Contents

Keys to Good Management Are Action and Enforcement   263
You Must Always Get the Money First   263
Good Tenant Records Are Essential   264
Don't Take Shortcuts with Formalities   264
The Application Form—What You Need to Know   264
Rental Contracts Don't Need to Be Complicated   266
Large Deposits Provide Added Protection   268
Tenant Urgency—Not My Urgency   268
Landlords Must Know the Law   269
Owners Should Do Evictions   269
Repairs and Customer Service   271
Obey the Laws of Habitability   272

22. Tips for Dealing with Tenants   **274**
Your Tenants Are Your Customers   275
Fewer Rules Are Best—but Be Sure to Enforce Them   278
Limit Improvements to What the Rent Can Support   278
Cut Down on Repair Visits—Get the Details over the Phone   279
Collecting the Rents and Knowing Where to Draw
    the Line with Deadbeats   280
Noncontact Management Works Quite Well   282

23. The Big Picture and Long-Term Wealth   **284**
Don't Get Bogged Down with Routine Stuff   284
Join the Real World of Investing: Find a Mentor   286
The Dream Alone Is Not Enough   287
Looking for Gold Buried in Mud   288
High Rent-to-Value Ratio Indicates Profits   288
I didn't Grow Up to Be a Landlord   290
Avoid Doom and Gloom like the Plague   291
Roadblocks—Your Momentum Will Carry You Around Them   292
Positive Cash Flow Makes It All Worthwhile   293

Appendix A. Income Property Analysis Form   **295**

Appendix B. Typical Property Sketch   **297**

Appendix C. Sample Co-Ownership Agreement   **299**

Appendix D. Resources for Real Estate Investors   **303**

Index   **307**

About the Author   **320**

Introduction

Starting my house-fixing career in Northern California, back in the 1970s, seemed like a perfect opportunity at the time! I had no idea back then that one of the worst real estate recessions since the end of World War II was lurking around the corner. I had no way of knowing that interest rates would suddenly shoot up to 22% and completely close the doors on traditional real estate financing.

I couldn't have picked a worse time if I had planned it. When interest rates began to climb, nearly all the real estate activity in town came to a screeching halt! Hardly anyone was interested in buying or selling. And yet, looking back now, I realize it was probably a good thing for me that I couldn't predict the future; otherwise, I would have likely kept on punching a time clock at the telephone company—and figuring how long before I could draw Social Security.

I still remember my early struggles. Friends and business associates kept telling me the same thing: "Jay, there is absolutely no way you can buy rundown houses today to fix up and expect to make any profits for yourself. To begin with," they told me, "most banks are not willing to finance real estate today, especially the kind you're buying. Besides that, you won't be able to sell your properties because there's no appreciation anymore! Obviously that means no future profits! You've got to face reality, Jay—the days of making money in real estate are over. The bubble has finally burst!"

I remember reading a book by William Nickerson, *How to Make a Fortune Today Starting from Scratch* (Simon & Schuster, 1963). In his book, Nickerson says:

> Although opportunities are much greater during boom times, I have come to the conclusion that opportunities are always present in good times or bad! Anyone who really wants to can make a fortune in real estate. To succeed one requires only the initiative to start and the determination to keep applying the three R's of renovating, refinancing and reinvesting.

Nickerson's words gave me the courage to ignore my critics.

Quite often I've found that things you don't understand too well can end up helping you more than the things you do understand! For example, I didn't understand why it was the wrong time to buy fixer houses, so I kept on writing offers and buying those kinds of properties anyway! I didn't understand that borrowing fix-up money at 20% interest was way too expensive, so I borrowed the money and fixed the houses anyway. Nearly everyone told me I couldn't sell the houses because it was such a terrible market for sellers! However, in just 13 months, I sold my Haywood houses (details in Chapter 2) and made a $150,000 profit.

Over the years, I have learned that it's far better to be a little bit dumb about things and to act than to be super intelligent and never accomplish anything! It may sound like I'm a little dumb when I tell you this, but I promise you, it's true! Good opportunities never disappear; people simply fail to recognize them! Action is the magic ingredient that separates successful people from those who can't figure out what to do.

My seminar students are always asking me this question: "Do you honestly believe there will always be an opportunity to make big money fixing rundown houses?" Let me answer this way: according to the latest government survey conducted by the U.S. Department of Housing and Urban Development (HUD), the need for decent, affordable rental housing exceeds production by at least 250,000 units annually. Adding to this problem is that more rental houses are deteriorating below habitability standards than are being rehabilitated. Translated, this means that fixing rundown houses is truly a golden opportunity for do-it-yourself real estate investors like me. Indeed, the future is brighter than ever and there's no end in sight.

People often say to me, "Jay, you sure are a lucky devil! You jumped head first into real estate investing at exactly the right time! Your timing was perfect, but tell me truthfully, do you still think the same things you've done for yourself can be done by others in today's economy?" My answer is a loud and clear "Yes!" Furthermore—as you'll discover by the time you've finished reading this book—the economy and timing have hardly anything to do with fixing houses for profits. Profits will come from adding value and your own personal skills. That's the real beauty of fixing houses: the only limits are your willingness to learn how and, of course, getting started!

Beginning with the first chapter, I'll share with you an exciting strategy about making big money! I'll show you how to set yourself up for life financially. You must be willing to learn a few new techniques and develop some special skills. There's no question—I can teach you how but, obviously, you must jump in and get the job done.

You'll be pleasantly surprised, as I was, to learn that money is not what you need most to be a successful real estate investor! Unless, of course, you're counting the cash expense to buy this book. Forget that right now, because I promise you'll earn it back many times over. To begin with, pay very close attention as you read the first chapter, because it takes only one property like my Hillcrest property to get your book cost back a thousand times over! Real estate profits can multiply like rabbits by using leverage, but they seldom get much better than my Hillcrest property.

Chapter 1 is important because it shows you that small-time investors can earn big-time profits doing fairly simple fix-up jobs. However, all chapters are important, because each one will teach you new and exciting ways to make money. By the time you're done reading the book, you should have enough knowledge to start turning "ugly duckling" properties, like my Hillcrest property, into beautiful "swans." When you do, your beautiful swans will start producing those lovely golden eggs I call cash flow!

If you're the kind of reader who highlights important information with a fluorescent marker, I fully expect this book to look like Walt Disney's doodling pad when you're done! If it doesn't, you should back up and start again, because you're skipping over way too much good stuff.

There's one final point I wish to make before I lead you through a money-making education. Do not expect me to tell you if a 10% loan is good or bad ... or which bank will loan you money ... or even where you should invest in fixer-upper houses. It's my hope you'll be able to tell me the answers by the time you've finished reading.

What I will show you are techniques and strategies that work anywhere, anytime—with or without bank loans. What you'll learn from me has been working for at least 100 years and—I'll guarantee you—it's going to work at least 100 more. I'm a firm believer in the age-old wisdom that argues, "Give a man a fish and you feed him for a day. Teach him how to fish and you feed him for a lifetime." If you agree, let's get on with our fishing lessons!

PART 1

Getting Started in Fixer-Uppers

1

How to Make $1,000,000 Working Smarter

Most people are too busy earning a living to make any serious money. I'm talking about the kind of money that can make you wealthy enough that financial problems will no longer be your biggest concern. Unfortunately, most folks simply don't know what to do or how to begin. The reason for this lack of knowledge is that Making Money 101 is not taught in traditional places of learning. The fact is, most educators are still preaching the age-old proposition that hard work, long hours, and a steady job at the mill are your best guarantee for a happy life and financial success. The problem is that today few facts support this theory.

To begin with, working harder and longer hours has strict limitations. For example, suppose you have a job that pays $200 per day for a regular 40-hour workweek. No matter how hard you work or how many hours you work, you can't possibly earn more than two or three times your normal paycheck.

Even if your employer would allow you to work another full 40-hour shift at double-time pay, it's likely your earnings would only be about 2½ times your regular pay after tax deductions. I would agree it's much better pay, but still pitifully short of what I would call serious money. To earn that, you need 10 or 20 times more income. Obviously, there are not enough hours in the week to earn this kind of money the old-fashioned way.

It is well within the reach of ordinary working-class folks, assuming they have the desire to learn, to become very successful and financially independent fixing up rundown houses. Earning a million dollars, if that should be your goal, is not an unreasonable target. Many achieve the goal in 10 to 15 years. Naturally, it goes without saying, you'll earn every nickel you make, but there's no limit to what your earnings can be. If your goal is to double your present income, that's easy enough to do. If your sights are set on becoming a millionaire, I suggest you just keep on reading and find out exactly how it's done.

White Picket Fences Provide Big Payback

One of the questions I'm most frequently asked at my seminars is "How much money can I make fixing up rundown houses the way you suggest?" Obviously, there's no single answer, because everyone who invests in fixer-upper properties will do it differently, with some, like building contractors, even upgrading foundations, adding rooms, and revamping walls.

However, I've discovered that my biggest paydays come from repairing things that need fixing and cleaning up. Hauling away junk and painting nearly everything that shows is always a top money-maker—and rejuvenating dead or dying yards by planting new shrubs and lawns is quite inexpensive compared with the profits you'll earn. As a finishing touch, to bring out the charm, I always like to add my signature improvement—a three-foot-high white picket fence enclosing the front yard. A white picket fence gives any house the "homey look" and, from a pure economics standpoint, fences will return $10 for every dollar you spend to build them.

That's exactly what I did to my Hillcrest Cottage property, which you will be reading a lot more about as we go along. I sold Hillcrest and five small rental houses together in a single package installment sale. I earned as much money for just this one sale by itself, with only two years' worth of fix-up work, as most people will earn during their entire working careers.

I never dreamed this would be possible, but let me assure you, it is. In fact, I'm still collecting payments to prove it. Let me show you why fixing rundown houses will beat the pants off working your life away down at the local sawmill. The chart below will help you see the big money difference between working for wages and working for yourself, like I do.

Fix-Up Profits vs. Wages at the Sawmill

As Figure 1-1 shows, working 40 years at the sawmill in my town will earn you $1,200,000. You will spend approximately 80,000 hours on the job (2,000 hours per year for 40 years). By dividing the total wages by the hours, you can see that sawmill workers average $15 per hour for working a lifetime at the sawmill. Naturally, income taxes will reduce their take-home pay.

By way of comparison, my Hillcrest sale earnings were $1,200,022, paid to me over a period of 26 years and one month. Obviously, I didn't work anywhere near 80,000 hours to earn my money, since I owned the property for only two years before I sold it. I have calculated that my fix-up work took about two years from start to finish. However, not all of my regular workdays were spent at Hillcrest. I was also fixing up several other properties during the same period of time.

Worker's Age in Years	Term in Years	Average Wages per Year	Total Wages
21 to 25	5	$21,000	$105,000
26 to 30	5	$23,000	$115,000
31 to 35	5	$26,000	$130,000
36 to 40	5	$28,500	$142,500
41 to 45	5	$31,000	$155,000
46 to 50	5	$33,500	$167,500
51 to 55	5	$37,000	$185,000
55 to 60	5	$40,000	$200,000
Totals	40		$1,200,000

Figure 1-1. Typical wages for sawmill worker—40 Years

Assuming that I had worked two full years at 2,000 hours per year, you can see rather quickly that my hourly rate of pay would be a little over $300 per hour. That's 20 times more earnings than the mill worker. Plus, I spent only two years of my life to earn the same amount of money it will take a mill worker 40 years to earn.

For the sake of comparison, I've shown you what the average sawmill worker in my hometown can expect to earn working 40 hours a week for the next 40 years. That's assuming the mill stays open. I don't believe there's any question which career you'd choose if you knew about fixing houses the way I do it. If there were some way the mill worker could increase his hourly pay to $300, like I earned fixing my Hillcrest property, he'd take home $24,000,000 in wages by the time his 40-year career was over.

My point is this: we all get exactly the same number of hours in a workday, the same number of days in a week, and so forth. The big difference between folks who earn modest wages and those who make millions is how they spend their time.

Making Serious Money Requires Extra Helpers: Compounding and Leveraging

Obviously, there's no way you can earn $300 an hour working at the sawmill. In order to make big money, you must spend your working hours doing the kind of things where your earnings can be tax-sheltered and leveraged. With the assistance of leveraged real estate and compound earnings, you can far exceed the limitations of a regular paycheck. Leverage and compounding will be your silent but powerful helpers when you fix up rundown properties like my Hillcrest Cottages. Probably the best news I can pass along is that there's absolutely no dollar limit on how much you can earn doing this. The sky's the limit.

Where Does All the Money Come From?

Many book writers seem to be very vague on this point. Some will tell you, "If you'll just follow the formulas in my book, the profits will take care of themselves." To me, that's simply not clear enough. I insist on knowing where the money is coming from, so I'll know exactly where to concentrate my efforts. Let me take the mystery out of the money. Profits and paydays come from three primary sources in this business. Naturally there are variations and combinations, such as selling partial payments on seller carryback notes and payments received from partnership buy-ins. We'll discuss these later.

Three Major Sources of Money Coming In

1. Monthly Rental Income—net cash flow
2. Property Sales
   a. Cash money from escrow at closing
   b. Seller carryback financing: monthly installment payments (receivables)
3. Borrowing
   a. Seller subordination at the time of purchase
   b. Equity loans during period of ownership

We'll discuss each of these sources in much more detail. But first, let me tell you how important I feel it is to have all three sources available as options at all times.

A Profitable Selling Plan Requires Proper Timing

Buying and selling fixer houses is not seasonal work, nor is it a fad. It works well anytime and it can be an extremely profitable business when you do it right. Many investors get very good at fix-up, but fall dreadfully short when it comes to developing a good management plan and marketing strategy. Some still make money, but not nearly as much as they could with decent planning.

Giving away hard-earned profits is not good business, so you must make plans to avoid it. There's a time to sell and a time to hold on. Cash flow is what allows you to hold on until the right time to sell. That's why it's so critical. Proper timing is very important for making big money in real estate. It's something like a surfboarder waiting to catch the biggest wave.

In real estate, we call this "selling during an up cycle." Ideally, you should plan for selling properties when great multitudes of buyers are out shopping for them. When buyers outnumber available properties, it drives up the selling prices. That's called a seller's market. This is the time to sell for the highest price and with the most favorable terms for you.

When you have sufficient monthly cash flow coming in from rentals, you're in the best position to wait for exactly the right time (up cycles) to make your sales. That's worth big bucks, even though it means you must learn landlording while you wait. Landlording and property management will take time to learn, but the benefits will far exceed the troubles of learning—I will guarantee you that.

Monthly Rental Income Keeps You Green and Growing

Most important to real estate wealth building is the steady flow of green cash. That means money you can depend on coming in monthly to pay the bills. Novice investors who think only of profits from selling often overlook cash flow. Borrowing the words of the famous hamburger millionaire, Ray Kroc, founder of McDonald's Corporation, it's most important to stay "green and growing." Staying green means having enough income to pay all the bills. Net cash flow from rents is your best guarantee for staying green.

Lack of cash flow is the biggest problem I have with trying to mix investing with speculation. Speculators are all too often willing to tolerate short-term difficulties, like little or no cash flow, in the hopes that they'll soon strike it rich from a big sale. More often than not, the big sale never happens and the speculator goes bankrupt or out of business.

It's for this reason that I strongly recommend owning and operating keeper rental units. By doing so, you'll always have cash flow generators to pay the bills. I also strongly recommend that cash flow rental units be your very first investment. It's most important to make investments that produce cash flow as quickly as possible. Cash flow must always be your number-one goal if you intend to stay in business and earn big profits doing this stuff.

Lump-Sum Cash vs. Monthly Payments

Whoever said, "Cash is king," was absolutely right. I would never disagree with that. However, there are many ways to skin a cat—and there are many ways to become wealthy without waiting around for large cash payments. It's well known that cash sales made without proper consideration of taxes or a plan for reinvesting can often cause a loss of capital. The loss of capital for any investor, especially in the early stages, can result in a serious growth problem. You could even end up going backwards—or, worse yet, going broke.

I've sold properties for thousands of dollars above the going market prices, because I've given excellent terms to buyers. When you consider those extra dollars earning two or three times more interest for me than most banks earn from their loans, it's easy to see why carryback paper is very good for your financial health. Obviously, notes don't appreciate, so you'll need to keep real estate in order to keep growing. A good balanced diet of rental houses and carryback notes with occasional equity borrowing sprinkled in provides a well-nourished investment program with a guaranteed monthly cash flow.

It Doesn't Cost a Ton of Money to Begin

I intend to show you that fixing rundown houses and small apartment buildings can earn you lots of money with very little up-front cash invested—sometimes none at all—when you learn to buy properties the way I teach you.

All of my early purchases had to meet two important investment criteria:

1. They had to be properties that I could acquire with minimum cash down payments—no more than 10% of the purchase price and sometimes less, whenever I could convince the seller. This first rule is not nearly so difficult as you might imagine, once you get targeted on the right type of properties.
2. The properties had to generate positive cash flow within six months to a year after I acquired them. This doesn't mean positive cash flow on paper. It means that green "foldin' money" I can stuff in my pockets every month, after I pay all the property expenses.

My goal was to acquire properties that would start producing earnings quickly, so I could quit my regular 9-5 job to invest in real estate full-time. If you learn to invest my way, but still wish to continue working at your regular job, rather than changing careers, that is perfectly all right. I'm sure the extra money you earn will prove you made a wise decision.

Why Fixers Are the Perfect Place to Start

The simple explanation is that fixers are easy to purchase and they offer the best potential to earn quick profits without having to wait for appreciation to help you.

The reason that fixing rundown houses offers such a high potential for making big profits is because investors can purchase them for only a fraction of what they're worth fixed up. Fixer properties also offer do-it-yourself investors a unique opportunity to substitute their personal handyperson skills in lieu of a normal cash down payment. Often this means a 20%-40% cash savings right up front. By quickly adding value—primarily from fixing and cleaning—they can transform ugly, rundown properties into attractive houses that renters and buyers are willing to pay big dollars for. Transforming ugly ducklings into beautiful swans is not complicated or scientific, and it pays handsomely once you get the hang of it.

With fixer-uppers buyers can enjoy the biggest profits with the least amount of risk and have almost total control over their investments. The primary reason is that sellers are forced to make more concessions in order to sell rundown real estate.

The "Adding Value" Strategy and Why Properties Must Have Potential

There are many different investment strategies for making money in real estate, but almost all of them depend on future appreciation for the lion's share of profit making. Appreciation is worth big bucks when you're fortunate enough to own properties during inflationary times. However, when you own real estate during a stagnant economy, you need a technique that makes money without appreciation—if you intend to stay in business very long. Let me tell you about my strategy where profits are not totally dependent on appreciation or even a growing economy. I call it the "adding value" strategy. In order to use this strategy, the property must have the potential for improvement.

Rundown properties with fix-up potential and properties that are poorly managed are the best candidates for adding the most value quickly.

Rundown apartments or junky houses that rent for $600 per month in a $750 marketplace are perfect examples of an opportunity for adding value. To start with, I would probably be willing to pay about six times the gross rents for houses renting at 25% below market value.

Let's say we have eight units renting for $600 per month, for a total of $4,800 per month, or $57,600 annually. My purchase offer would be six times $57,600, or $345,600.

The value of a property that commands top market rents of $750 per month doesn't stay valued at six times gross (as when it's under-rented). Instead the value will increase to something like eight times the gross rents when the property is fixed up and looks good. As you will see, that can represent a big value difference. Eight units renting for $750 a month equals a total of $6,000 per month or $72,000 annually. Eight times $72,000 equals a new value of $576,000.

When you learn to acquire under-performing properties like this example, you can quickly make yourself $230,400 richer. Suppose it takes you a year or so to complete the work. It still beats working for $15 an hour at the sawmill, don't you agree?

Limited Handyperson Skills Are All You Need

Plus, starting out with an ugly or problem property provides you with an opportunity to learn what you can and cannot do. If you purchase a house or small apartment building that's already rundown, ask yourself this question: "How can I possibly make it worse?" Even with very limited skills, your efforts are still likely to make some worthwhile improvements. If you don't do things exactly right the first time, so what! Who cares! No one but you will probably even notice. Simply do it over again until you get it right.

Doing ordinary cleanup work, which almost everyone can do fairly well, is likely to result in a major upgrading. Most certainly it will improve the looks. When you tackle the more sophisticated improvements or repairs, take your time. Read a book or two and look at the how-to pictures. I promise, you'll be pleasantly surprised to find out how many things you can actually do if you make the effort.

Less Competition Always Equals Better Bargains

When you set your sights on acquiring rundown properties and poorly managed real estate, you are automatically putting yourself in the "profit mode" right from the start. That's because there's far less competition. Most buyers are turned off by properties that are ugly or rundown and have management problems. This means there are fewer buyers for these investments. Naturally, less competition allows you to control the purchase price and terms—especially when no one else is making offers when you are. There have been many occasions where my offer to purchase a rundown property was the only offer. Obviously, sellers are receptive to most any reasonable offer under these circumstances, if they're really serious about ridding themselves of their problem.

The following profit-making terms and conditions are generally always available to buyers of problem properties:

1. Low purchase price (20%-40% below fixed-up market value)
2. Minimum cash down payment required
3. Liberal seller financing for all or most of the mortgage debt
4. Opportunity to increase income quickly (under-performing properties)
5. Chance to reduce operating expenses and improve the bottom line immediately
6. Cash flow improved quickly by eliminating deadbeat tenants

Let me explain why these six terms and conditions are worth big bucks to investors who have the skill and know-how to fix the problems.

1. Low Purchase Price

Obviously when you can purchase a rundown property for 20%-40% under the potential market value, you are building in a sizable profit to start with. It also means your debt service (financing) will be much less than for comparable non-fixer properties and most likely can be held to 50% or less of the gross income. If you can acquire properties with 10%-15% down payments (high leverage) and keep the monthly payments less than 50% of the gross income, you'll be in the positive cash flow mode right from the outset.

2. Minimum Cash Down Payment

Sellers of fix-up real estate and properties with management problems are in no position to hold out for normal down payments, if they expect to sell their problems. I have seldom paid more than 15% down for any property. Also, many of my down payments have been for less cash because they were "lemonade down payments." Lemonade down payments are part sugar—which is the cash—and part lemon—which is something else of value, like my old ski boat or used camping trailer. Even junk furniture stored in the garage will work sometimes.

For example, my offer on a $100,000 fixer property might be 15% down—consisting of $5,000 cash and $10,000 worth of ski boat, motor, and equipment. Chances are, my boat setup would not sell for a nickel more than $5,000 through the classifieds, but to a motivated property seller, a value of $10,000 seems reasonable. Besides, how many "burned-out" property owners are boat appraisers? For the best results, execute this plan during hot, sunny months—near a lake, if possible.

3. Seller Financing All or Part

Seller financing is the Cadillac of all financing when you learn to negotiate good terms like the following list:

- Long-term payoff (15-30 years).
- Low interest rates, 6%-9% range, today's market.
- No "due on sale" clause in note or mortgage.
- No prepayment penalty in note or mortgage.
- No late fee in note, unless the seller insists on having one.
- No other restrictive terms or conditions, such as buyer agreeing to repave common roadway when holes or ruts appear. (This condition was actually one of the terms in a promissory note I assumed. It's not really enforceable, however.)

Seller financing is better than FHA loans, GI loans, or any other type of institutional financing when you structure it properly. Naturally, fix-up property sales are perfect for this, because most banks simply won't write loans for this type of real estate. Sellers must finance the sale themselves or they can't sell in many cases. Motivated sellers who own properties that won't qualify for bank financing have no choice other than carry back a mortgage or sell for cash (which is not too likely).

4. Opportunity to Increase Income Quickly by Adding Value

Investment properties that are not producing the amount of income they should are truly "gold mine opportunities" for investors who can spot the problems and fix them. The reason this technique is so lucrative is that the purchase price is based on current income production, which is low (under-performing). This price will generally be much less than its fixed-up value. The key here is to be able to clearly understand what is wrong and have the knowledge to fix it. It takes several properties (practice) to get good at this, but when you do, it's like taking candy from a baby.

When you have the ability to increase the income stream by whatever means you use, you will automatically increase the property value. This is the essence of my "adding value" strategy. It's routine business for me to upgrade small, multiple-unit properties by doing physical cleanup and fix-up work. At the same time, I'm gradually moving in new tenants who are willing to pay higher rents for a clean, fixed-up apartment.

5. Chance to Reduce Operating Expenses and Improve the Bottom Line Immediately

Start-out investors will often rush out and purchase leveraged properties at retail prices. Next, they hire professional property managers to run them. It doesn't take long before they learn a painful lesson about excessive expenses. To begin with, inexperienced investors and professional managers are almost the perfect recipe for bankruptcy. If there's a single most important experience that every new investor needs, it's the experience of operating his or her first investment property hands-on. This is the best way to learn firsthand how much things cost and where the biggest savings can be found. Most smaller income properties with a 50% or greater monthly debt service will not support hired services.

As a general rule, operating expenses for older fix-up properties—which include management, taxes, insurance, repairs, and maintenance—will cost anywhere between 45% and 60% of the total monthly income. It's not uncommon to find new investors making mortgage payments (debt service) in excess of 60% of the total monthly income. It shouldn't be very difficult to see there's a serious problem here. The first rule is: Don't do this. The second rule is: When you find properties with these kinds of financial problems, they may very well be excellent opportunities for ring-wise operators who know how to reduce the expenses. Also, you can often renegotiate high mortgage payments with private note-holders, once you are able to determine that they really don't want the property back. Many will take lower payments instead.

6. Improve Cash Flow Quickly by Eliminating Deadbeat Tenants

Unruly tenants will often frighten potential buyers away from high-profit deals. Investors who will spend the time necessary to learn local landlord-tenant laws can put themselves in a money-making mode. Education is worth big bucks here—it arms you with the special know-how to handle tenant problems that often scare away most of your competition.

Many years ago I acquired a seven-unit property filled with hostile-looking bikers. The purchase price was about half of what I felt the value could be. The owner was even afraid to show me the property—he was scared to death of his own tenants. I simply filed eviction papers and had the marshal serve all the tenants. Several weeks later, all the bikers were seen rolling down the interstate only minutes ahead of the marshal, who had gone back out to evict them. All I had to do was clean up the jumbo mess they left in order to earn a handsome profit of almost $60,000. The evictions were hardly more than a short-term inconvenience for me, which unlocked the doors to long-term profits and cash flow. It's a very worthwhile trade-off, believe me.

2

The Haywood Houses: A Textbook Fixer-Upper

My Haywood houses were a textbook example of the kind of property that can make poor investors a whole lot richer in a reasonably short time. As investors often say, "This property had all the right things wrong with it."

Classified Ads Can Sometimes Lead to the Gold Mine

I found Haywood in the classified ads one Saturday morning. The ad read as though it were written especially for me. The described property sounded almost perfect. I responded quicker than flies to a picnic.

By the way, let me pause to emphasize an important point here—speed pays off. When you hear about a deal that sounds really good, check it out quickly, especially if other people will know about it—like in the classifieds.

Here's how the Haywood ad was worded:

Income property for sale—2 duplexes plus 7 older cottages on

2 acres in city limits. Growth area—future commercial zoning. Property needs work—low down payment. Owner will finance for 10% interest. Price $189,000. Capital Real Estate Co. 413-4567.

The first thing I did was call the real estate office. The agent was off that day, so I called him at home. Somewhat reluctantly—after I promised that, if I liked what I saw, I would immediately call him back—he finally gave me the property address. He wanted to represent me if I decided to write an offer; he was the listing agent and had high hopes of representing me, too. That way he would get a 100% sales commission.

After looking at the property and deciding it was definitely what I was looking for, I called him back to set up an appointment. I was ready to make an offer. But first, allow me to flash-back to what I saw at Haywood.

The location was excellent. It was in the east area of town where all new growth was headed. Although nothing exciting was going on at the time, I could sense future commercial zoning. Naturally, I'm always happy to have commercial potential when I buy properties; however, I won't pay extra for "pie in the sky"—and neither should you. That's called *speculating*. What I'm doing is *investing*.

I was pleasantly surprised to discover that the "duplexes" in the ad were really four individual, two-bedroom houses. Detached houses have more appeal to tenants because they offer more privacy and individual living. Also, the older cottages were not actually cottages. Rather, they were older houses of various shapes and sizes. Some even had garages. On the issue of "property needs work," no one would have questioned that. The tall weeds and brush growing among and around the houses was so high it nearly hid them. Several junk cars were scattered about, fortunately hidden by the weeds.

Find What You're Looking For and Act Quickly

The one word that best described the Haywood houses would be "neglect." And, as you will soon learn, neglect is worth big bucks for us do-it-yourself fix-up investors. As you might guess, it's easy to procrastinate or fiddle around too long with an offer on ugly properties like this. Don't—because you'll lose them.

Besides the high weeds at Haywood, there were a host of other things that made the property ugly. Let me list them, so you'll know what to look for next time you visit a potential money-making opportunity.

1. Unsightly yards, dead grass, unkept trees, high weeds.
2. No painting done for many years, bare wood, peeling paint, or repulsive colors on buildings.
3. Broken-down fences, porches, sheds, carports.
4. Ugly roofs that distract from looks of houses or buildings.
5. Broken and bent, nonworking garage doors—or lack of doors.
6. Exposed "pier-type" foundations with accumulated junk shoved underneath the houses.
7. Falling-down fencing and ugly entrance porches that looked like tenant "add-ons."
8. Inoperative vehicles or, even worse, vehicles sitting on blocks with no wheels.
9. Piles of junk strewn about property, including stolen shopping carts.
10. External fixtures falling off houses—like gutters, fascia boards, gates, window trim, shutters, screen doors, porch lights, ugly amateur-built add-ons, and broken windows covered with cardboard.
11. Unsightly pens built with chicken or hog wire and scavenger materials.
12. Unsupervised dogs and stray cats running around everywhere.
13. "Spider-web" wires, overhead electrical and telephone lines running in all directions. Very unsightly.

Fixing People Problems Is Worth Big Bucks

Besides the physical things wrong with the Haywood property, there were also people problems. Fixing people problems pays big bucks—the same as fixing house problems. In many cases, owners become so fed up or intimidated by their tenants that they are willing to sell out for much less than the potential value. Here are the most common types of people problems I've encountered.

1. Scary-looking people with tattoos who hang around property drinking beer and working on junk cars.

2. The motorcycle crowd—where one or two legal tenants move in, then all their biker friends become permanent guests.
3. Loudmouth renters who constantly yell, fight, and scream, causing good tenants to move out.
4. Deadbeat tenants who pay only when you chase them down or catch them with cash. Most are always behind with rents.
5. Renters who attract a constant stream of visitors, especially nights and weekends. (Dopers do this.)
6. Uncontrollable tenants who routinely violate the owner's rules. Examples: allowing unauthorized live-ins to occupy premises, hauling junk cars onto property, and doing substandard alterations to living units (houses or apartments) without the owner's permission.

I'm sure I could think of several more; however, the six I've listed here should be enough to acquaint you with the basic people problems. They are the main sources of fuel for what I call "the fed-up factor." Many owners become sellers because they get fed up. They simply get sick and tired of nonconforming, deadbeat tenants robbing them of the earnings they anticipated. Their dreams are shattered.

The Haywood owner had a mild case of "people problems" when I arrived—and it helped me a great deal in negotiating an excellent price and terms. Sellers will make big concessions when they lose interest in their property. In this particular case, the seller had moved to another town and asked me if I would mind overseeing the property while we waited for escrow to close. He had no interest in even visiting his property again. Whatever his real estate sales rep and I decided to do was perfectly all right with him.

Smart investors in this situation can fix short-term people problems in exchange for receiving valuable long-term benefits. For example, I could remove and replace every tenant within six months—maybe less. That's a short-term problem easily corrected by a knowledgeable landlord.

In exchange for knowing how to solve tenant problems, I will expect to purchase the property for anywhere from 20% to 40% under the normal market price, with a small down payment (5% to 10%). I am also expecting long-term owner financing (10 to 20 years). These are excellent benefits for a buyer—plus, they are long-lasting. They're exactly the right ingredients for making a bundle of money with a fixer property.

Flexible Sellers Provide High-Profit Opportunities

The seller wanted $30,000 cash down, which I didn't have. I offered $195,000, with $15,000 down and two additional principal payments of $5,000 each, the first due one year after close of escrow and the second due two years after close. You'll notice that my offer is $6,000 more than the asking price in the newspaper ad. I was hoping that, if I paid a higher price, the seller would accept a lower down payment and give me good terms on the seller financing.

The owner counteroffered, asking $20,000 cash down. He wanted three $5,000 lump payments instead of two. He also agreed to carry back a note for $175,000, for 15 years, at 9.5% interest. One big concession I asked for and got was that my payments for the first three years would only be $1,200 per month. After three years, I would increase the payments to $1,500 per month, which was the amount the seller wanted initially. I explained that $1,200 was all I could afford based on present rents; later, after I upgraded the property and increased the rents, $1,500 per month payments would be acceptable to me. The seller agreed and we signed the deal.

Flexible Financing Made Haywood Work

My Haywood houses were a perfect example of seller flexibility. He originally wanted a $30,000 cash down payment, which I didn't have. I was lucky to scrape together $20,000 cash. To come up with even that amount, I had to borrow on my overloaded Visa card. You'll notice that the seller allowed me to make a smaller down payment if I agreed to make three future principal payments. I agreed to pay $5,000 payments at the end of the first, second, and third years following the close of escrow.

The seller originally wanted 10% interest on his carryback note—I offered 9.0% and we compromised at 9.5%. That seemed fair enough at the time. However, even at 9.5%, the interest payments alone on a $175,000 promissory note were more than I could afford starting out. Here again, the seller was very flexible. He allowed me to make reduced payments of only $1,200 per month for the first 36 months. I agreed to increase the payments to $1,500 or more per month starting at 37 months after close of escrow.

Obviously, during the first three years, the monthly payments were less than the 9.5% interest stated on the note. There were no accumulated payments or add-on interest to this deal: we simply agreed to reduce the monthly payments to $1,200 for the first 36 months. Until then, the seller would not start receiving his full 9.5% interest rate on the note. This concession alone saved me over $6,600 in interest. Now you can understand the reason why I agreed to the extra $5,000 principal payment.

If you will recall, my original offer specified only two $5,000 principal payments. As it worked out, the interest rate I paid during the first three years was slightly over 8.0% and not the 9.5% interest stated on the note. The lower mortgage payment ($1,200 per month) was extremely beneficial to me, because my rental income was quite low to begin with. I knew that after I cleaned up and fixed the property, it wouldn't take long to increase the rents to market level. I felt that the current rents were about half of what they would be after two years of my ownership.

Good Financing Sets the Stage for Big Profits

The good seller financing I was able to obtain was the key that would allow me to unlock big profits later on. I did not try to beat the seller down on his asking price. In fact, I paid him more than he was asking, but the terms he gave me were well worth the extra money.

The terms of the financing you get when you purchase a property will directly affect your profits when you sell. They will also determine whether or not you'll get cash flow from the rental income. A 15-year mortgage term is about my average seller carryback. In my view, anything less than 10 years should be avoided, unless there are special circumstances involved. Examples might be purchasing property for a very substantial discount—say 40% or perhaps zero-interest financing.

Several years ago, I started acquiring larger single-family houses with my extra rental income. My objective was to buy them for 10% cash down and get the sellers to carry back mortgages for their equity (owner financing). I prefer situations where I can assume loans, because I don't like to refinance the property. My plan with these larger houses is to break even on the rents and expenses starting on the day I acquire them. These types of properties appreciate much faster than my small houses and make excellent long-term investments. They can also be sold to users (homeowners) as well as to investors. Users buy with their hearts rather than their heads and will often pay 10% to 15% more.

It's much easier, with seller carryback mortgages, to customize the payments in order to balance out the income with the expenses. Owners are much more flexible than banks. My longer-range plan is to completely pay off one house every year. Naturally, I always allow myself an extra year or so for miscalculations.

Clobbered Financing Won't Work

A common mistake that far too many investors make is becoming overly concerned about how much they pay, rather than how much time they have to pay it. Here's what happens: It's very difficult to sell properties with "clobbered" financing (lousy terms). Buyers will shy away from lousy terms. Typically, buyers want to pay so much cash down and assume some "nice and easy" long-term financing. If you cannot offer that, it generally makes your property less desirable to the buyers. It also means your profits will be less than they could be. When the financing is short-term, it's likely the monthly payments will be so high that it's impossible to ever achieve cash flow. Also, most buyers are very leery of big balloon payments that are due three to five years after they purchase the property.

Looking for Loans in All the Wrong Places

Many deals I've witnessed will go like this. The investor buys an older property for $50,000. He's able to buy it for $1,000 cash down, because it's a real "dirtbag" property. However, the seller wants the $49,000 balance in five short years. Older properties are always tough candidates for acquiring conventional bank financing, even when the loans are variable-rate with extra high points and low loan-to-value (LTV) ratios. The seller in this case agrees to take $500 monthly payments, including principal and interest (mostly interest). Obviously, there will be a large balloon payment of over $40,000 at the end of five years.

The buyer figures he can clean up the property and fix whatever needs fixing. After that, he intends to sell or refinance the deal to make his profit. The problem with this strategy is that few buyers will purchase an older property with a $40,000 loan due in just five years. That means refinancing is necessary and that can be very expensive.

If you sell to a homeowner, he or she will need to qualify personally for the loan, as well as the property. This can be a real hassle and it often takes a long time. Worse yet, there can be many added expenses before everything is done. Obviously this means less profit for you.

If you sell to an investor, you can almost forget a refinance with non-owner occupancy lending rules. Naturally, it's tougher with older properties. Even if you find a lender, chances are the only type of loan you'll get is one where you are personally liable, in addition to securing the loan with the property. It will also be a short loan, which means 50% to 65% of the lender's conservative appraisal.

Many lenders will not allow sellers to carry back a note for any part of the financing. This means the buyer must have a larger down payment. Investors don't usually pay large down payments. Before you're through, this seemingly simple straightforward transaction can turn into a real horror story. Worse yet, with $500 monthly loan payments, there's a good chance you'll never be able to rent this property high enough to have cash flow, should you keep it. *My advice*: Don't do deals like this—they're much too risky for such a limited profit potential.

Fixer Skills Turn Ugly Duckling into Beautiful Swan

Let's get back to my Haywood houses. I want you to see how just one property can be enough to give your real estate career a tremendous financial boost. In terms of plain old profit making from start to finish, I earned a respectable $8,000 a month for my "hands-on" fix-up skills and management.

I want you to understand that the skills I'm talking about are skills easily learned by anyone. Mostly, my skills involve cleanup, hauling junk, and various other jobs that make a property look bright and shiny when I'm done. I call it "grunt work." Equally important is my technique of rearranging the tenants, a management technique that I call "tenant cycling."

When I buy a property in rundown, junky condition, I most always inherit tenants who are similar in condition to the property. You can't fix one without the other, because they go together like a pair of shoes. They are different parts of the same problem.

Getting a Tan and Building Your Bank Account

I spent the better part of one full summer doing outdoor work on my Haywood property. Sometimes, I would hire a handyman to help me. Several houses were in desperate need of major cleanup from top to bottom. They all needed painting. I started my inside fix-up on the first vacant house after a nonpaying renter decided it was better to move.

The most dramatic change was the cleaned-up appearance of the property as you drove in—a job that took about two months to complete. Mostly, this process consisted of lots of cleanup and cutting down the overgrown trees and bushes. First, we chopped down the high grass and weeds around the houses, then we started watering all day. We sprinkled on new lawn seed to speed up the process—and, after four months, all the yards were green as the city park. Like I tell my seminar students, it's extremely important to first make the kind of improvements that show. That means you should always haul away the junk, clean up the yards, evict the junky tenants, paint the building exteriors and fences, and anything else that shows, first, when you drive up.

People passing by the property will notice your work immediately, especially if the property has been a real "scumbag" for a long time. Often passersby have stopped to tell me how nice the property looks since I started working on it. Everyone appreciates seeing ugly, rundown houses fixed up and made attractive again. Occasionally a deadbeat tenant I've just evicted for nonpayment of rent will stop by and say to me, "This place really looks great. I don't guess I'd mind paying the rent now." Unfortunately, most deadbeat tenants seldom mean what they say.

To Make Big Money You Need a Profit Plan

Before I completed my Haywood purchase, I had already penciled out my profit plan several times. My "ballpark" estimate for fix-up was $20,000. That amount included all the painting, fencing for several front yards, and wood-panel siding on three houses to improve their looks. I also planned to replace four garage doors and install new carpets in six houses. I always install new window coverings, either drapes or mini-blinds, when I "rehab." There were several leaking water lines to fix and several new sewer clean-outs that had to be installed to open up sluggish lines. Naturally, as with most fix-up houses, the maintenance and repairs were long overdue. According to the tenants, no one, including the owner, had ever been seen fixing anything. The tenants who stayed with me (only three) were delighted with the change of ownership.

The End of a Very Profitable Season

Two wonderful things happened to me during that summer. First, I got one of the best suntans I've ever had. Second, I earned about $75 an hour while I got the tan. By Christmas time, I had eight new tenants and my rents had increased from $1,650 a month to $2,940. In case you need help with the math, that's $1,290 a month more than when I started. I considered that to be a very sweet return for my fix-up work. By the way, my actual fix-up costs eventually totaled about $18,000, which even included the interest charges on my Visa cards. I was very pleased with the way things turned out—and even more satisfied that I accomplished the task for less money than I had estimated.

Waiting for "Mr. Good Buyer"

Haywood survived the winter nicely and suddenly it was summer again. Income properties in my town were scarce, and it seemed like the timing was about right to make a decent sale. I ran the following classified ad to test the water:

> 11 houses 2 AC. Commercial—good tenants—annual income $38,400—low dn. Great terms—10% owner financing $350,000. Call Jay today—won't last long.

The ad was right—it didn't last long. The second offer turned out to be the buyer. The selling price was $345,000.

I sold Haywood with the following terms: $50,000 cash down payment with an "all-inclusive" note and trust deed (wraparound) for the balance of $295,000. Payments to me were $2500 or more per month, all due in 13 years. You may recall the payoff date on my $175,000 note when I purchased Haywood was 15 years from close of escrow. I timed my carryback note to match the balloon payment I would face in 13 years.

I hope you can see the financial benefits of buying the right kind of property—property that can be improved quickly, inexpensively, and with owner financing. Haywood was almost the perfect handyperson property. When it sold, I got back my $20,000 cash down payment, along with the $18,000 fix-up costs and a little extra cash to boot. Also, I was now the beneficiary on a wraparound promissory note that paid me $1,000 a month net income for the next 13 years.

Remember Haywood the next time you drive by a junky property with ugly houses and high weeds. Think about the hidden profits. Would you take on a summer's worth of work for $150,000 profit? I've had many jobs in my lifetime that paid me substantially less.

3

The Profit Advantage Using Fix-Up Skills

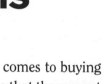

Many people have a serious mental block when it comes to buying ugly rundown houses. Somehow they just assume that the present looks of a house have something to do with its long-term value. Nothing could be further from the truth. I'll explain as we go along.

Learn to See the Money-Making Potential in Ugly Houses

I have watched many seemingly smart investor types, including real estate sales professionals, walk away from junker deals or advise clients to do so. Quite often that can be a bad financial decision, especially for the smaller, mom-and-pop investors who usually have very limited funds to begin with. Limited funds can earn much higher profits and earn profits a lot faster when they are wisely invested in ugly ducklings. Let's discuss basic money-making techniques in this business.

Only Two Methods to Make Money in Real Estate

There are basically two ways to make big profits in real estate. The first method is to locate and purchase a quality property at substantially less than its current market value—not necessarily the appraisal value, but rather its true value in terms of how much money it can earn for you. The second method is to use the fix-up, "adding value" method, which I've described in previous chapters. Earnings from the first method would be a monthly cash flow now or as soon as possible, in addition to longer-term profits from a sale or exchange in the future.

My personal view is that the highest priority should always be cash flow now. The reason is rather simple: investors must buy groceries on what they earn now; otherwise, they won't be around to reap any profits in the future.

Big Sharks Can Bite Harder Than Small Ones

The difficulties with this first method become painfully clear the minute you hit the marketplace in search of a bargain. What you'll notice first, right away, is that there are a lot of investors out there with you. The competition is fierce. Not only that, but you'll also discover there's a bunch of dummies out there, with a lot more money to buy real estate than you have. I don't need to remind you: cash always wins. Just in case that doesn't bother you too much, I think you should also understand there are many experienced "real estate sharks," who continually prowl the market in search of a bargain. They are smart investors who can move lightning-quick when they spot a good buy. Some are real estate agents who buy up listings before the general public gets out of bed.

Selecting the Right Strategy Is Key to Success

I think you can understand what you're up against, if you are just starting or don't have much money. The odds that you'll find decent quality properties at a profitable discount and be able to snap them up quicker than the real estate sharks seem low, to say the least. But, don't despair: there's still hope for poor investors who don't know much about the game yet. It's the second method I mentioned for making big money—the "adding value" method.

This method works just as well. It's my method of choice and certainly the one I recommend for do-it-yourself investors. Finding rundown ugly houses and fixing them up is the fastest way you can add value. It means that you will be able to buy cheap and sell for a profit in the shortest time. You can also increase rents and develop a positive monthly cash flow much more rapidly with these properties. With fixer properties, you can force values up by making improvements. Upgrading the property automatically increases its value. This way you don't need to wait nearly so long to earn your profits.

Fixing Up Looks and Management Earns Profits

The fix-up, "adding value" method of investing comes in two flavors. The first flavor is where the property needs physical fix-up work—things like painting, landscaping, fixing leaky roofs, and building white picket fences. In addition to physical work on the outside, you may need to upgrade inside, things like plumbing fixtures and new flooring. Obviously, these will add immediate value to any property. The second flavor is changing the operating procedures generally brought about by bad management.

Improving Management Means Higher Earnings in the Future

A good example of poor management is when out-of-town owners allow the tenants to manage themselves. Tenants who manage themselves will eventually manage the owner right out of business. Once an owner realizes he or she is losing serious money every month, it doesn't take long before a real estate bargain is available on the market.

Quite often, unwary owners learn the hard way that poor management not only robs them of everyday profits and cash flow, but it also costs them most of their long-term profits.

A good example of this would be buying a building like the one previously mentioned or one that's always half empty because not enough effort is made to rent the vacant units. The seller of such a building will probably not be able to obtain the highest price possible because his or her income is artificially low. Income properties or rental units generally sell for a price that's largely determined by the income they generate. Most often a factor called *gross rent multiplier* is used to establish a selling price.

For example, if a six-unit building—fully occupied most of the time—is earning $400 per month per unit (six times $400, or $2,400 a month and $28,800 annually) and if the gross rent multiplier for the local area is eight, all other things being equal, the building will likely sell for about $230,000. It's figured like this: $28,800 (annually rental revenue) multiplied by eight (gross rent multiplier) equals a $230,400 selling price ($230,000, rounded).

Obviously, $230,000 is a "ballpark" number. Many factors will come into play during sale negotiations—such as location, economic climate (is anyone buying?), financing, condition of building, and motivation of the seller. However, remember this point—skilled buyers will pay pretty much in line with the building's actual earning record, not its potential earnings in the future. Higher earnings in the future should be your reward for better management.

However, if the property is always partially empty, the value and selling price change. For example, let's say an average of two units were not rented all last year. In that case, two times $400, or $800, per month times 12 months equals $9,600 in lost income. The reason doesn't matter. What's important is that the actual income earned is only $19,200, rather than $28,800 when all units are full. Now, when we calculate the selling price, it will be eight times $19,200—$153,600. That's a big difference: $80,000.

Real estate agents will often do their best to conceal or downplay the actual income because it makes a tremendous difference in the asking price of properties.

Fixing Houses Is Equal Opportunity for All

There are those who incorrectly believe that fixing houses is a job that only experienced carpenters or contractors can do. Nothing could be further from the truth. Almost anyone can do this job. And, as a general rule, owners who fix up houses for themselves do not need licenses. However, if you do it for someone else—for example, as an employee or independent contractor—that's different. It's very likely you will need a license to be perfectly legal.

Fixing up houses, physically *doing the work*, is much easier than most people imagine. It's also much more profitable than most folks realize at first. It's not the least bit uncommon to earn back double the amount of money invested for a down payment and fix-up costs in a very short time. Quick, 100% returns are commonplace among experienced fixers. Obviously, you'll need to get the hang of it first. Fixing houses is the best "fast track" wealth strategy for common, everyday people. It's also the most inexpensive and safest way to invest in real estate today.

The Women's Advantage Shows Up

Fixing houses is definitely equal opportunity. The job is not gender-sensitive, with perhaps one small exception—I think women understand living space better than most men I'm acquainted with. Take as an example cupboards and closets, cabinet space, and electrical outlets in the bathroom. My male fixer team often ignores or overlooks the importance of these items. They are often called to our attention when a female renter calls to complain about having only one cabinet or not enough electrical outlets for all her bathroom goodies. Women seem to have a natural instinct for house remodeling and I suspect this comes from their homemaking abilities. I have caught my male fix-up crew building a bedroom closet just large enough for three wire hangers; female fixers seem to know better than that.

Most everyone can eventually stop a leak in the toilet. Likewise, everyone can do a halfway decent paint job if they really try. Knowing how to turn those chores into cash is a horse of a whole different color. In the final analysis, it matters very little who performs the physical fix-up work, as long as the right things get done.

Save 70% Doing Your Own Fix-Up

Fix-up work has two parts that cost money. First, and most expensive, is the labor. On average, labor will cost about 70¢ of every fix-up dollar you spend. Supplies and material will cost 30¢ of every dollar. Certainly these numbers can vary a little for jobs such as adding or overlaying exterior siding, where the siding materials (4- x 8-foot sheets) are expensive and the labor involved is relatively quick and simple. However, the 70/30 split is well within the ballpark for estimating average fix-up jobs.

Let's say that you are able to purchase a fixer property for 30% under the estimated "fixed-up" market value—for example, a house with a market value of $70,000 for $49,000—and you estimate it will cost $10,000 to fix it up to its full market value of $70,000. The 70/30 split means that it will cost you somewhere around $3,000 for material and supplies. If you do all the labor yourself, you can expect to have about $18,000 equity in the property when the job is done: that's the $70,000 value minus the $49,000 purchase price and the $3,000 for materials. Doing fix-up or "adding value," as it's called, means you won't need to play the inflation game to make profits in this business.

Fix-Up Skills Earn Average Wages but Knowledge Builds Fortunes

Owners doing their own fix-up work will enjoy a money-saving advantage only if they fix the right things at the right time. This is very important. As you will learn, *knowledge* is what makes the big money. Having fix-up skills can certainly be an advantage, because it's one less thing you'll need to learn about, but swinging a hammer or swishing paintbrushes will merely earn you average wages or save a few bucks in the short run.

To illustrate my point, just think about all the thousands of licensed building contractors who can do almost anything to a building—they have plenty of skills. Now think about what most of them don't have plenty of. If you answered, "Money," you're right. *Big paydays do not come from fix-up skills; they come from real estate skills and specialized "how-to" knowledge.* When I started out in this business, I had no idea how important this really was, although now it makes perfect sense to me.

Sizzle Fix-Ups Provide High Investment Returns

When I talk about fixing for dollars, I'm primarily referring to what I call "sizzle items"—things like white picket fences, fresh paint, window coverings, and ceiling fans. These items have lots of customer appeal. This appeal translates into big dollars at the box office (a.k.a. my rental office). The very same appeal makes selling your properties much more profitable because they look better. It's not uncommon to get three or four dollars back—in the form of higher rents from tenants—for each fix-up dollar you spend on these items, which puts you into the high-profit mode.

Biggest Payday Comes from Knowing Where to Kick

Allow me to share the story of an electrician who repaired sawmill motors. He specialized in heavy-duty electrical motors and his job was to keep the big, high-speed machines running smoothly. Large crews of mill workers and their families depended on the giant motors; when they didn't run, the crews were sent home. Obviously, their paychecks stopped at the same time the motors stopped.

One afternoon the repairman got an emergency call. The biggest motor at the mill had quit running.

"Come quick," they pleaded. "We had to send all the men home. We're losing thousands of dollars' worth of business. We need you right now."

The repairman arrived shortly thereafter, carrying only a small leather tool pouch. Very methodically, he opened the pouch and pulled out a weird-looking wrench; then he stood there a moment staring at the lifeless machine. When he finished looking, he began adjusting the bolts and turning a couple of screws. In less than 10 minutes, he was done and yelled to his helper to turn on the switch. The helper did, but nothing happened. Once again the repairman paused and stared at the giant motor. Suddenly, with a renewed sense of direction, he walked around to the other side of the motor and gave it a swift kick with his hard-toed work boot. With a loud pop and a couple of squeaks, the giant machine began to turn. Within seconds it was running at full speed again. Everyone smiled and the crew was called back to work.

Several days later, the repairman's bill arrived in the mail, and the mill owner, who had stood by and observed the complete repair job, stared at the bill in total disbelief. "$500 for only 10 minutes' work," he screamed. "That's outrageous. I demand an itemized statement of the charges. I demand some explanation. *Why so much?*"

Two days later, the amended bill arrived in the mail. It was itemized as requested:

Travel time	$30.00
Adjustment to motor	$20.00
Knowing where to kick	$450.00
Please remit promptly	$500.00
Thank you.	

Almost anyone can eventually fix a leaky toilet and most folks can do a halfway decent paint job, if they really try—but knowing how to turn these chores into big paydays is the real secret to fixing for profits. *Understanding where to kick is what pays the big bucks.*

Size Yourself Up—What Are You Capable of?

You can't build big bank accounts on what you think you can do, only on what you really can do. You can save yourself a lot of time and effort by sizing yourself up correctly to start with.

For example, when I began buying houses, I was not really a very skilled investor. I was actually a telephone man. I had over 23 years' experience doing telephone work. People still thought of me as a telephone man even when I owned 18 houses. It took three or four years after I quit my telephone job before people began to think of me as a real estate investor.

You're probably thinking, "What does all this have to do with investing?" The answer is "Plenty." You can benefit yourself a great deal by doing an honest self-evaluation. Figure out what you're really capable of doing right now, not what you imagine you can do. In other words, level with yourself. It's not wrong to know almost nothing about real estate investing when you're starting out. What is wrong is to fool yourself into thinking you do. This is a serious mistake that can hold you back, permanently. Also, it makes you an ideal target for any "snake oil salesman" with a "get rich" program to peddle.

It's most certainly true: you can make a ton of money investing in real estate. You can do it gradually, at home, part-time, on your kitchen table. You can build an unbelievable amount of wealth and security for yourself and your family. You can also be your own boss and insulate yourself from the ups and downs of a shaky economy that besets most ordinary people. I'm convinced you can do all of this, but you must be completely honest with yourself when you start.

4

How to Get Started Investing in Fixer-Uppers

Everything we do begins with "the first time." It's not necessary to be fully trained and have years of experience before getting started. On-the-job training has long been recognized as one of the most effective methods for gaining competence quickly. Getting started is always top priority. First, find out what you must do. Then, go out and do it. Keep learning how to do it better as you are *actually doing it*. Live combat training with real bullets will speed up your education by tenfold.

Getting Started Ranks First

Getting started also ranks higher than finding the best deal in town when you start out. Don't look forever trying to find a "blue ribbon" property. When you start, chances are you will stumble past the right deal on the way down to see it, without even realizing you were there. Most of us don't really know enough at the start to distinguish a good bargain from a "Grade B" dirty deal. (By the way, that's poultry jargon from my old chicken farming days.) The best approach in the beginning is to *special-*

ize in whatever type of property you decide works best for you. I recommend the older fix-up types, because profits can be earned much faster by adding value than with the nicer-looking units.

Continuing Education—A Must

In my own particular case, I specialize in fixer (rundown) houses and apartments. That's how I started and I'm still doing the same kind of deals today. I've gotten used to the money. I also invest in other types of properties now, but only if the projects are good enough to meet my financial objectives. Also, I've gained lots of experience from buying properties over the years. I've already paid my dues. I'm an educated buyer now, thanks to what I've learned from others, attending many educational seminars, reading several hundred books (many over several times), and spending literally thousands of hours practicing my first love—*fixing rundown houses.*

Specialization Is the Quickest Way to Learn This Job

Specialization is the best way I know to learn this job quickly and rise above your competition. When I started buying rundown houses, most of my competition was from agents and owners who looked at every property listed for sale. I looked only at fix-up properties and could, therefore, concentrate all my efforts on just *my specialty*.

After a few deals, I became very knowledgeable and soon learned how to beat my competitors on many of the best money-making properties. Later on, agents started calling me as soon as they listed good fix-up properties. Needless to say, you're in the driver's seat when you're the first one to know about a good deal. It took a while to build my credibility; however, by concentrating in just one area of the market, I soon became recognized as the local authority on *fixer houses*.

Real Estate Investors Must Think Like Business Folks

Can you guess the similarities among real estate investing, cattle ranching, and running a railroad? At first thought, you might not think there are any. However, let me assure you, there are. They are all specialized businesses that must be operated using good sound business principles if they are going to be successful. A negative similarity is that if they fail to earn a profit, they'll all go broke about the same way.

A fault common to many speculators is they tend to see themselves as "dashing real estate tycoons." Operating a business—using time-tested methods and a well-defined plan—sounds like a "real drag" to most tycoons, so they simply don't bother learning. "Let the accountants figure out my taxes and worry about employees and payroll," they say. When a tenant sues a tycoon over some management violation, which, of course, he or she didn't bother learning about, it's no big deal. That's what attorneys are for, right? As for setting up the books necessary for good operating records, tycoons never have enough time to worry about things like that. "Someone can do the records later when we need them," they claim. Speculators and tycoons often think like that. However, it's a very poor plan for real estate investors who would like to be around long-term and enjoy their wealth.

Building Real Estate Wealth Doesn't Happen by Accident

Every so often, speculators will make a killer deal. They need a dump truck to haul their money home. But I've noticed they never stay rich very long. When they do deals that don't work out, they're always back to zero again. When you study wealth building, you'll quickly discover—as I have—this is not the best way to achieve it. You need a plan that takes you from where you are right now to where you'd like to be later on. It must be simple and easy to follow, because complicated schemes seldom work.

The "no-money-down" craze of the early 1980s was based on simplicity, which is exactly why it was so popular. No-down seminars sold out everywhere. It was a simple idea all right, but it had a serious flaw: the debt was too expensive for the income. The plan was not achievable for most people. Even the instructors couldn't make it work well enough to stay out of the bankruptcy court.

Always Invest Where Demand Is Highest

It's very important to stay within your means financially and to acquire the type of properties you can handle yourself. If you do that, you can almost write off the risk factor. Inexpensive rental houses and small apartment buildings will always have long waiting lists of qualified tenants if you keep the properties looking attractive and in good repair.

According to the U.S. Department of Housing and Urban Development (HUD), thousands of lower-income rental units are disappearing in this country annually. Some are torn down for urban expansion, some are converted into condominiums, and some just fall down. The reasons don't matter much. The point is that they are becoming scarce as hens' teeth. The next thing you know, the federal government might start subsidizing landlords and landladies who own what's left. Certainly that would make as much sense as paying farmers to plow their tomatoes under so they don't flood the market and bring the prices down.

Because they are scarce and in such high demand, the risk of owning and operating inexpensive rental houses is almost nonexistent. That is exactly what new investors need, *no risk*. There are plenty of other things to worry about.

Jay's Formula for Making Money in Real Estate

My wealth formula is designed for do-it-yourself investors. If your goal is similar to mine—that is, to build long-term real estate wealth for yourself and your family—my strategies can help you. I never speculate unless I have extra money to gamble. Even then, I always insist on favorable odds to tilt the scales a bit my way. For the record, however, let me simply say I'm truly an investor at heart. Once I earn profits in this business, I get very possessive and have no intention whatsoever of giving them back. That's the way most investors think and it's also the key to staying in business for the long term. Let me tell you the four basic ingredients to my formula—then we'll analyze each one.

Investing My Way—Four Basic Ingredients

My formula for successful investing is simple. It's easy to do. Only four ingredients make it work. If you use them all, you'll find as I have that they're all you'll need.

1. **A workable plan**—You must have achievable goals and allow yourself reasonable time to achieve them.
2. **Action**—You must do the work necessary to execute the plan. Periodic adjustments are OK, but quitting is not an option.
3. **Investing**—You must invest continuously, in profit-making real estate. Speculation is never allowed in the early stages.
4. **Compounding**—You must keep your money continuously in the earning mode (that means fully invested). Your knowledge will compound automatically as you follow steps 2 and 3.

Now let's discuss each one individually to make sure you understand what I'm suggesting here.

1. A Workable Plan–Setting Achievable Goals

A workable plan does not mean you need a complicated computer study with stacks of printouts, to support some preconceived notion that all real estate is bound to make money no matter what—because that's not true. All real estate does not make money. The simple fact that many banks and savings and loan associations have thick files crammed full of "take-back" properties (REOs—real estate owned by banks after foreclosure) should offer sufficient proof of that.

A basic truism you can bet your boots on—nobody ever gives property back if it's making money for them. People who give properties back do so because they are losing money. Chances are they jumped into a deal quickly, without doing the proper research. Many new investors start out before having sufficient knowledge to operate the property after they own it. Still others buy properties without the foggiest idea of how to make a profit. In short, the lack of advance planning is the number-one reason investors go broke.

The Investment Plan Must Be Simple with Achievable Goals. My basic business plan has always been to acquire rental houses that will earn a reasonable operating income. To achieve my monthly income (cash flow), I buy houses that will return 18% to 24% annually. That's a realistic and workable plan.

For example, let's say I purchase four older, two-bedroom houses or small apartments on a large city lot for $110,000. To get that low purchase price in my town, I'll need to buy rundown, junker houses to fix up. Assume my fix-up costs are $10,000. That means my total cost, or basis, in the property will be $120,000. (Don't confuse this example with tax basis information. This is for the income analysis only.)

Once the four rental units are fixed up, the basis for each house will be $30,000 ($120,000 divided by four equals $30,000). After fix-up, my target rents will be a minimum of 18% annual return, which equals $450 per month ($30,000 times 18%—$5,400—divided by 12 months). If market rents are $500 per month, my return will be 20%; with $600 rents I'll earn 24% annually.

Once you learn this business well enough to consistently earn rent returns of 20% or higher, you'll begin to visualize more opportunities—perhaps diversify your portfolio. This strategy is a major advantage for investors who follow my advice. The idea is to go for cash flow first—then acquire the better houses after you've established a steady monthly income. Folks who do this in reverse are always fighting the cash flow battle—and many lose the ranch.

2. Action–the Magic That Makes It All Happen

It goes without saying, you'll never make any serious money in the real estate business unless you do something—you must make this happen. I've briefly described my plan of action, to give you an idea about how I earn my money. Without question, the most important ingredient in any success formula is *action*. Nothing moves forward without it; even the most brilliant idea will fail without action to make it happen.

Once I discovered I could make more money than other investors by fixing and renting rundown houses, I just kept doing it. I became a *specialist* at finding the right properties, fixing them up economically, and renting them out quickly. Folks often say, "Jay, fixing your type of houses seems like a lot of work. How do you fix them so fast?" Two things will automatically happen as you gain experience. First, you get to be very good when you specialize at doing something. You become more and more efficient, as you eliminate needless work. Second, with cash flow coming in, you're quickly in a position to hire help. You can furnish the knowledge, while your help does the work. This allows you to expand at a much faster pace.

3. Investing—and Knowing Exactly How You Will Profit

Obviously, in order to make money in real estate, you must invest. However, that's not all there is to it. You must invest only in those properties that will earn income and produce profits. Buying property is the easy part. Earning income and profits requires a good thorough analysis before you sign the deal.

So far, I've told you how I started out by investing in inexpensive rental houses. I did this not because I'm cheap, but because I discovered that inexpensive rental houses will earn a lot more money than higher-priced houses. What that means is more cash flow. Many people ask me about the long-term profits from inexpensive rental houses. Will they be as good as the profits from the more expensive, single-family houses? Probably not, from an appreciation standpoint. But appreciation was not my top priority when I started. Appreciation is a luxury for folks who have extra money in their wallets to buy groceries while they wait for it to happen.

Write Your Profit Plan—Then Get a Second Opinion. My highest priority when starting out was to have a little cash left over at the end of every month. Appreciation often takes too long, so I made it my second priority. That strategy has served me very well over many years of investing. It's tried and tested and—best of all—it works!

Determining how you will earn profits on a property you plan to acquire can be done best with an ordinary pencil and a yellow legal pad. That means manually, by hand. Writing numbers out longhand helps reveal flaws quickly, I've found.

4. Compounding—the Secret to Building a Fortune

Compounding is a silent but powerful wealth-building ingredient that works continuously around the clock to make you richer as you invest, almost without you noticing. A money-growing cycle begins when each one of your investment dollars starts earning money from itself. Those earnings, in turn, join forces with more invested dollars to keep repeating the wealth-building process. Rich folks can tell you that real wealth comes from *repeating the compounding cycle* over and over.

Compounding money at extra high rates of return is perhaps the greatest single advantage of investing in real estate. Small investors who learn how to make compounding work for themselves can quickly move up to "wealthy tycoon" status.

I have personally completed transactions that have exceeded 100% compounding. However, it's difficult to do this for very long. Still, experienced investors can keep their dollars earning consistently in the 25% to 50% range. If you were to invest $20,000 today and compound at 50% annually, after 10 years you'd be a millionaire. If you average just 30% annually, it will take you only about five years longer to get there. Compounding is very powerful medicine for your financial health and well-being.

It's Important to Position Yourself to Make Money

For hands-on investors like me, I've long held the notion that the best type of real estate to buy, when you are just starting out, is something between rundown and ugly and a complete junker. The degree of rundown or ugliness will depend mostly upon how brave you choose to be. Personally, I think the braver you are, the better off you'll be with your first several acquisitions.

Evaluate Your Personal Financial Status

As you might suspect, how you invest will depend on your present financial situation. Do you have a regular job right now? How long will it last? Are you planning to quit or retire? Do you have some cash available? Do you own a home with borrowing equity? Are you flat broke with nothing but determination and a pretty face? Each individual's situation will be different to start. However, do not despair if you don't have much money right now; many have done fine without any.

Guts, *determination*, and *desire* to succeed are the top priorities. They are necessary with or without money. Money simply adds some comfort. Remember that just as many flat-broke investors make it big as those who can easily borrow start-up money from their mothers-in-law.

The methods for selecting your first property will be the same whether you are currently employed and hoping to change careers down the road or presently unemployed and desperately in need of work that will produce some spendable income right now.

If You're Short on Knowledge or Money, "Adding Value" Strategy Is a Perfect Opportunity

I have used exactly the same advice I'm passing along to you. The day I started investing, I knew there were two important things I was short of—*knowledge* and *money*. Do-it-yourself investors just can't lack a whole lot more than these two things.

On the positive side, I had two good things going for me. First, I had a very strong desire to learn everything I could about real estate investing as quickly as I could do it. Second, I was 100% ready and willing to substitute my own personal efforts, whatever was needed, to make up for my lack of money. Those two things can level the playing field if you don't renege on them. Also, they work absolutely perfectly with my "adding value" strategy.

The following is an actual classified ad from my local newspaper that seems to fit my plan:

Will trade, sell, or whatever
Small duplex unoccupied on 3/4 acre. Partly remodeled. Ran out of money. Each unit 2 bedrooms and detached garage. City services. Good potential for fix-up. Assume $21,000–$167 per month. Will take vehicle, lot paid for, motor home, boat, etc. for equity. Call 227-3414. Leave message for owner.

When I read this ad, I can pretty much tell that the two things I don't have much of, *knowledge* and *money*, will not likely be too important in doing a deal. Conversely, my two strong suits would seem to fit this property quite nicely, namely a *strong desire to learn* and *100% willingness to contribute personal efforts*. My thinking went something like this.

Agreed, I'm not very knowledgeable about real estate transactions because I'm just getting started here. It looks as if I'll be dealing directly with an owner who probably doesn't know much more than I do; otherwise, why would he or she be stuck with such a mess? Also, I don't have much money, but it doesn't seem like I need very much to acquire this property. The owner says he or she is willing to take almost anything for his equity. Obviously, my personal efforts (saw, hammer, and labor) can be substituted for lack of fix-up cash.

Pending further investigation, this property sounds very exciting to me because it seems almost tailor-made for what I am able to contribute. If an ad sounds interesting, you should immediately make contact and start talking with the owner. This is how high-profit deals start out.

I realize we're merely discussing the ad at this early stage, but try to envision what you might quickly uncover here. Some things are written; others you must interpret by reading between the lines. Also important to note is the ad appears to be written by the owner, rather than a real estate broker office. Most generally, owners tend to state the truth because they're not professional ad writers.

Looking for Mr. Right, Not Mr. Perfect

The first property you buy should be the largest one (in terms of the number of rental units) that you can acquire based on your available resources. Resources can include cash, trades, or sweat equity (working on the property in exchange for the normal cash down payment). Trades can be boats, trailers, cars—even your personal residence, bare land, or whatever. If you're a good negotiator, perhaps a no-cash-down deal is possible. However, be very careful with large mortgage payments and short-term financing with large lump sums or balloon payments due in a year or so. Don't get yourself trapped by either one, especially when you're just starting out and you don't have extra cash reserves.

Zeroing in on the Target

The target purchase should be a rundown property with management problems and a very discouraged owner. The location and condition are not nearly so important as seller motivation and the potential for property improvements or upgrades. Improvement means the ability to increase the property value and in turn increase the rental income. Obviously, there are properties in some locations that are good only for tearing down and starting over. However, the vast majority of older rental units suffer only from poor management and neglect by owners who simply milk the property and do little or nothing about upkeep or improvements.

Selecting a Property That's Right

Your first property purchase and the next several after that will be extremely important to your investing career, although it's very likely you won't realize just how important at the time. There are right properties and wrong properties on the market. What I'm talking about is choosing those that earn *long-term profits* and *short-term cash flow*.

Making a good, solid first selection can easily spell the difference between establishing a strong permanent launching pad for your investment career and creating a deep financial hole in which you will quickly find yourself buried. Your dreams of wealth can quickly fizzle out and die if you purchase properties that cost you more than they'll ever be worth. Buying the right property is the first step—and it's extremely important because it's usually make-or-break for new investors. What I tell you next will provide valuable information on how to buy your first properties right and what to look for before you sign the deal.

Finding Sellers Who Truly Want to Sell

Before you start looking at the specific properties to purchase, it's time to pause and think. Ask yourself this question: "Who is most likely to sell their property at the best price and with the best terms?"

I can assure you, motivated sellers are out there. You must purchase properties from sellers who are really serious about wanting to sell—*not from sellers who* might *want to sell*. That little five-letter word, "might," makes a very big difference. The seller you must find should have a strong reason for selling. It can be one of many reasons. However, I've found the most common of these to be financial problems, management problems, divorce, and job transfers or moving. It's not uncommon to find all four of these problems existing at the same time.

Don't Be Stopped by Lack of Cash

Perhaps the most used—or overworked—excuse given for not investing in real estate today is "I'm waiting until I get enough money together to start." Money is not what you need most. What you need is *creative thinking*. There are numerous completely legitimate and respectable ways to acquire real estate without waiting for your financial ship to come in. And besides, who's to say if it ever will?

No Money Down Is Not the Goal

Now let me also explain why it's not always best to buy for no money down. Years ago, a highly popular book directed novice investors to buy real estate for little or no money down. This strategy will often work when employed by savvier, more sophisticated investors; however, in the hands of the uneducated, it's almost a sure path to disaster. The inherent problem is that financing 100% of anything will most likely cause the monthly mortgage payment to eat up all the income generated, sometimes even more. Investing is not much fun when you have to pay additional out-of-pocket money each month, just to keep the property operating.

Plus, quite often a little cash, inserted at just the proper moment, will hasten the desired results and will more than make up for the problem of finding the money somewhere. You normally get far better terms. Obviously, you must have some cash or you must find it somewhere.

Many no-down investors attempt to use what I call the "Christopher Columbus technique." When they begin their investment voyage, they have no idea where they're going or what they should buy. When they finally acquire a property, they seldom know much about it until after they close the deal. Finally, they seem to think the entire transaction should be financed, using someone else's money. Quite often they go broke before they ever realize where they've been or what they've done. Hopefully, by learning a few basics, you can avoid such a fate. A little early planning can make your maiden investment voyage smoother sailing and more profitable.

Don't Buy Until You Know How Much to Pay

The only way to avoid overpaying for your first property—or any property you plan to purchase—is to determine how much the property is worth and then make an offer. Use my *income property analysis form* (see Chapter 9) to help determine the operating income and monthly cash flow you can expect from the property. It will force you to dig out the information you need. It's an excellent checklist. And, of course, everyone should use some kind of checklist so as not to overlook expenses.

Perhaps the most important use for my form is as a negotiating tool. With all *income* and *expense* numbers on the table, it quickly becomes apparent if the property will make any money. This form tends to take away the emotional aspects of negotiating. For example, if the seller argues that the expense numbers I'm showing are too high, I say, "Fine. You show me what they really are, then prove it." When the form is properly filled out, it will show you and the seller exactly how much money is needed for operating expenses and how much is left over to pay the mortgage debt. When you can see all the income and all the expenses in one place, at the same time, it helps you avoid paying too much for a property.

Spreading the Risk

The other thing to keep in mind when considering properties to purchase is that the more units there are the better the financial leverage and percentages. For example, it's often just as easy to purchase 10 rundown houses with the same down payment as a four-unit, nicer-looking apartment building. The seller with the nicer-looking units can obviously be more selective and hold out longer for top price and terms, because a lot more buyers are interested in buying nicer-looking properties. Assuming all the important numbers (price and terms) fit, it's always better to pay the least down per unit as possible in order to obtain maximum returns on your up-front money (down payment). If you buy 10 rundown houses, a $20,000 cash down payment would equal $2,000 per unit for the 10 apartments. The same down payment would equal $5,000 each for just four nicer-looking units. Again, always try for the least down and the most units.

Buying Properties Is a Numbers Game

The same logic applies for vacancies: the more units, the better. One vacancy in a 10-unit group is only a 10% vacancy, while one vacancy in the four-unit property means 25% of the total units are available for rent. Obviously, this percentage is not conclusive by itself, because other important details have not been considered. I'm merely trying to show you that bigger numbers mean spreading the risk. With more units, it's cheaper to operate per unit as well as cheaper to purchase. You'll be getting a lot more bang for your investment buck. If this doesn't seem clear now, I promise you, it will later on. If I can help you buy the first property correctly, so that you can actually experience success, I will have achieved my purpose. After that, you'll do just fine by yourself, the same as me.

Diversification Later Is the Best Strategy

Once you've become established financially and, even more importantly, become more knowledgeable about real estate investing, you may then enjoy the luxury of diversification. You might even venture out and buy several "pride of ownership" properties. After all, money's not everything. Besides, you might want to own a good-looking property to drive by with friends or your mother-in-law so you can show off a bit. It's important to remember that most of the world judges by looks. Most of my advice is about making money. Once you have all the money you need, who cares what you do? You might even consider buying property that just breaks even.

The Greatest Seven-Inch Fisherman

TV minister Robert Schuller tells the story of a young boy watching an old man who is fishing off the river bridge and doing quite well. The young boy couldn't help noticing something very strange about the old fisherman. It seems that ever time he would catch a really nice trout, 10 or 12 inches long, he would very methodically take it off the hook and toss it back into the river. Each time he would catch a small fish, he would take it from the hook and carefully place it inside his fishing basket, making sure to close the lid each time.

After several hours of watching the old man fish, the boy's curiosity got the best of him. He walked out on the bridge and told the old fisherman what he'd observed. "Why," he asked, "do you keep all the small fish and throw the big ones back into the river?" The old man looked at the boy, slightly amused and smiling, then answered, "Because I only have a seven-inch frying pan. The bigger fish won't fit in my pan." The old fisherman had already determined ahead of time what worked best for him. Now he was merely working his proven plan.

Most beginning investors would be much better off using a single-size pan to begin with—in other words, specialize. Nothing fits seven-inch pans better than seven-inch trout. Once you become famous for your seven-inch trout dinners and understand exactly how to make money serving them, only then would I recommend getting another frying pan. It's far more rewarding and profitable to be good at doing one thing very well than to be just mediocre trying to be good at everything. Besides, it's a lot easier to learn just one thing at a time. Your life will be much less complicated, believe me.

If, by now, you get the feeling I want you to specialize in the early stages of your investment career, then give yourself an "A" for perception. You may also move up to the front of my investor training class. Who knows? With any luck at all, you might even become the teacher's pet someday.

The Best Odds for Your Success

William Nickerson, author and rehab millionaire, began fixing rental houses over 50 years ago. Bill quite accurately concludes in his best-selling book, *How I Turned $1,000 into Five Million in Real Estate in My Spare Time* (revised, New York: Simon and Schuster, 1980), "The chances for success are 1,600 times better owning and operating rental properties than for starting another type of business." If you need more convincing, I suggest you write to Bank of America Business Services Dept. or Dun & Bradstreet Credit Rating Service, Inc. The information they provide about starting other businesses and the odds of success are quite gloomy by comparison.

10 Must-Do's That Will Speed Up Your Success

1. Develop a total investment plan from start to finish. I recommend specializing to begin. Say you plan to buy four rental fix-up properties each year for five years. Each one must produce a cash flow of $100 per month. That's a reasonable plan.

2. Learn your local market. Know what properties should cost and what they can reasonably sell for. Learn how much rent you can get. Do this step before you buy, not afterward.

3. Develop a business sense. Think like a retailer. That will help you to pay wholesale prices when you buy. Buying at retail prices and selling for retail prices simply won't work.

4. Learn to identify hidden bargains quickly, then act fast to acquire them. Remember: competition is keen. You must develop a sixth sense for sniffing out hidden money makers. Become a house detective.

5. Learn landlording, firsthand, from doing it. Manage your own customers (tenants). Many inexperienced investors farm this function out to professional property managers. I consider this a serious mistake for new investors. Maybe it's OK later on, but owners should first know the job inside and out.

6. Invest, don't speculate. Investing is a plan to make money. You must be able to identify exactly how you will do it. That's why step 1 is necessary. Spectators are guessing without a plan.

7. Establish local trade accounts. Most building supply stores will give you 10% discounts. It's not automatic; you must ask for the discounts. Besides saving money, you build a solid credit history. Another benefit is you don't need to always have a pocket full of money. Paying monthly statements is better for bookkeeping.

8. Learn to live on tax-free or tax-sheltered income. Rents you collect are normally tax-sheltered. Rehab loans, like Title One loans, are tax-free, the same as borrowing on equity or refinancing. When you collect $100 rent, you get to keep $100. When you earn $100 in wages, you keep only $60. Taxes eat up the rest.

9. Learn how to do deals where you have as close to 100% control as

possible. Basically, this means owner financing and doing the management yourself. Avoid short payback notes and variable-rate mortgages offered by institutional lenders.

10. Once you've developed a plan that works well and consistently makes money for you, stick with it until it stops working. Most investors suffer from a common weakness—they are suckers for a better mousetrap. Avoid the "too good to be true" temptation—it generally is.

Throughout this chapter, I've told you about many things that will help get you started purchasing and fixing up property. Getting started, specializing in fixer-uppers, developing and acting on a financial plan—these things are necessary for becoming a successful fix-up specialist. That's what I recommend for you, at least in the initial years of your investing. Later on, you'll have many more options—but never forget that monthly net income is what you want first. With it, you'll continue to grow and become successful. Without it, you won't. It's as simple as that.

5

Finding the Right Properties and a Motivated Seller

The House Detective Approach

Part of being a house detective means finding out about the availability of a property before anyone else. More specifically, your offer to purchase the property should be the only offer. The most important thing to remember here is that the more potential buyers who know about the deal, the less chance you can snag a bargain. If you can secretly find out about property that's for sale and get there with the only offer, it puts you in the driver's seat. Without any competition, your offer will be the only game in town. You must learn how to be a house detective and find good deals before the competition arrives. That's one of the secrets to buying property substantially below market.

You'll soon discover, as I have, it's nearly impossible to buy properties cheap enough or get really good terms when there are lots of eager bidders for the same property. Acquiring cash flow properties should be as private as you can make it. You can tell the whole world about the deal—after you own it.

The Secret Path to the Gold Mine

As a house detective, you must possess the ability to spot hidden profit potential. That means you must have special knowledge and the skills to increase the property's income, or value, that other competing buyers don't have. These special sleuthing skills can be developed only through experience. Obviously, new investors will need to own and operate several properties in order to get that kind of experience. Generally, novice investors without much real estate experience will not be able to recognize a property's gold mine potential, even if they get close enough to fall down the shaft. *Education* and *experience* will take some time. Completing several actual deals will provide the necessary experience. I do not know of any shortcuts to develop these skills.

Before You Invest, Do Your Homework—Obtain a Property Profile

Before you invest one penny, do your homework and check things out. The first thing I do is visit the title company where I do most of my business. I request a parcel map, the tax bill, and copies of all the deeds or mortgages recorded on the property. Many title companies provide this service free for repeat customers and real estate agents. Some folks refer to this information as a property profile. Obtaining the property profile documents is a good way to start a file on property you are interested in, because they will provide you with the following information:

- The parcel map gives you the lot size and often shows easements and right-of-ways, as well as location.
- The tax bill shows who owns the property and where the current tax bill is being mailed each year. It also shows how much the taxes are now and how high the county assessor has appraised the value of land, improvements (buildings), and personal property (dollar amounts).
- With a parcel map and the tax index (owner names), you can find out who owns the properties around the parcel you're investigating.
- Copies of mortgages or trust deeds show the amount of debt against the property at the time of the last sale or transfer of title. They also

show who owes the debt (trustor) and who receives payment (beneficiary). Any due-on-sale clauses will normally show up on trust deeds or mortgages. Deeds and mortgages will show the chain of title, with recording dates and notarized signatures.

- The grant deed shows the documentary transfer tax—a state tax on the sale of real property, generally stamped on the grant deed. The tax is computed on the full selling price or selling price less the liens remaining at the time of sale. So, if you know the tax rate in your state, you can easily determine what the current owner paid for the property, based on the tax amount. For example, if the property is in California, where the rate is currently $1.10 per $1,000, and the documentary tax is $46.75, computed on the full value, then the purchase price would be $42,500 ($46.75 divided by $1.10 times $1,000 equals $42,500). Sometimes, knowing what the owner paid can help you develop your own offer to purchase. Remember that sellers dislike offers for less than what they paid, no matter how motivated they are to sell. Always keep this in mind when negotiating.

Information Hunting Is Valuable and Free

All this information can be found at your local county courthouse or a title company and it's easy, if you happen to know someone who will help you. Assuming you don't know who owns the property, first take a look at the key location map. It will direct you to the proper assessor plat map where you'll find the parcel, or lot, you're looking for. Once you locate the parcel number, you can go to the name index file and find the owner. Both the courthouse and the title company will assist you with this chore.

My research consists, primarily, of finding out who owns the property and where they live. It's generally the address where the tax bills are mailed. I want to know how many mortgages or trust deeds are secured by the property and what their original amounts were. Also, the tax bill will show me the "value for tax purposes." I like to know if my estimate of value is somewhere in line with the county appraiser's view. I always like to get an idea of how much mortgage debt is still owed because I'm looking for properties with a lot of equity. Also, I'm looking for the opportunity to create a long-term seller carryback mortgage, should I be successful purchasing the property. Obviously, this sets the stage for buying back the mortgage at a sizable discount sometime in the future.

The Four Basic Methods of Finding and Buying Fixers

I like to keep things simple. Others may tend to embellish these four fundamental methods I'll discuss here, but my experience has proven that these are solid methods that continually work. Naturally, you must make them work for you. Nothing will help if you simply sit back and watch TV while you wait for others to make you rich. First, I'll tell you what these four methods are. Then, we'll dissect each one to show what makes it work.

1. Watch the daily classified ads.
2. Use a real estate agent.
3. Work the multiple-listing book.
4. Initiate written cold calls.

Before we get into these four methods, let me simply make this statement. Once you become proficient at doing this stuff, you'll begin to understand that there is no shortage of fix-up real estate anywhere. The problem is that the right fix-up properties are seldom located where the public can find them and most real estate agents don't know "good deal" fixer properties from overpriced junk. True bargains rarely reach the multiple-listing books because they get sold by listing agents to a handful of "pet buyers" who can cut a deal before the agent is required to submit his or her listing to the multiple service. They're called pocket listings and listing agents see no point in splitting commissions when they have a "slam dunk" deal.

1. Watch the Daily Classified Ads

This is the method I have found least profitable for finding and buying fixers. Yet, I consider it worthwhile, because it doesn't take a lot of time and it keeps you tuned into what's for sale in your buying area. I read the classifieds everyday and have done so for years. I always read "Income Properties for Sale," "Investment Properties," and "Commercial Real Estate." I also keep an eye on "Houses for Sale" because occasionally, mom-

and-pop owners will list their six little duplexes under that classification. Agents almost always list properties under the correct classified heading.

The location where you find the ad might tell you if you're dealing with a sophisticated seller or a do-it-yourself property owner who has decided to retire. Naturally, mom-and-pop deals can be very productive because, quite often, they will sell for less if they like you. Also, many are trying to sell on their own (for sale by owner) to avoid paying commissions. Perhaps more importantly, older, retired sellers are much more likely to carry back a mortgage. It will pay you to watch classified ads regularly to catch an owner-seller bargain.

Another benefit of calling the interesting classified ads is that it helps you become more knowledgeable about prices, gross multipliers, and what terms and conditions are important to sellers. Many times it turns out the property I call about is not what I'm looking for; however, during the conversation, the seller mentions other property that's not advertised in the paper or that he knows someone who wants to sell another property. Telephone calling generates leads. One good lead can make you big bucks.

I purchased my Haywood property (Chapter 2) through a classified ad. The property comprised 11 junky houses on a two-acre lot. With this one fix-up project alone, I earned $150,000 for just 13 months of part-time fixing. Classified ads have accounted for about 10% of all my deals—that's $400,000 worth.

When you read your local newspaper classifieds, you'll see all of the various reasons for selling over and over again—owner moving, poor health forces sale, ground-floor opportunity, owner retiring, divorce spells my loss but your gain. These are typical classified statements in the real estate "For Sale" sections of any regular newspaper. Obviously, the ads are written to persuade potential buyers that the owners are motivated to sell. Some ads are true; most are not. It's nearly impossible to tell about true motivation from an ad. Still, it's a starting point.

2. Use a Real Estate Agent

This method for finding properties and making deals has been, by far, the most productive for me. I acquired at least 60% of my properties with the help of a real estate agent. However, not just any agent will do. I've had only two since 1977—Merv and Fred. Merv passed away in 1985 and Fred is still working with me today.

You must work hard to find the right real estate agent. Agents won't hang around for long if you're just a "looky-loo"—a person who wants to see everything, but never seems to find anything that meets his or her approval. No agent can afford that nonsense. Fred works for me for one simple reason—it's profitable for him. He knows I can close deals fast if he does his job. Fred's job is to know exactly what I will buy. He doesn't call me about every property for sale in Redding. A good agent will immediately qualify the property to determine if it has potential. Fred knows I don't normally want deals that require new bank financing. He also knows I want sellers who will carry paper and that I rate small, multiple-unit properties—like four to six houses on a single lot or a bunch of ugly, rundown duplexes—at the top of my buying list. When he hears about these kinds of properties, he acts quickly.

Fred's job is to qualify the property. Is the seller in any sort of financial trouble? Does he or she live out of town? Is the property managed for him or her? Are the tenants causing the owner problems? Fred tries to determine if there are reasons for the seller to be motivated, such as retirement, going broke, dying, etc. It's detective work like Columbo does on TV. He obtains a property profile. He asks for copies of notes (mortgages) on the property. He verifies rents, vacancies, and liens. All this takes time and it costs Fred money. The only way he gets paid for his work is if I buy the property.

Fred doesn't make a lot of dry runs. He knows what I want and determines quickly if a property has the right stuff. How did Fred get so smart? How did he ever learn this detective business? Well, when Fred and I started, we spent a lot of time discussing what I wanted. Investors must be very clear about which properties they will buy when one comes along. Otherwise, agents will attempt to show them everything.

To start with, I would recommend that you simply walk into five or six realty offices, sit down with an agent who is on the floor, and discuss the kind of properties you would like to acquire. Some agents will jump through hoops to help you. Others will shine you on. Personalities will naturally play a role. You like some people; others, you don't.

Using this method, it shouldn't take too long to find one agent who seems more interested than others. He or she will call you more and bring you property profiles to look at. When this special interest develops, you might have found the right agent. If not, keep repeating the process until you do.

3. Work the Multiple-Listing Book

Only licensed real estate agents can have multiple-listing books. That's the reason I've always kept my copy out of sight. It seems like month-old copies somehow find their way to my desk. It's perfectly OK with me if they're a month, two months, or even a year old. Here's why.

First, understand that most income properties in the multiple-listing book would have sold before they ever got listed if they were really bargains. Remember what I told you about pocket listings: they never get published. What you normally find in the "Income Property" section in the multiple-listing book are overpriced apartments and "dog properties."

The multiple-listing service contract provides for selling agents to split commissions with the listing office when a sale takes place. Obviously, the multiple-listing book provides the maximum exposure for the property owner: every licensed agent is a potential seller. The value to me is keeping an eye on properties that stay in the book for a long time, say six months or even a year. Sellers who can't sell in that length of time often become extremely motivated. Offers they never dreamed they'd accept when they listed the property somehow become much more acceptable to them after a long dry spell.

I've had pretty good luck buying properties that nobody seems to want from old multiple-listing books. On several deals, the listing had already expired and I was able to purchase directly from highly motivated sellers. Picture yourself in the seller's position: if you can't sell a property in six months with all the exposure of the multiple-listing book, obviously it calls for more drastic measures—usually, lower price and better terms. I've done about 10% to 15% of my business as a result of tracking down multiple listings. It's well worth the effort.

4. Initiate Written Cold Calls

Real estate investors often complain that their wealth-building plans are seriously hampered because too few properties are available in the areas where they invest. You can't buy real estate and build much wealth if nobody will sell you a property, right? Obviously, it takes both buyers and sellers to complete transactions. So, the big question is "Where do you find real estate sellers when it seems like nothing is for sale?" Cold calling is a technique by which you contact property owners who own the kind of properties you'd like to acquire and try to persuade them to sell.

One of the first questions I'm always asked is "Why in the world would people consider selling their property to me merely because I contacted them and asked?" There are more reasons than you might imagine, but first let me confess to you that I did not invent cold calling. Real estate agents have been doing it for years and with enough success to keep doing it. The problem that many real estate agents have with cold calling is that it's too much work. It's much easier when sellers walk through the door and hand them a listing. A big percentage of agents are willing to wait.

How I Make Cold Calling Work. Naturally, there's a big difference between investors who operate properties for profits and real estate agents who sell them for commissions. Cold calling can be different, too. For example, agents will sit at the telephone for hours calling long lists of owners. Obviously, that's got to be very boring. The way I do cold calling is much different.

To begin with, I write letters to property owners rather than make telephone calls. I also do some research before I make any contact with property owners. This allows me to customize my cold calls (letters) to fit the property and address any special circumstances pertaining to the owner.

Not every rental property is a candidate for my "cold call" letters. To start with, my specialty is the fix-up real estate. I make money by acquiring properties I can fix up. My strategy is to quickly increase the value. Average looking properties, without any visible signs of being rundown or neglected, do not fit my profit plan; therefore, I automatically eliminate those properties from my cold calling list.

When I'm driving around, I always keep an eye out for interesting properties I would like to own—assuming I could buy them for a reasonable price and terms. I keep a little notebook in my car to write down the address, number of units, and the condition. I also jot down my own estimate of their current market value—and the amount I would be willing to pay. I find it very helpful to draw a little sketch of the lot and then take a measurement from the nearest street intersection to the lot. A sketch will help you locate the property on the county assessor's map when you visit the courthouse. Assessor maps don't have street addresses, so the measurement will help you find the right location on a scaled map.

Cold Call Letter Strategy Requires a Plan. First, let me tell you what you shouldn't do—don't insult or offend the owner because his or her property looks like junk. I sympathize with the owner and attempt to establish my credentials as an experienced property owner, but not as a "hotshot real estate tycoon." Remember: owners of troubled properties who might be willing to finance a sale will not put much trust in a buyer with no experience. They can easily visualize the property coming back to them in even worse condition.

If the owner hasn't been around the property much, especially if he or she lives out of the area, I try to paint a picture of a property that is poorly managed and in need of immediate attention. I often give the owner an idea of what it might cost to get the property up to snuff. Note that the sample letter in this chapter refers to "a $20,000 lesson I will never forget." I let the owner know that I'm a local landlord and I buy fixer properties. I generally write something like the following in my letters.

- "Each day when I drive by your place, I can't help noticing how many jacked-up cars the tenants have accumulated."
- "I can't help noticing the lawns have all died in the past few months."
- "I notice the houses need a lot of work and I'm wondering if you ever thought about selling the property."

You'll notice my reason for writing says nothing about buying the property. I try to keep my offer to purchase as an alternate solution to his problems. I even ask him to check me out: "Drive by my houses and see what you think." This reinforces my credibility with him. It also proves I'm a real landlord, as I say in my opening sentence. Out-of-town owners generally know about management problems and high expenses. My letter merely reminds them that it's true and owners are the only ones who can make a difference. I think every owner will agree with that.

I like the owner to start thinking about his or her monthly net income, especially out-of-town owners who receive a monthly check from a property manager for the amount that is left after fees and expenses are paid. When I tell the owner about earning more net spendable income; that generally grabs his or her attention. Again, I never say that my intention is to purchase. I only ask the owner to keep me in mind if he or she should sell. I offer my financial statement and tell the owner how to save a big commission.

When I discover that the property owner lives out of town and his or her property is not being maintained, I will try to emphasize things that indicate how—unless changes are made immediately—the property value will decline and his or her income will suffer. These are very compelling reasons for an owner to take some action. Several times in my career, cold call letters have worked long after I've written them. In one case, an owner worked desperately to fix his problems. He hired three managers in a 12-month period. Finally, 16 months after I wrote him a letter, I bought his property for $41,000 less than my initial drive-by estimate of value. If your cold call letters don't work overnight, just be patient and don't give up.

How to Write a Cold Call Letter. The sample letter here is an example of how I do cold calling. Read it several times and try to picture yourself as John P. and Mary Jones. How would you feel if you owned the property on West Street and received this letter from me? Would my letter start you thinking?

John P. and Mary Jones	RE: 2020 West Street
1234 Easy Street	AP# 07-360-14
Lake Camanche, CA 95640	Shasta County

Dear Mr. and Mrs. Jones:

I am a local property owner and landlord in Redding. I own several rental houses in the same neighborhood as your property on West Street. I drive by your property at least once every week on my way to check out my rentals.

Apparently, you're having the same kind of problems I have with tenants who own junk cars. Last week, I noticed a car motor hanging in the tree in front of your duplexes in the back. I would guess it belongs to that old rusty blue sedan with no wheels, parked between the two pink houses.

I realize it's difficult to manage properties from 200 miles away. I did it only briefly before moving to Redding, but never again. The management company I had hired allowed the tenants to take over everything. I had junk cars and dead grass—and you wouldn't believe what the houses looked like inside. It was a $20,000 lesson I will never forget. That's why I visit my properties at least once a week now.

The reason I'm writing is because my company does fix-up and repairs for rental property owners. We just rehabbed the three light blue houses on the NW corner of West and 17th Avenue. Drive by the next time you're in town. I think you'll be impressed. Keep me in mind if you need work done.

When I spoke with your tenant in the front house, Judy, to find out who owned the property, she said the owners were retired, but she pays rent to the Ace Management Company on Hilltop Drive. I hope they are better than the managers I had, but by the looks of things, they don't seem much better.

I found out the hard way: owners are the only ones who really keep the property up and watch what the tenants do. I would never again own property in a town where I didn't live.

By the way, if you should ever think about selling out, keep me in mind. I'd be happy to show you my financial statement and several of my Redding properties, so you can see how I do business. Quite often, you can earn more spendable income from mortgage payments than from rents and, of course, you don't have to worry about tenants and property managers.

Drop me a line or call if I can be of any service. Call me direct if you should ever decide to sell. You can save a bundle without paying a big commission.

Sincerely,
Jay P. DeCima
(916) 221-0123

Never say anything about the condition of his property that puts the blame on the owner. Always put the blame on lousy tenants, bad luck, poor property managers, or something other than the owner. The whole idea is to not alienate the owner. Instead you should sympathize with him or her, perhaps explaining that you have the same problems yourself, but you have more time to spend with your tenants. If any owner thinks that spending time with tenants is necessary to make his property get better, he or she may just give it to you. Of course, that's wishful thinking, but you get the idea, I think.

Your letter should not mention price, cash down payment, or terms. It should state that you are a serious buyer who moves quickly if a sale can be worked out. You should also point out that, by dealing with you directly, he or she can save a large sales commission. If your letter is timed properly (obviously this is mostly luck and intuition), you can develop the selling idea in the mind of a "leaning" owner. "Leaning" means he or she has been thinking about selling, off and on, but has never gotten around to doing anything yet. Be sure to include your telephone number in your letter, so he or she can call. If you get a call, you're all set to grab your sketch of his property and follow along as he explains details over the phone.

Many owners have called and thanked me for my nice letter, then told me they weren't interested in selling right now. But, you can probably guess who they'll call first when they are ready to sell. Believe me, they'll never throw your letter away. One of my best properties was acquired exactly this way. The owner was not interested when he first read my letter; however, a month later he was interested and we closed the deal.

Cold call letter writing puts you in a position to buy a property that no one knows about, except you and the seller. Finding a good deal that no one else knows anything about puts you in the driver's seat. It's like going to an auction where you're the only bidder. Cold calls have accounted for about 20% of all my acquisitions.

Finding Sellers Who Truly Need to Sell

Contrary to what many novices think, the most difficult part of buying the right properties has nothing to do with contracts, paperwork, escrow instructions, and presenting offers—it's finding sellers who really and truly desire to sell their properties. It's called discovery.

You're looking for sellers who have very compelling reasons to sell. Sometimes, fear of losing the property in a foreclosure creates the right pressure. That's an obvious reason. Many other reasons are hidden, however, or not so visible. Always remember this: a real need situation must exist for the seller, or you will have great difficulty meeting your purchase objectives—that is, buying the property with the kind of flexible terms you need to make the transaction profitable for you. Again, I will repeat myself here because it's so important.

You must locate sellers who, for whatever reason, have a real need or a very strong desire to sell. Nothing short of this will work—don't forget this part. Also, there is no point pursuing sellers who don't seem to have any urgency to sell; you'll be wasting your valuable time. In the long run, you'll discover your time is more valuable than money.

Know the Real Reason a Seller Wants to Sell

Initially, it's quite likely that you won't know the seller's real needs because he or she won't tell you about them. Eventually, as you gain more knowledge from practice and experience, your detective instincts will improve and you will learn how to dig out the information you need more easily. Knowing the real reason a seller wants to sell can be a tremendous advantage when negotiating the kinds of terms that you must have to be successful—that means profitable real estate that pays you back for all your efforts.

For example, "lease with option to own" might really mean the owner doesn't want to be bothered for at least a year or more. Most out-of-town owners don't like long distance renting, especially with problem tenants, but will seldom say it that way. Owners who inherit properties often think rental houses are too much of a hassle. Obviously, they weren't the ones who bought the property. Owners with financial problems or two mortgage payments will seldom tell you they're hurting when, in fact, they sometimes are.

You must learn to dig out this kind of information in order to make offers that will generate a reasonable level of interest from potential sellers. You can make very profitable offers or proposals once you find the right property and a motivated seller. The big money comes from doing your homework before ever making an offer. Always learn everything you can about the seller. Do it fast, though, so you don't lose the deal.

Most Common Reasons That Motivate Sellers

Sellers get motivated for many reasons. Here's a list of the most common reasons, all except one, which we'll tackle separately in a minute.

1. Owners live out of town.
2. Owners have financial problems.
3. Owners have family problems (divorce, death, life-style change).
4. Owners are advertising "for sale by owner" (all newspapers).
5. Owners have lost their jobs.
6. Owners are elderly, disabled, retired, or in poor health and can't work on the property any longer.
7. Owners inherited the property.
8. Owners are advertising the lease-option or even houses for rent.
9. Owners have moved (job transfers) and are now making two house payments.
10. Owners have changed investment goals, found a better mousetrap.

"For Sale" Often Means "I Need Help"

I know from experience there are many owners of small rental properties—the kind I recommend—who have their properties for sale, but in reality the "For Sale" sign really means "I Need Help." These sellers have various problems; many of them need some serious help. Their solution is to sell the property. Owners in this situation can provide big financial opportunities for investors who are willing to help solve their problems—namely, they can give you a great price with seller carryback financing.

"Don't Wanters"–Most Don't Know How to Manage

Many real estate instructors refer to sellers who don't know how to manage their property as "don't wanters." The number-one reason most sellers of small income properties are "don't wanters" is because they cannot manage their own properties. For the most part, they can't stand the hassle of dealing with their tenants. The reason for this failure is that most of them have never taken the time to educate themselves to pre-pare for this most important task. They are victims of what I described in Chapter 4 as the "Christopher Columbus technique." They don't understand what they're doing and they have little or no idea where they're going. They are simply drifting without direction. Since they have no plan and very little knowledge, they are unable to fix the things that are wrong. You won't find yourself in this situation if you do as I suggest and learn how to be a landlord or landlady (manage your prop-erties) right from the first day you start investing.

Violation of Habitability Laws–a Motivator

Many owners become very motivated to sell when needed repairs stack up or when the tenants "gang up" and refuse to continue paying rents until something is done. Quite often city or county housing officials add extra tension when habitability laws are violated. Housing authorities can pro-vide tremendous motivation to owners who neglect their properties. Many of these owners become highly motivated sellers when they find out what building officials require them to do. Out-of-town owners often panic and decide to sell at the first chance they get. You can find these properties by attending abatement committee meetings in your local buying area.

Offer Relief from Pain in Lieu of Cash

The reason you're looking for ugly, distressed properties is because they're most likely to be big problems for their owners. The strategy here is to use your time and your efforts to fix these problems in lieu of the normal cash down payment. Fixing seller problems has a cash value. Often the value of fixing big problems will add up to a higher dollar amount than the normal down payment might have been. Your willingness and your ability to fix problems for others can create a very lucrative opportunity for you.

Many investors, including me, have used this wealth-building tech-nique to quickly develop large real estate portfolios. It's an excellent strat-egy for investors who have very little cash for a down payment, which includes most of us when we're just starting out.

When I check out a rundown property, I try to find out if the tenants are basically running the place. There's a good chance that poor management or lack of landlording skill is really the reason the property is for sale. If this is the case, sellers are often willing to give very favorable terms in exchange for immediate "pain relief."

Problem tenants who are out of control are worth big bucks to investors who know how to establish law and order. Many sellers who find themselves in this predicament are willing to forgo traditional cash down payments in order to rid themselves of the unpleasant situation. People pay handsome rewards to investors who can straighten out the mess.

Key Factors for Making a Bargain Purchase

When you're looking for a bargain, here are 14 factors to consider:

1. It's easy to purchase. Very little cash is required; trades are acceptable.
2. It's OK to assume existing financing, if there is any.
3. Private notes (mortgages) are much better than institutional lenders (banks and mortgage companies).
4. The seller is willing to carry back financing on good terms (minimum of 10 years).
5. Mortgage payments (total of loans) are 65% or less of total income.
6. The rents are low and can be increased with property cleanup.
7. The property is dirty, rundown, or ugly, which means less competition.
8. The seller is motivated for any of the reasons listed earlier.
9. There are tenant problems (motorcycles, junk autos, deadbeats).
10. The property is empty (tall weeds, broken glass, garbage everywhere).
11. There are financial problems (foreclosure, bankruptcy, bank repossession).
12. The building is only partially completed (all activity stopped).
13. You have the skills to fix up physical problems.
14. You believe that the property will function OK as is, allowing adequate time to upgrade and force the value up.

These 14 items are certainly not everything to consider, nor will any of them necessarily guarantee the property is a bargain. They are, however, excellent factors for making a profitable deal.

Beware of Over-Financed Property

In order to acquire properties at bargain prices or at least for prices that will allow you to make a reasonable profit, you must first determine if you can actually purchase the property for a reasonable price. I imagine you are thinking to yourself, "That doesn't seem so tough. Why not simply ask the seller? Certainly he or she can tell me in a minute." Here's a bit of advice: sellers may not know why they have problems, especially if they paid too much themselves.

Many times I've found properties for sale that are very desirable, but seriously over-financed. Owners who have over-financed properties are often extremely anxious to sell—many times for low or no cash down payments—because they need to stop their negative cash flow. You must be wary of these kinds of properties. An over-financed property can spell big trouble, no matter how low the down payment. Once you determine how much you can afford to pay for a property and still make money for yourself, you should forget the whole idea if it looks like the price will exceed your estimate. Sellers with too much existing debt have very limited flexibility for negotiating the price downward. Conversely, sellers with lots of equity have room to reduce their asking prices. Those are the sellers you're looking for.

Look for Owners with Equity

Properties that the seller has owned for a substantial time—six to 10 years or more—will offer far greater opportunities for negotiating the selling price downward. This is because the owner has most likely paid down the existing mortgage debt over the years. Always look for sellers who have a substantial amount of equity in the property, because they can discount that equity.

For example, let's say the seller is asking $250,000 for her property. You can assume the existing mortgage of $195,000. The balance of the asking price ($55,000) is the seller's equity. You've already filled out your income property analysis form and concluded that $210,000 is the right price to pay. If the seller accepts your offer, she will receive $15,000 for her equity. She may not like the low price, but she still receives some money from the sale.

Now consider a similar situation where the seller purchased the property just a year ago for $235,000, with a down payment of $20,000. Obviously, she still owes almost $215,000 on the mortgage. Your chances of buying this property for $210,000 just flew out the window, because the seller would need to pay you $5,000 to make the sale work. Even if this transaction would help the seller financially, it's almost too much of an obstacle for him to overcome emotionally. Sellers will seldom pay buyers to take their property. In short, this seller is not in a position to make you a good deal!

Avoid Deals Like HUD, FHA, and VA Foreclosures

Don't be surprised when I tell you that most HUD, FHA, and VA foreclosures or take-back properties are not very good deals for investors—especially investors who have visions of becoming rich anytime soon. You're probably thinking, "How can that be?"

The answer is really quite simple. You need to understand the public is composed of countless "dummies" willing to bid up the price. Well-advertised properties are seldom sold at prices low enough to be considered substantially below the market. Their normal selling prices are not discounted nearly enough to allow you to make anywhere near a *substantial profit*. You probably won't even be able to get cash flow if you rent the property. The truth is that sellers don't need to cut prices very much when the entire public is notified about the sale.

Your only consolation, if you do decide to purchase a government-owned foreclosure, is that you'll also receive a heaping supply of top-grade plywood as a bonus. Both the FHA and HUD use tons of plywood to board up all the windows when they foreclose properties. However, the selling price rarely ends up less than 10% to 15% under true market value. To me, that's simply not enough discount for a cash flow investment.

It Pays to Be Snoopy

The very first thing I do, when I hear that property I'm interested in becomes available, is to begin my "detective work." Sometimes my broker,

Fred, will perform this task—but it took four years with my coaching before he became "snoopy" (skilled) enough to suit my taste. Brokers and sales agents, typically, don't do the exhaustive research or "snooping around" I insist must be done.

The biggest difference between most sales agents and me is that they will accept the word of sellers as being mostly true. I accept it as being mostly exaggerated and often untrue. It's never considered true until it's proven true to me.

I'm not trying to be overly critical, but you must never forget this important fact of investment life—once the escrow closes and everybody gets paid, it's you, alone, by yourself, who must live with the deal you signed. If, somehow, you've failed to uncover the true property expenses and it turns out they're considerably higher than you were led to believe, guess what? It's you, alone, who is now stuck. That's the reason I learned to become a very snoopy house detective early in my investment career.

Verify Income Plus the Market Rents

If you plan to rent your properties to average tenants at prevailing market rents, you must first know exactly what those rents should be. You can do this by matching the rents in classified ads to comparable properties in the same neighborhood as your rentals (or soon to be yours). This exercise will provide you with some valuable information. First, you'll learn if the rents for the property you're negotiating to purchase are currently too high or too low. You hope they're low, so you can raise them. Perhaps, equally important, you will quickly discover how much income is the right amount for the property. When you know exactly what the true market income should be for a particular property, it becomes a lot easier to figure out how much you can pay for it—and still make a profit.

When the Rents Seem Unreasonably High

Always investigate if you think the tenants are paying way more than appears reasonable. I have found tenants who are paying $500 rent for a $400 house. A little detective work will show you the type of tenants who are willing to do this and why. In one particular case, four occupants were listed on the rental agreement, but I counted 12 coming out one morning when I was inspecting the property. Sometimes you can get an idea about who lives there by checking out the cars after dark. When I feel that negotiations to purchase a property are going my way, I spend more time driving by and observing what goes on at the property. The word that best describes how I conduct these observations is "sneaky"—I don't bother calling ahead for a formal visit. You can't find out what's really happening at the property unless you snoop around.

When the Rents Seem Low

Over the years, I've had good luck finding properties that were *under-rented* (under-market rents). Here are two common situations to look for.

The first situation is with older owners of small income properties—perhaps six or seven small houses or apartments—who take care of everything, including maintenance, rent collection, and dealing with the tenants. Often, these owners will live in one of the houses on the same property. It's quite common, in this situation, for an owner to allow the rents to remain low or lag behind the market value, hoping this will keep the tenants from asking for repairs or maintenance. These owners simply don't want to be bothered. Tenants understand full well when their rents are low, if they're smart—and they generally are about their own rents. They don't call the landlord with complaints. They simply let things be. The problem for these owners doesn't become apparent until they sell. Income property selling prices are based on the rental income the property generates. Low rents mean a lower price when it's time to sell.

The second situation is somewhat like the first. It frequently occurs when owners have no mortgage payments on the property; it's free and clear of loans. Quite often, the original owner will pass away, leaving the rental property to the kids. Because there is no mortgage payment, the rents on the property provide a large net monthly income.

(Typically, the mortgage on income properties will eat up 50% to 70% of all the rent monies. Those properties must be tightly managed or there will be very little or no net income. In fact, these owners must sometimes dig into their wallets each month just to keep their rental operation afloat.)

When the net income is so high, it's easy for a complacent owner to get careless with property management—vacancies are not nearly so crit-

ical, raising rents annually is not really necessary, and routine maintenance expenses are easy to pay from the rental income. So, these properties must also be sold for lower prices, because they're generating less net
income than they should.

Sophisticated buyers will expect to purchase under-rented properties
using the capitalization method to determine the value. The cap rate valuation method, as it's called, is based on the *net income only*: the capitalization rate for a property is determined by dividing net operating income
by purchase price. If the net income is low due to poor landlording, the
sale price will be lower as a result. As a buyer, you should look very hard
for both low rents and poor management when trying to find the properties that will generate cash flow quickly—after you fix the problems.

What to Do When You Find the Right Property

Let's look at a hypothetical situation, but one that's very common today.
The property is totally trashed with broken windows and junk inside and
out. The county ownership records reveal that tax bills are being sent to
out-of-town owners. We learn, after writing to them, that the owners are
a middle-aged working couple with two children. The trashed house is a
rental property. The last tenants left in the middle of the night without
paying rent. A close friend who oversees the property is trying to get fix-
up bids for the owners, but hasn't had much time lately, so the house just
sits. Nothing is happening.

The general area is residential. Houses are worth about $60,000 and
20% of them are rentals. The neighborhood is an older, established tract
approximately 25 years old. Rents average about $500 per month for a
three-bedroom, one-bath house. We learn the mortgage balance is $29,500,
with payments of $216.47 per month at 8% interest. We determine that fix-
up work will cost $7,500 ($2,500 for materials and $5,000 for labor). Labor
generally runs about 70% of the total fix-up costs, the way I do it.

Here's the proposal we'll make. We offer $54,000. (For this type of deal,
I generally offer 10% under the average market price in the area.) There
will be no cash down payment. Instead, I'll jump right in and provide all
labor and materials to restore the house within 30 days. The sellers will

allow me $7,500 credit (down payment) for my personal efforts to restore the property. This deal will solve all of their problems in one big swoop.

I make a down payment of fix-up (labor and material) worth $7,500.

I assume or take over the existing mortgage of $29,500 (monthly payment, $216.47).

The owner carries back a private note for the balance of the sale price (10-year term at 8%) (interest-only payments) of $17,000 (monthly payment, $113.33).

I normally agree to pay closing costs—because sellers should not be saddled with out-of-pocket costs. Remember, there is *no cash* down payment to the owner for escrow expenses. This small item will upset most sellers, so I strongly advise you to pay the closing expenses, if possible. It's an excellent exchange for maximum concessions by the owner. Don't irritate the owner when you're asking him or her to carry a long-term note with very favorable terms (below market). It's not a smart move to try and get everything; you should just be concerned about the most important things.

Small Deals Build Large Bank Accounts

This deal is just a plain and simple "garden variety" transaction. It's not very hard to do at all. If the seller accepts your offer, you will need $2,500 for materials, plus closing costs. Use your credit card or split the deal with a friend who has the money. You can do the fix-up labor yourself.

I'll be the first to agree that this "two-bit" transaction will certainly not make you a millionaire; however, what's important is that you now own a property. You've started. Starting is like making a touchdown in football, going on your first date, or getting a jump-start when your car battery is dead. It provides the momentum you need to move forward. Now you're beyond the thinking stage—you're in the action mode.

When the dust settles, you'll have $10,000 equity and rental income of $500 per month. Your mortgage payment will be $329.80. After taxes and insurance you might even have enough left to make payments on your overloaded Visa card. When you've completed five or 10 of these deals, you'll be on your way to an exciting future in real estate. After you have completed 15 or 20, you can start carrying around a briefcase instead of a toilet plunger.

As you gain more experience and learn how to quickly sniff out the high-potential *profit makers*, this business will get much more exciting. It's sort of like being a private detective, but it pays much better and you'll seldom have to dodge bullets.

Equity and Profits Are Greater with Larger Properties

Larger properties have exactly the same problems and the same motivated owners as single houses. However, percentage-wise, the equity and profits are much greater. Your financial statement grows bigger and faster with multiple units. Also, don't forget groups of older houses and duplexes in rundown condition can be purchased for much larger discounts because fewer investors want them, so there's *less competition.*

The Courage to Look Where Others Don't: Nontraditional Properties

People constantly ask me how I find these kinds of properties—"diamonds in the rough," some call them. The complaint I hear most often is "There are no properties in my hometown like you write about." With very few exceptions, I must disagree. The properties are there. You simply haven't found them yet—and there are several good reasons why you haven't.

I've found most folks are not looking around nearly enough. Most investors I know do the traditional kind of search for properties—if they wish to be apartment owners, they tend to look at traditional apartment buildings; if they want to invest in single houses, they generally search through the suburbs. Hardly anyone is willing to look at slaughterhouses or an old motor lodge. My suggestion is to broaden your vision a bit. After all, nontraditional properties are a lot more fun and, quite often, a lot more profitable.

Break Ranks with the Typical Buyer

Frequently, you'll find the biggest rewards are found a little ways off the beaten path. Rich gold mines are seldom in plain view to all who would seek them. Think about investing a little differently. Isn't it the folks with vision who always seem to be the ones who make the most money? Followers are always lagging behind and never quite sure what they're looking for. Most often, they show up too late, after competitors have already bid up the prices. My suggestion—don't follow, lead.

Finding the right properties, with a high potential for profits and cash flow, is the first step for developing a successful investment plan. It's most important to break away from traditional thinking and stop following the average investor crowd. Serious money is made by those who study the marketplace and develop the ability to spot bargains that others simply fail to see. You don't need to buy slaughterhouses, but you do need to develop buying skills and open up your vision to different possibilities. Be especially "tuned in" if you run the numbers and a rundown property shows good cash flow.

6

My Yellow Court Houses:
The Right Property and Seller Make for a Profitable Deal

Yellow Court did not look like the kind of property you see on the late-night cable TV show *How to Get Rich Without Cash or Credit*. There were no Rolls-Royces, no testimonials from slick pitchmen, and certainly no bikini-clad women frolicking on the deck of an expensive yacht.

Yellow Court was five ugly houses repossessed by an out-of-town bank for nonpayment of the mortgages. When a bank forecloses on real estate, as you recall from Chapter 4, it's called an "REO" (or "real estate owned"). Banks don't like REOs because they're in the business of lending out money for interest, not managing houses. When you learn how much money they lose on them, you'll clearly understand why REOs are poison to the banker's balance sheet and profitability.

In the case of Yellow Court, the bank had foreclosed on five junky houses that had been completely trashed by wave after wave of deadbeat tenants. The city had formally advised the bank that the houses had become a public nuisance. Finally, after continuous nonpayment of utilities, the city shut off all services and "red-tagged" the houses, deeming them unsafe for human occupancy. The tenants moved out, taking everything they could tear loose—medicine cabinets, plumbing fixtures, carpets, interior doors, and even the kitchen sinks and toilets.

When I first heard about Yellow Court, the tenants had been gone for nearly 18 months. All the houses had long since been boarded up. The windows and doors were covered over with plywood that was bolted in place. There were nearly enough boards and bolts to build another house. It's like you see on those "trashed-out" HUD-foreclosed houses—they look like forts under enemy attack.

Why Banks Want to Unload REOs

Banks not only despise REO properties because the mortgages are nonperforming, but also because they now own a liability, rather than an asset. To cover their loss, they must set aside funds that they could otherwise be lending. Also, they must now shoulder the liability costs involved when they become the owner. That means fire insurance and management fees. It costs them even more when no one is living there. After an extended period of ownership with continuous cash losses, even the richest banks will become extremely motivated to dump a property.

Timing Is Everything, from Wine-Making to Real Estate

Winemaker Paul Masson claims to sell no wine before its time. That claim is based on simple economics. Obviously, they can't sell unfermented grape juice or they would, believe me.

Life is full of events that require perfect timing. With real estate investing, you must have proper timing if you expect to make serious money. For example, if you decide to purchase a property simply because "you want to own it right now," you might be doing exactly the wrong thing unless, of course, you have a special plan worked out in advance. Buying right requires a good plan. Buying property and having a good plan go together like a pair of purple socks.

By the way, I make exactly this same argument when I discuss selling properties. You simply cannot make maximum profits unless you time your sales properly. Buying low and selling high will happen only when you learn how to properly time both events.

Determining How Much to Pay

I cannot overemphasize the importance of knowing your particular marketplace. You must know what properties are worth, either to sell or to rent. You will also need special knowledge about repairs and fix-ups. This may sound a bit more difficult than it really is. However, estimating fix-up work on a house is really no more difficult than learning grocery prices at your local supermarket. Once you've done the first one and compared the actual expenses with your initial estimate, you'll catch on very quickly.

I always submit my bid for REO properties written on plain paper or on the bank's forms. Verbal communications back and forth by telephone are often misunderstood, sometimes on purpose. They are also not binding. If a bank accepts my bid, I want to see a piece of paper with a bank officer's signature on it. That way all my time and hard work won't be lost in the event a higher bidder shows up and the bank suddenly forgets all its verbal promises to me. With fax machines, signatures are just as easy to get as verbal commitments—and much safer for investors.

Making an Offer

I first learned about the five houses on Yellow Court when I saw the "Do Not Enter" notices posted on the buildings. The bank ran several classified ads in my local paper. No price was listed, so I immediately called the bank's REO department and asked how much they wanted. No prices had been set yet; however, they sent me their forms to submit a bid.

The five Yellow Court houses were three-bedroom, two-bath properties with approximately 1,350 square feet of living space. They each had double-car garages and large backyards. That's the good news.

The bad news was everything inside the houses was totally trashed. There were giant holes in the plasterboard walls and holes in the floors, doors were ripped off cabinets, windows and sliding glass doors were broken, the roofs were leaking, and every hot water heater had been stolen.

There was great potential for overpaying, because every system needed major repairs or replacement. I knew full well that if I paid too much I would end up working my tail off several months for no profits. I had estimated it would take my crew and me the full summer (approximately three months) to rehab all five houses. That's a ton of labor, not including the licensed contractors I would need to reroof the houses, install new gas lines, and rebuild the electrical services. It was also necessary to install brand-new fuse boxes, because former occupants had completely stripped them.

Overpaying can destroy dreams for wide-eyed, inexperienced investors. Take my advice seriously here: work the numbers, backwards and forwards, then over and over. Always use Murphy's Law of Estimating—"If something else can go wrong, it will." If it can possibly cost more than you thought, it always will. If there's the slightest chance you missed something in your cost estimate, you did."

My Bid and the Reaction

I called in my numbers first, then I mailed the written offer. The REO manager did not like my numbers: I could hear it in his voice.

Before I could even speak a word, he advised me that the bank would need $42,000 per house just to come out even. "However," he said, "any offer you make will receive our serious consideration." I've always been fond of those words—*serious consideration*—so I told him my offer and terms:

Offer: $100,000 *full purchase price* for the five houses. $20,000 *cash down payment* to be paid to seller upon acceptance of offer.

Terms:

1. Buyer to purchase property in "as is" condition with no contingencies.
2. Seller to finance balance of purchase price ($80,000 mortgage), for 10 years, 10% interest-only payments.
3. Seller to provide a six-month moratorium on the mortgage payments to allow buyer time to repair houses and begin generating income.
4. Buyer will provide required financial statements necessary for seller

to approve carryback mortgage ($80,000) for buyer.

I recall that telephone conversation vividly. There was a rather long pause at the other end of the line. I had to ask, "Are you still there?"

Then came sort of a muffled whisper: "But that's only $20,000 per house!"

"That's correct," I agreed.

Just before he hung up, the REO manager said, "Jay, I'll need to get back to you on this. There could be some problems, but I will tell you right now, our bank never allows moratoriums. Also, if we provide carryback loans, they are always written at 12% interest for five years maximum."

Unknown to me, at the time, several local building contractors had also submitted bids to purchase Yellow Court. The bank knows that competition makes for a better horse race. Looking back now, I imagine they probably mailed out information packages to everyone they knew.

The REO manager finally called me back. He sounded a bit too gleeful. He told me that the bank had not accepted my offer. It had accepted a higher purchase price. He thanked me for my participation, made some joke about "maybe next time," and said, "Goodbye." And that was it. I never expected to hear about Yellow Court again.

Keep Records

Here's a tip for all investors: never throw away your notes or cost estimates. I've learned this lesson the hard way—several times. Keep files on every property you have an interest in. If it's worth your efforts the first time, chances are it will be the second or third time, too. Good notes last forever. Besides that, you will develop a good history about the property that allows you to act quickly if there should be another round of bidding. Dedicate a special file for this purpose, "Pending Property Deals." It will pay big dividends over time, believe me. Now back to our exciting Yellow Court episode.

The REO Man Rings Twice Sometimes

Three weeks later, the phone rang. When I answered, I recognized the REO manager's voice immediately. This time the gleefulness was missing.

"Jay," he began, "would you reconsider your Yellow Court offer?"

"I most certainly would," I told him, "with the same terms as I submitted before."

He once again explained how the bank had this policy about no moratoriums and no carryback loans for more than five years.

"The deal can't work that way," I said. "I need more time."

He said, "Let me check with the loan committee and get right back to you on this."

It wasn't even two hours before my phone rang again.

"We've just had a new policy revision for REOs," the manager said. "We can allow up to a six months moratorium for mortgage payments and we'll extend our financing for up to 10 years."

"Gee, that's wonderful." I said "That's exactly how my offer is written; therefore, I accept. We've got ourselves a deal."

About a year later, I learned that the contractor who had bid higher than me lost out because he had lousy credit. The bank would not approve financing for him. My persistence had finally won out.

My cost estimate to fix Yellow Court was $12,500 for each house. Since there were five houses, the total estimated cost was $62,500. Fix-up expenses quickly add up for trashed-out properties.

Affording the Fix-Up

In this case, I was financially able to pay the bills as I did the work. This is not a job you should attempt without money. You must purchase these properties and fix them up within your own financial limitations. Obviously, this was not my first fix-up experience. My first fix-ups were much smaller and took a whole lot less cash, believe me. By the time Yellow Court came along in my career, I was doing pretty well with my other properties.

Everybody starts with small steps. If you don't trip, you'll soon have the money to be doing five-house jobs like Yellow Court.

Success!

The Yellow Court job took all summer, like I'd thought. It was, indeed, a lot of work, but the houses turned out simply beautiful, I'm proud to say.

I often take my "Fixer Camp" seminar students over to see them. I like to brag about the way the houses look today. The students are always interested to hear about the financial rewards at Yellow Court.

Was it worth all that effort? I'll let you judge for yourself.

Do you remember the mortgage payment moratorium I worked so hard to get? Well, I never needed the full six months they gave me. Instead, I completed all the work in half that time and refinanced the entire property (all five houses) with a local savings bank. My new appraisals averaged $62,500 per house. I placed new $40,000 mortgages on each house. That was enough to pay off the existing mortgage debt and pay back all my fix-up money. There were even a few bucks left over for me. By the way, my actual expenses to fix each house were $15,000—not $12,500 as I had estimated. That's how Murphy's Law works.

Here's a quick view of the financial picture at Yellow Court. You'll recall that I paid $100,000 total cost ($20,000 per house), with $20,000 cash down payment. My new financing paid off the $80,000 loan carried back by the REO seller.

Purchase and Fix-Up—Five Houses:
Purchase price for each house: $20,000
Cash down payment by Jay: $4,000
Mortgage carried back by seller: $16,000
Fix-up costs, paid out over three months by Jay, out-of-pocket:
   $15,000

Completion—Six Months Later:
New appraisal value of each house: $62,500
Income from rents: $550 per month
New 30-year mortgage on each house: $40,000
Mortgage payment: $305 per month
Pay off REO loan: $16,000
Pay back Jay for fix-up costs: $15,000
Return of down payment to Jay: $4,000
Cost of loan—escrow expenses: $1,250
Balance of loan proceeds from escrow: $3,750
Leftover funds, returned to Jay's pocket

The bottom line: I have all my money back, plus I get to keep $3,750 for each house (leftover loan proceeds), for a total of $18,750. My equity after the refinance was $22,500 per house, for a total of $112,500. The monthly rental income, less mortgage payment, was $245 per house, for a total of $1,225.

You won't need a computer to figure out the return on this investment. I've got all my money back—my fix-up money, my down payment, and all financing costs—plus I put $18,750 in my pocket. I no longer have one thin dime invested, yet I end up with $112,500 equity and $1,225 per month cash flow. When you own properties like this, all you need to do is hang onto them and start looking for more.

The Goal Is Finding Profitable Deals

Good properties are always available, but it takes a little creative effort to find them. Finding the right properties—the kind that will produce monthly cash flow and long-term profits—is one of the most important skills you must develop to enjoy any success in this business. Remember: if this was too easy, everybody would be doing it and all would be getting rich. Finding properties that will earn reasonable profits is one of the biggest challenges for every investor, regardless of how many properties are for sale in the buying area.

You must always keep in mind that the goal is finding profitable deals, not finding lots of deals. You should pattern your buying strategy somewhat like the old Hills Brothers TV commercial. The buyer in the ad says, "90% of all the world's coffee beans are rejected by Hills Brothers. They're simply not good enough for Hills Brothers, so they're sold to the other guys." I would guess about the same percentage should apply to investors looking for the right properties—unless, of course, they're buying property as a hobby. Quality deals are the ones that make money. Don't substitute your profits for volume. It makes little sense to hurry up and buy a loser.

7

Good Realty Agents Don't Cost You Money—They Help You Make It

A skilled real estate agent can be a valuable asset to every investor. And, much like building a strong and successful marriage, you will need to spend some time and effort finding exactly the right agent who fits your style. Chances are you won't find Mr. or Ms. Right on the very first date, so don't be hesitant to dump a few along the way. That's how it works for everyone during the hunt.

The worst part is always breaking the ice, introducing yourself to complete strangers who you think might be able to help you. There's no way to shortcut this process, so it's best to simply charge ahead and do it. When you eventually find an agent who can appreciate your goals and is willing to spend time helping you achieve them, you'll suddenly realize you've added a powerful new tool to your "wealth builder's kit."

Real estate agents are the eyes and ears of the real estate business. Approximately 96% of all sales and trades involve licensed salespeople and their brokers. It would be very foolish, indeed, to harbor any serious notions about excluding them from your investment plans. The best thing you can do for yourself is to begin diligently searching for a good one.

Before I get started on the hows and whys of selecting the agent who's right for you, let me first discuss the issue of commissions. Those are what agents earn when they help you buy and sell real estate. You must first understand there is no such thing as a standard one-size-fits-all commission. They come in different sizes and are often negotiated.

For example, most agents in my town charge about a 6% commission for selling houses. However, that's not the market I'm a part of. House buyers generally represent one-time transactions for most agents. I'm a buyer and sometimes a seller whenever the opportunity arises. Unlike the folks who buy a house and that's it, I'm good for many transactions. Naturally, I represent a greater source of income for my agent.

Understandably, agents can work for smaller-percentage commissions when multiple transactions are anticipated. To give you an idea of what I'm saying here, I'll share my own experience.

The average commission I've paid out for all my transactions during the past several years is slightly less than 3% of the purchase price. That's roughly half of the so-called going rate. I find it best to negotiate the commission in advance of every deal I make. Just remember: it must be fair for the amount of work involved.

How to Find an Agent Who's Right for You

The first thing is to visit the local real estate offices in the area where you plan to invest. Ask the receptionist if he or she knows which agent sells the most apartment buildings or income properties. Get yourself introduced and tell the agent exactly what you're trying to accomplish. The interview will be your opportunity to learn what the agent thinks he or she can do for you. But remember: the agent must know exactly what you want done in order to respond in a meaningful way.

Once you're face to face with the agent, be as specific as you can. In my situation, I might tell him or her the following:

I'm interested in "fixer-type," rundown properties. I prefer detached houses on a single lot. For example, 10 or 12 older houses on an acre of land would be something I'm very interested in. I'm also looking for properties with owner financing. I'm particularly interested in properties that have several private notes or mortgages that I can assume. Deferred maintenance (rundown), problem tenants, and properties that need major cleanup are my specialty. I wish to avoid new bank financing whenever possible and I'm trying to purchase properties with 10% cash down. I can also add notes or other properties in trade.

This description of what I'm looking for and my special preferences should be enough to give most any agent a fairly decent idea of what I'm in the market for. Naturally, the price will have to fit the deal, but don't ever forget that the asking price seldom has much to do with the final purchase price, particularly in the fixer business.

Look for Experience and Likeability

Just like a budding romance, the chemistry has to work. It will do you no good in the long run to force yourself to work with an agent who disgusts you, no matter how good you think he or she may be. Obnoxious agents are best left to service obnoxious home buyers, since there's no shortage of either one out there. I mention this because it's very important to develop a relationship that can last a long time. A lasting relationship is much easier when you like each other. I've had just two agents in the last 20 years or so.

Additionally, if you're relatively new to investing, you will need a more experienced person to help you. You also need to seek out an agent whose specialty is income property or investment sales. In the larger brokerages, you'll find more specialists. But, then, larger firms always have a ton of new agents cycling through to get experience. In the smaller offices, sales people take on everything that comes through the door. On the other hand, many times you'll find the more experienced agents working by themselves or in smaller offices.

What About Agents Who Shop for Themselves?

I often hear seminar leaders tell investors to seek out real estate agents who buy and sell properties for their personal investment accounts. This advice is akin to leaving your fiancée at an all-night bachelor party, hoping your friends will always do what's right for her.

I can see no advantage to having my own agent competing with me to acquire bargain properties. I once accused my current agent, Fred, of doing exactly that. We were both looking at the numbers on a small, subsidized (HUD) apartment building for sale, when I unexpectedly had to leave town for a week. When I returned, Fred had purchased the building. He said that since I hadn't advised him that I was interested, he assumed that I wasn't. What he couldn't explain very well was why he didn't wait until I returned before he made the purchase. Fred started treating me extra nice and bought me many lunches for a year or so trying to make me forget. Finally, I did and it's never happened again.

Five Important Benefits an Agent Provides

Once you find an agent who seems to talk your language and, of course, demonstrates some honest action, like jumping right in and finding a few properties that seem to fit your search instructions, you'll be off to a running start.

One thing to remember here: both you and your agent are new to each other. Don't make your agent do all the work. You should help in every way you can, especially in the "getting acquainted" phase. For example, if the agent is showing you properties in good condition and you have told him or her you want junkers, reiterate your instructions so you get what you want. By helping your agent, who is trying to help you, you'll end up the big winner.

The benefits you'll receive by taking the time to develop this relationship will be worth big bucks to you in the long term. Here are five of the most important benefits:

1. Your agent has immediate "pipeline" knowledge of when a bargain property is listed for sale, either as a member of the multiple-listing service or by networking through associates and contacts. You'll get the information quickly, so you can write an offer fast if the property is right for you. Being first, or near first, is very important in this business.

2. A good agent will automatically "weed out" properties for you once he or she becomes accustomed with what you really want. My agent

Fred always brings me everything I need for making an educated evaluation on each deal. The information provided is normally a property profile, copies of existing promissory notes, and either a filled-out income property analysis form (see the last page of Chapter 10) or at least the necessary data to fill one out. This is valuable, time-saving work for an investor, needed before any intelligent buying decision can be made. Obviously, it puts Fred closer to a commission if his help results in an offer to purchase.

3. My agent provides an intermediary "buffer" between the buyer (me) and the seller. This is a valuable service to me. Mom-and-pop real estate owners (the kind I buy most properties from) often feel intimidated negotiating with me one on one. They seem to feel that because I own so many properties and I'm successful, they'll automatically end up on the short end of the stick. It's a perception that's hard to overcome, regardless of whether it's true or not. Fred can generally reduce this problem for me in his capacity as a neutral third party. Sellers often feel that a licensed person will be more sensitive to their needs, as opposed to direct, face-to-face negotiating with a savvy real estate investor who owns multiple properties.

4. A good agent will never let the commission block a sale. The good ones are creative and will take a fraction of what they have coming in order to close the sale. They'll let you pay the balance later on, perhaps in monthly payments. My first agent, Merv, allowed me to pay 50% of his commission at closing and then agreed to take a promissory note for the balance, with monthly payments anywhere from $50 to $250, depending on my projected cash flow. At one point, I was paying monthly commissions of $1,250 to Merv. The arrangement helped me and Merv was very happy to have the steady monthly income plus 8% interest.

5. A good agent can put you in contact with moneylenders, both private "hard money" guys and institutional lenders with programs that fit what you're doing. Lenders shop real estate offices looking for qualified buyers among their clients. This is a valuable benefit to investors who are always in need of funds for upgrading and acquisitions. Naturally, you and your project must qualify in order to take

advantage of this opportunity. Nonetheless, money is always the ammunition that keeps investors in the hunt.

No-No's to Avoid If You Expect Loyalty

As you might guess, the benefits must flow both ways between the agent and investor. Here's what you should not do if you want to develop a profitable relationship.

1. Don't jump from agent to agent. Use your agent for all your transactions, unless the two of you have previously agreed upon special exceptions. Loyalty will move mountains.

2. Don't try to squeeze the commissions. If you're like me—that is, you negotiate commissions—do it before the agent goes to work, not after the deal is written up and in escrow.

3. Don't send agents on "wild goose" chases. The veterans will dump you if you try, but don't even do it to the inexperienced dummies. They will soon catch on and will have nothing more to do with you. I've heard so-called real estate experts tell novices to instruct their agents to draft up and present dozens of lowball shotgun offers to purchase properties from the multiple-listing book. Ask any respectable agent what he or she thinks of that advice. Take it from me: don't waste your agent's time with such nonsense.

4. Don't make a ton of offers without ever closing anything. No agent can survive without paydays any more than you can. Take better aim so you'll hit the target and close the deals.

5. Don't deal directly with just any agent who calls you. Always refer them to your agent. Also, some sellers will insist on dealing directly with potential buyers and they don't want to involve an agent. That's fine, but tell your agent about the exception. Sometimes, I pay Fred a small fee, say $500 to $1,000, to help me do the legwork in the background. If you take good care of your agent, you'll benefit in the long run, believe me.

Your Real Estate Agent Can Help You Build Wealth

Real estate agents are the eyes and ears of the real estate business. A sales commission is peanuts compared with the value of having a good agent working to help you achieve your financial goals. I've heard seminar instructors tell their participants, "It's best to avoid agents whenever you can, to save commissions. Use them only for free appraisals and advice or to write up dozens of offers from the multiple-listing book for a mass mailing." In general, the suggestion is to get free service, but avoid commissions. I must tell you, friend, this is poor advice. If you think it's right, pretend you're the agent for a moment. Would this treatment seem satisfactory to you?

Here's the deal: try to find an agent who shows some interest in working with you. Take your time: you don't have to choose the first one you meet. But when you find one that clicks, you'll both likely know it. Clearly explain in detail what you will buy if the agent finds it for you. And remember: no agent can work for you very long without a payday.

8

The Price Is Determined by Income and Location

Complex Formulas Are Not Necessary

Figuring out how much to pay for a property and how to estimate the profits does not require a complicated, lengthy set of financial calculations! If it did, I can assure you there's a whole bunch of millionaires out there who would never have made it.

After many years of doing this work, I'm convinced that simple formulas are the best. But, before I tell you how and why this is true, I must warn you to be very skeptical of "high-tech" computer programs that tend to bowl you over with tons of elaborate financial computations. Hyped-up input data that shows rent increases year after year can make any property look like a gold mine. However, any experienced landlord or landlady will tell you that rents don't always go up—and neither do values!

Too many people get all obsessive about complicated strategies. They seem to have the same mindset as body builders who insist, "No pain, no gain." If you want pain, I suggest you buy a $100,000 house with a $850 mortgage payment and rent it out for $600 a month. If that doesn't hurt enough, keep doing it. If you need higher levels of pain, buy a motel or small business opportunity. That should be enough.

Another trap that nails inexperienced buyers is relying too much on financial information supplied by selling agents. I have found the income data they provide is nearly always overly generous, while the expenses are usually understated. Before you put too much faith in the income and expense data printed in the multiple-listing book, let me remind you of the words you'll find printed somewhere on each of the pages—"*This information deemed reliable but not guaranteed.*" You can get more assurance than that for a kidney transplant! Take my advice: pay very little attention to any financial numbers that can't be verified. If they can't be proven, they just aren't so.

What Are Gross Rent Multipliers and Why Are They Important?

It's vital that you understand gross rent multipliers (GRM), as mentioned in Chapter 3, because they will help you to determine the value of a property—both before you make your purchase and after you've fixed the place up. A GRM expresses the relationship or ratio between the sale price or value of a property and its gross rental income. GRM numbers reflect the quality, condition, and location of a property and the average rental income that can be expected for each unit. They directly impact your cash flow and profits.

GRM numbers are not the same for every location. For example, in Redding, California, the numbers vary from four on the low end to 10 for premium-grade buildings; the average is seven. Just 250 miles away, in the San Francisco Bay area, average apartments sell for 12 times their gross income. If a building is managed poorly, the GRM will be lower. Remember: the GRM numbers are set by buyers. When there are many buyers wanting to purchase a very limited number of available properties, the GRM goes up because of the competition. Conversely, during a buyer's market, when there's a glut of available buildings, the GRM goes down.

GRMs are not precision measurements; they would not work for brain surgery or splitting neutrons, but they work well enough for making money with fix-up real estate. You must, however, know how to use them properly. It goes without saying that any investment must ultimately be valued on the net income it produces—not the gross. However, as you will see, there's a direct correlation between the gross income and what's left over.

In order to establish values and estimate future profits, the first thing I must do is determine the range of multiplier numbers for my particular buying area. This is the essence of knowing how much I can pay, as well as estimating how much profit I can eventually earn. The following chart shows you the range of GRMs in my town. But remember that all locations are different. You must develop your own chart based upon where you invest!

GRM	Description of Property	Rent
10	Premium-grade. Long-term tenants. Excellent owner management. Shows pride of ownership every day.	$525
9	Good property, tenants drive nice cars. Management very good. Quality maintenance.	$500
8	Solid rentals. Most tenants have jobs. Management satisfactory. Little deferred maintenance.	$475
7	Decent condition. Blue–collar tenants. Management OK. Average deferred maintenance.	$450
6	Generally older buildings–trashy, rundown. Marginal tenants. Poor management. Needs work.	$425
5	Older properties–ugly, junky. Deadbeat tenants. Lousy management. Heavy fix-up.	$400
4	Older, "falling down" construction–"pigsty," Hell's Angels tenants. No management. Complete rebuild necessary.	$375

Selecting the Right Location

As we've discussed, location can influence the GRM and the overall value of a property, so be sure to ask yourself these five basic questions before making a selection. If you answer "Yes" to all five, it's OK to proceed.

1. Would I personally feel comfortable (safe) working in this part of town?

The Price Is Determined by Income and Location

2. Do I think this particular location is safe at night, relative to other sections or areas of town?
3. Does this area look like it's reasonably stable, i.e., not going downhill, in terms of renter desirability?
4. Are city or private services—like buses, police protection, schools, fire department, hospitals, and decent shopping—available within a reasonable distance from the property?
5. Does this location look like a normal rental area, where I can easily attract the kind of tenants I'm looking for—for example, low-income families, HUD-assisted, working class or rich tycoons with Cadillac Sevilles and speedboats?

Cheap Deals in Bad Areas Are Not Worth the Hassle

Don't buy property near the Beirut Airport or in locations where you'll need a Bradley armored vehicle to drive through the neighborhood just because it's cheap. It's not that you can't make money in a combat zone, because you can! But you'll find that houses like the ones I'm recommending are not scarce in decent areas once you develop your "star search" network. Bad areas are simply not worth all the hassle or anxiety. Save your energy for painting!

In determining whether the location is suitable for purchase, many inexperienced investors develop tunnel vision. They zero in only on what they perceive to be a cheap price. Remember: if the price is cheap, compared with other properties the surrounding area, there's always a reason. The secret here is to not get sucked in by a cheap price. Make sure the answers to the five basic location questions above are "Yes" before you jump in!

Here's an illustration of what I'm telling you. Say you negotiate to purchase a duplex in a particular area for $70,000. We'll say that comparable duplexes in the area are selling for somewhere between $85,000 and $90,000. On the surface, without knowing anything else about the deal, it would seem as though you've found a property 20% below the average market. That part sounds great! 20% is an excellent discount, under normal circumstances. However, remember that everything that glitters isn't necessarily gold. Fool's gold glitters, too!

Will Your Location Attract the Kind of Tenants You Want?

If you answered "No" to any one of the five location questions, you could be buying a problem, regardless of the 20% discount. For instance, a 20% discount is not nearly enough, in my opinion, if you don't feel comfortable working on your own property. If you as the owner are not comfortable being there, I assure you no one else will be either. Worst of all, neither will any potential renters. If the property is in a rough area, only rough tenants will live there.

In the case of a "No" answer on Question 5, you should ask yourself, "How could I ever make money with the property if I'm not able to attract the kind of tenants I want to live there?" Generally speaking, working-class tenants desire to live around other working folks. That's mainly what they have in common! Conversely, they would not likely be happy for very long living next to nonworking renters who stay up listening to screaming music until 3:00 in the morning. In case you are planning to rent duplexes to the BMW crowd, you better figure on garage doors that open without anybody touching them.

You Can't Get There (Wealthy) Starting From Here

In my town, basic three-bedroom starter houses cost $105,000. Rented, they'll bring in $750 per month, tops. With a 30-year, $8\frac{1}{2}$% fixed FHA mortgage, the payments are $692.03 per month for principal and interest. That's after paying $15,000 cash down, plus an additional $5,000 for all the other costs. When you add in the taxes and fire insurance policy, we're talking $820 per month without a single nickel for repairs and management. It's easy to see that total monthly expenses could average somewhere around $900 if I bought this house!

I don't know about your financial means, but to me this kind of deal doesn't make much sense! Worse yet, it may not make any profits for years to come. The only thing I can see happening here is continually paying out hard cash every month, waiting for the value to go up or hoping to increase the rent enough to cover monthly operating expenses.

Five Common Locations and Their Investment Potential

Often seminar students quiz me about where to purchase ugly, rundown houses for cheap prices, when I tell them that undesirable areas are off limits and that the newer, tract houses are most likely too expensive to ever produce cash flow! "Where on earth is there left for us to go?" they ask. Here's the answer, so pay close attention.

Most towns and cities, both large and small, have five separate, but distinguishable, sections where residential properties exist. There are obviously overlapping and combination locations; but, for the most part, the sections are quite separated and, if you think about it, you'll know exactly where I'm talking about in your town. Here are the five locations. You'll recognize them, I'm sure.

1. Snob Hill—where the wealthiest folks in town reside.
2. Downtown commercial—mostly businesses with acres of concrete and blacktop.
3. Older residential—surrounding downtown area, generally 50 years and older.
4. Dense slums—downtown or pocket areas, often older, plus newer projects, most notably HUD projects.
5. Suburbia—sprawling subdivisions, tract houses, mostly owner-occupied.

Let's take these five locations, one at a time, and discuss what's right and wrong with each in terms of investing:

Snob Hill

This is the place to live once you make it! It's not the kind of real estate to make money with. It's most certainly prime residential property and will undoubtedly increase in value over time. If inflation breaks loose, obviously, this type of real estate will soar in value, which is exactly what happened years ago in Southern California. Many who bought homes to live in and raise their families watched the values increase 20 times or more during the life of their mortgage.

Still, when all is said and done, modestly priced rental houses did about the same thing with respect to jumping values; but, of course, as their values shot up, they earned their owners steadily increasing rents. Naturally, the big difference between owning a home and owning rental houses is that tenants pay all the bills for the rentals. A home is an excellent investment for a family, but the houses you see on Snob Hill will seldom achieve cash flow, so long as there's a mortgage to pay. Even without one, the investment returns are not satisfactory for most investors.

Downtown Commercial

Cagey sellers will often attempt to market houses in the downtown areas using the proposition that zoning is commercial; therefore, the property is much more valuable because it has unlimited future potential. Do not fall for this! There's no such thing as unlimited potential and, although an older house in the downtown area may be an excellent rental property, it's still a fish in the wrong pond. Only speculators should buy for the future. Investors should always buy properties and pay for them on the basis of their earning capacity right now. I'm always happy to buy properties with commercial zoning, but I'll buy them only for the same price that I'd pay without the zoning.

Older Residential

This is the best location to buy for cash flow, the older residential sections surrounding the downtown area. Many of these older properties are functionally obsolete, with three bedrooms and one bath or single-car garages. Today's homeowners are shopping for two bathrooms and double garages, so investors won't find as much competition for these properties. Less competition means lower prices, since the owners have fewer selling opportunities. Many long-term owners are in the retirement age group, with mortgage-free properties. There are great possibilities for seller financing—*a real plus!*

Many of these older properties consist of several (multiple) units on one lot. Often there's a duplex in the back or a "granny" apartment above the garage. Renters are willing to pay top prices, because they're close to shopping, yet still able to enjoy the privacy of residential neighborhoods. There's also a bustling first-time homeowner market when these older properties are cleaned up, rejuvenated, and sold to young couples or families. This is the area where rundown properties can be fine-tuned and rented for cash flow or sold on easy terms to a first-time buyer.

Dense Slums

I do not recommend investing in slum areas, even if the property is dirt-cheap or half the regular price. They violate some or all of the five basic location questions listed earlier. The bottom line: when there are doubts about personal safety and marketing opportunities are very restricted, you're simply taking on too much risk, in my opinion. There are always exceptions, of course, but not very many.

Suburbia

This is the location most investors choose when they decide to acquire residential properties—the giant subdivisions and sprawling tracts of houses, most generally located a few miles from the city core, tied together by express lanes and freeways. Most subdivisions are occupied by middle-class America.

Buying middle-class houses in these locations makes perfect sense, but very little cash flow. The only opportunity to make any serious money is during inflationary periods or after holding the property 20 years or more until the mortgage is paid off. Few investors I know are able to quit their day jobs anytime soon when they invest in subdivision houses. To me, building a dependable cash flow income is first priority! Tract houses purchased at reasonable discount prices are an excellent long-term investment when properly managed. But, if you're in need of monthly income, this is not the investment to start with.

My suggestion is to concentrate on older residential areas first. Build a solid income and then gradually transition out to the suburbs, if that's what suits you.

There is no one-size-fits-all in the real estate investment business. You must choose how and where to invest, based on your skills and available funds.

The Myth of Location, Location, Location

When I first started investing in real estate, old-timers always used to tell me, "Son, there are only three things you've got to think about when you buy real estate—*location, location, and location*. If you do that," they told me, "you'll end up filthy rich someday."

But without money coming in every month, small-time investors like me would not likely last long enough to reap the benefits of choice locations. Not only that, but early on I didn't have the green stuff to outbid my competition, even if choice locations had been my first priority. Don't get me wrong here. I'm not knocking good locations. I'm merely suggesting that you may need to broaden your vision when it comes to buying income properties. After all, you invest in income properties for ... income!

How to Calculate What You Should Pay

To show how to calculate what you should pay, we'll use a six-unit apartment as our example. The property, however, can be two buildings, six detached houses, duplexes, or any combination. (One single-family house is not well suited for the GRM value measurement.) I'll use the numbers from the GRM chart earlier in this chapter to illustrate how you can put big bucks in your pocket, once you get the hang of this.

Let's assume we find a rundown fixer property in Redding that can be purchased for five times the gross rents. In Redding, as you can see by referring to the GRM chart, apartments valued at five times gross are renting for $325 per month. That means the purchase price will be approximately $117,000 (six apartments times $325 rents equals $1,950 per month, times 12 months for $23,400 annually, times a GRM of 5). As the chart shows, you can expect the property to be older, ugly, and junky with deadbeat tenants and lousy management. Heavy fix-up is needed— that's the challenge, but it's also an opportunity.

So, we buy and fix up the six-unit apartment. Rents are now $450 and the building is worth seven times gross rents. What's a small, two-point increase in the GRM worth? I think you'll be pleasantly surprised to find out that the new value is $226,000—almost double the price we paid. Also, the rents have increased $9,000 annually, which should put us well into positive cash flow! These are the kinds of numbers that turn poor fix-up investors into wealthy tycoons in the shortest time.

Don't Count the Pennies Doing Fix-Up

By the way, most beginners figure too close when determining how much to pay and how much profit is involved. You can't count the pennies in this business! That's much too close for estimating. It's quite common for rental property owners to get stiffed by tenants who don't pay rent. Deadbeats almost always come with the purchase of low GRM properties. Still, all in all, low GRM properties are by far the most profitable properties—when you know how to fix the problems.

The Value Difference Between Quality Buildings and Rundown Properties

Most folks are really surprised to learn how much difference in value there is between quality buildings and rundown properties. Playing with GRM numbers and figuring values will give you a good idea why fixers are such an attractive opportunity for profit-making.

There's a tremendous markup in value between a 5-GRM property and one that sells for 10 times the gross rents. I will tell you now, before you start trying to calculate the numbers, that fixing up or attempting to convert a 5-GRM property to a 10 is generally out of the question. That's far too much change to expect. You simply can't make a silk purse out of a sow's ear.

For one thing, the location of the property will limit you! For example, on the low-income side of the tracks, it's quite reasonable that the highest GRM sale you could ever expect to find would be seven times gross rents—but that's where the biggest profits are made. Conversely, in the Snob Hill section of town, you can't buy a piece of property for less than nine or 10 times gross, even if it needs some fixing up. Furthermore, if you insist on acquiring properties in a more upscale part of town, you'll certainly be pleased with the beautiful glossy pictures they make; however, you'll be a lot less happy with the money in your bank account! Folks who buy this type of property lust after prestige and those plaster of paris plaques you get from the Rotary Club!

Cheapest Property Will Likely Offer Best Selling Terms and Biggest Profits

It goes without saying, if you live in a trashy apartment, your rent will be a lot lower than if you live on Snob Hill. Naturally, apartment buildings on Snob Hill are worth much more than the ones at Scumbag Villa. Suppose there's a six-unit property for sale at both locations. Scumbag has a GRM value of five times gross and units rent for $325 each. (Refer to the GRM chart earlier in this chapter.) The indicated value would be six units times $325 rent equals $1,950 per month, which is $23,400 annually. Multiply this annual gross times a GRM of 5 for $117,000. Thus, each unit is worth $19,500. Doing exactly the same math for Snob Hill, which is valued at 10 times gross with rents of $525, you'll find that each unit is worth $63,000.

Let me ask you this question: Which property do you think is more profitable—the $19,500 apartments that earn $3,900 annually or the $63,000 units that earn $6,300 annually? Looking at rent returns, you'll see it takes five years at $3,900 to pay off the $19,500 units, but 10 years (twice as long) at $6,300 to pay off the $63,000 units. Although it's very important, the "quickest rent pay back" is only one consideration.

Which property owner would you imagine is likely to offer the best selling terms; which would require the smallest down payment and provide long-term seller financing? Which one would be the most motivated to sell? I'm sure you guessed right—it's the owner who is selling the property with the most potential for upgrading and improving the cash flow.

Baseball legend Yogi Berra used to say, "Baseball is 90% physical, but the other half is mental." Real estate investing is something like that! Buying income properties at the right price and terms is about 90% of a successful transaction The other half is doing all the things you need to do to make the property a profitable investment.

Jay's Super Simple Profit Strategy: Up the Rents and Improve the GRM

My investment strategy is super simple: fix up rundown properties enough to improve the GRM by at least two full points and increase the rents by 40%—and that's it! Increasing the rents and improving the GRM work together like two singers harmonizing. If one improves, it helps the other.

For example, in my town you couldn't rent your apartment that's worth five times gross for $450 per month. The value wouldn't be there. That's why $325 is the most you can get. Conversely, apartments that rent for $450 per month are worth much more than five times gross value when they sell. To be exact, they're worth seven times gross rents, as the GRM chart shows.

If you do it right, you can almost double the value of a property without waiting around for regular appreciation or the passage of time! My strategy is called *forced appreciation*, because I force the property value to increase by improving the GRM.

By increasing the GRM value by two points, I can automatically raise my rental income by 40%. Both improvements result from four basic actions on my part:

1. I clean up the ugly property to make it more attractive in appearance.
2. I evict the problem tenants and the deadbeats.
3. I fix up deferred maintenance and make improvements to attract better tenants.
4. I provide the proper management to operate the property more efficiently.

That's it! See how easy it is? In order to achieve maximum results with this strategy, it's necessary to purchase low-GRM properties—maybe not the very bottom, but as near the bottom as your fix-up skills will allow. Naturally, your skills will improve with each new purchase and, eventually, you'll end up just like me. *No property is too bad, no problem is too tough, if the price and terms are low enough.*

There's a Time to Sell and a Time to Buy

Investing in real estate the way I do it—that is, buying fixer houses and so forth—will not be a profitable venture unless you can properly time your acquisitions and sales. Proper timing is worth big bucks!

For example, today in Southern California, three-bedroom houses that once sold for $375,000 might be a tough sale at $325,000! Some are down by $100,000 in areas where big defense contractors have laid off thousands of employees. The point is, you shouldn't plan on selling when prices are down. Obviously, if you don't sell now, you will need to rent your properties until the market improves.

Real Estate Prices Go Up and Down

The real estate market is cyclical! It goes up and down, like a yo-yo, and it always has! A 20% swing in the cycle can be worth as much as $40,000. That's because, in a seller's market, $100,000 properties can often be sold for $120,000. This happens when many buyers are chasing too few properties. Conversely, the same properties can be acquired for $80,000 when times are tough and buyers are scarce. It goes without saying that owners who tailor their investment plan (buying and selling) to match the real estate cycles can greatly benefit their bank accounts.

I have long supported the proposition that mom-and-pop investors must learn good landlording skills in order to earn serious real estate profits. When the market is down, you want paying tenants renting your houses. Paying tenants will afford you the luxury of continuous income while you ride out the low cycles. With income, you can patiently wait to time your sales properly. Many investors continue to ignore this wisdom, hoping to earn big profits, regardless of what real estate cycle they are in! This strategy, if you can call it one, is akin to driving your car through stop signs everyday, hoping that no other driver will be coming the other way.

Rely on Cash Flow, Not Speculation About the Future

Most new investors spend far too much time trying to figure out the future of properties they're interested in buying. This is actually unproductive for novice buyers who have very limited knowledge about real estate growth and development.

I've purchased some dandy properties with future commercial zoning, which I thought would pay off big-time, like slot machines, whenever development came my way. Development came all right—but on the opposite side of town. My rental houses are still just sitting there doing the same thing they've been doing for years—producing cash flow!

When I look back at all the properties I've acquired over the years, it occurs to me that picking locations has not been my greatest strength. It's not that I don't have some good locations; I do. But, to be perfectly honest, they weren't so hot when I bought the property. What happened in several cases was that new development sprang up around my older houses, creating much more desirable surroundings. There is simply no way I could have predicted this would happen when I bought them 10 or 15 years ago.

As I look back over 20 years or so, the most important thing I've ever accomplished with my real estate holdings was to buy them so they would pay me money every month—producing cash flow!

Overpaying—The Deadliest Investor Sin

Overpaying for income properties is probably the biggest single mistake an investor can make—especially investors who lack sufficient knowledge to recuperate from such an error! It's not just new investors or first-time buyers who make this mistake. Many buyers with years of experience fall victim to overpaying when they purchase properties in unfamiliar territory. It's absolutely essential to heed the old adage about buying wholesale and selling at retail if you intend to make any serious money in real estate.

Here's the bottom line—you can't expect to make money in real estate unless you learn to pick out *bargains* and buy them at *wholesale prices*. You must lock in profits and future equity buildup at the time you buy. Learning to master this technique is not optional.

Let's suppose you're just starting out, like many others who seek my advice. You don't have much money, knowledge, or experience. However, you're sold on the idea that investing in real estate will make you wealthy and you're very excited. You can't wait to get your feet wet, so you race out and find a seller who will accept no down payment or very little cash. However, in your haste, you forget what I told you about the price—you pay the seller retail. That's not what you should do. That's what dummies do!

If you do start out paying retail, chances are you'll never make a profit on the deal. To make matters worse, you'll most likely have a negative cash flow every month. Plus, if you're married, it will certainly put a strain on that relationship. The worst mistake income property buyers make, in my judgment, is buying income property that won't produce income. Overpaying is like a fatal disease for many investors; but, unlike other fatal diseases, science is not working on a cure for this one.

Almost every investor I know has paid too much for income properties. It happens quite frequently when we first start out. There is almost no defense against paying too much as least once or twice. I've done it more times than I care to admit. However, in my case, buying fix-up properties allowed me to add value and improve the income stream more quickly than if I had overpaid for average non-fixer properties. By fixing and adding value to properties, I've always been able to recover from my overpaying errors much faster.

Investing Long Term for Future Growth

Life is full of compromises—and it's the same way for investing! I'll be the first one to agree that beautiful properties in top locations will increase more in value over the long haul. The sacrifice, of course, is that these same properties will pay you nothing while you wait!

You can overcome the problem by adopting a strategy to acquire two different kinds of properties. Why not start out with fixer-type properties that can provide a solid monthly income? You may call this Phase One. Phase Two can be a gradual transition into nicer properties, with better long-term profit potential. However, do this only after you've secured the money to buy groceries.

Each type of property has good and bad features. For example, small rental houses can earn twice as much net income as larger homes. Repairs and fix-ups are much more economical in small, not so perfect houses. Rough tenants can do far less damage in smaller units that are not equipped with modern amenities like many of the larger and newer houses.

For most of us, it makes more sense to buy cash flow properties with uncertain futures than to acquire high-potential properties without enough cash flow to operate them right now.

The top three reasons for owning and operating income properties are *income, income, and income.* Everything else starts with number four.

9

Thoroughly Analyze the Deal Before Making an Offer

Throughout this book, I will refer to average costs plus several rules of thumb I use to determine whether a property is a good candidate to consider purchasing. The ones I most commonly use are *gross rent multipliers* (see previous chapter), *cost per unit*, and *annual rent returns*. One of the most important worksheets you'll use is the *income property analysis form*. I always use the form to help uncover the answers in an important financial examination of a property.

Study the Numbers and Keep It Simple

Everyone who knows me or seeks my advice understands rather quickly how strongly I feel about doing the basics. That means buying properties that will start returning profits before very long.

I determine this by studying all the dollar numbers before I make the purchase. Most of my longhand studies are done on yellow legal pads. They usually take the form of a sketch with a bunch of dollar numbers plotted in year by year. I want to visualize clearly, in picture form, how much money I'll be putting into the deal to start (down payment). Next, I figure how much more for fix-up and what my monthly fixed costs of operations will be when I'm done. After that, I calculate my expected income, month by month, usually for five or 10 years, or sometimes to a predetermined sale date.

My yellow pad studies are purposely simple. I'm interested only in cash returns. The two questions I ask myself are "Will I make profits on this deal if I spend X number of dollars?" and "When do I get to have those profits in my hand?" That's what most investors need to know.

Keep it simple and keep it basic. You don't need to know the *internal rate of return* (IRR) on a duplex to make a profit. You're far better off knowing if both toilets flush. Later on when the money rolls in, let your accountant explain about the IRR. Perhaps he or she might even agree to do your plumbing when not doing the books.

Unit Cost and Rent-to-Value Ratios: How to Determine if a Property Will Be Profitable

As I've already told you, fixers can be purchased for substantially less than comparably sized properties in good condition. After rehabilitation, however, fixers will normally rent for almost the same monthly rates as the better properties. By converting this information into numbers, it becomes easy to determine future profits for a property.

There are two key numbers I consider to be most important because they will tell me the expected *cash flow* and *profitability* of a property. And by the way, income property is supposed to provide cash flow regardless of what your real estate professional tells you about the extra tax breaks you'll receive. As far as I'm concerned, tax benefits are merely a bonus for investing in real estate.

The first number I'm always concerned about is the *unit cost*. How much will it cost to purchase and rehabilitate each house or apartment? Let's say I purchase a four-unit property for $72,000. That means I'll pay $18,000 per unit. Next, I estimate it will cost $6,000 each to rehabilitate the units. My total unit cost will be $24,000 when my fix-up work is completed.

The second important number has to do with rental income return. I call it *rent-to-value ratio*. If you don't remember some of the other things I tell you here, try not to forget about this part. It's very important to your financial future, because it's the difference between having cash flow and not—ultimately, between success and failure. The rent-to-value ratio is a number that expresses the percentage of monthly rent as related to the unit cost or my assigned value to the property.

For example, if I own an apartment that rents for $300 per month and the apartment has my assigned value or unit cost of $24,000, then the rent-to-value ratio would be expressed as 1.25%. To arrive at that number, you divide the rent by the unit cost ($300 ÷ $24,000 = 0.0125) and then move the decimal two places right.

My goal is to achieve a minimum ratio of 1.25, but when you really get the hang of this stuff, 2.0 and more is well within your reach. It's also lots more fun going to the bank.

Jay's Income Property Analysis Form

The income property analysis form helps me discover many easy-to-overlook property expenses. It also provides an excellent tool for negotiating with sellers. I consider the negotiating value of the form just as important as its use in assessing the income and expense data for a property. Even though the form is quite simple to use and filling in the blanks shouldn't require an MBA degree, it's still easy to overlook important information, believe me. Therefore, I'll guide you, line by line, and explain my reasoning, as well as how I came up with the numbers. The example I'm using is an actual case history for an eight-unit property I negotiated to purchase several years ago. Let's call the property "Jay's Rundown Houses," Elm Street. (A blank copy of my income property analysis form can be found in the Appendix.)

The information I'll need is the actual *income* and *expenses* that will transfer to me if I should purchase the property. Notice that the income and expense data is shown on a monthly basis.

Line No. 1—Total Gross Income. This figure is the total income from all sources, including rents, laundry, storage, or whatever else is earned by the property when it's fully rented. That is, 100% of all the income.

Line No. 2—Vacancy Allowance. Allow a minimum of 5% of total gross income for this line, even if the units are 100% rented at the time of purchase. The reason is that no rental property stays 100% rented all the time. If the seller suggests it does, request a copy of his or her tax forms, 1040 Schedule E, for the past two years. Simply divide the income each year by 12 to establish the average monthly income reported to Uncle Sam. This check proves very enlightening to most buyers.

Line No. 3—Uncollectable or Credit Losses. Allow a minimum of 5% of total gross income for this line. Generally it's more for rundown properties, like I purchase, because people problems are likely to be present with property problems. This line reflects losses from tenants who skip out without paying and evicted tenants who are forced to leave after a judgment. Chances of collecting any money from them are slim to none.

It's difficult to argue against vacancies (Line 2) and credit losses (Line 3). That's because all rental properties have vacancies from time to time and tenants who don't pay rent for one reason or another. The combined total of 10% for both of these occurrences is not the least bit exaggerated. Some properties consistently operate at much higher losses.

Line No. 4—Net Rental Income. This line represents the actual net amount of money you have left to operate the property—sometimes referred to as *gross operating income*. It's the actual money you get to hold in your hand each month.

Now let's talk about all those nasty expenses.

Line No. 5—Taxes, Real Property. This line needs to show what the property taxes will be per month on the day you acquire the property. First, you'll need to estimate approximately what you think you'll end up paying for the property, then apply your local county tax rate to the estimate. For example, for the Elm Street houses, I anticipate paying approximately $195,000. My county taxes will be slightly over 1% of that. $195,000 times 1% equals $1,950 in annual taxes. This amount divided by 12 months equals $162.50 (rounded to $165) per month.

In California, the seller may have been enjoying low property taxes if he or she has owned the property for a length of time. However, because of Proposition 13, the purchaser's taxes will immediately jump to 1% of the selling price as soon as the property transfers title. Don't use the seller's lower tax bill when computing your expenses on this line.

It's easy to check out property taxes. To determine the tax expense, call the tax assessor's office. Ask what the taxes will be if you purchase a property for $195,000. Don't tell them the exact location of the property; just the dollar amount and the proposed purchase date will be enough.

Line No. 6—Fire and Liability Insurance. You must apply the same logic on this line as for Line 5 taxes. Ask yourself, "What will insurance cost me based on the condition of the property and the amount of fire and liability coverage I will need for proper protection?" Some sellers I've bought properties from have been grossly underinsured because it's cheaper.

Fire policies are based on footage construction costs to rebuild the property in case you suffer a loss. If actual construction costs are 60¢ per square foot in your area and you decide to take over or assume the seller's policy calculated at 30¢ per foot, you'll quickly become stuck if you ever suffer a loss. Line 6 should be the monthly amount for insurance that provides you with adequate protection if you become the new property owner. Don't be caught underinsured after the fire trucks leave.

To find out the insurance cost, call an agent and ask him or her to give you a "quickie" cost estimate for a policy covering both fire and liability on the proposed purchase. The agent will need to know the property address, but he or she needn't go inside the houses to give you a ballpark figure. Provide the agent with the approximate square footage of each unit and an estimate of the age.

Line No. 7—Management. I personally charge 10% for my management services because I'm worth it! Professional managers charge anywhere from 5% to 10% for the job. At any rate, properties don't manage themselves. People must do it and, obviously, it costs money. It's a very legitimate property expense.

Here's the problem you will always encounter when you negotiate to buy properties from owners who do their own management. They don't understand this expense and will always ask, "Why are you showing a property management expense of $250? Aren't you planning on managing the property yourself?"

I always tell them, "Yes, but I don't plan on doing it for nothing."

They usually respond, "We do our own management and we don't take a fee."

I ask, "Are you trying to tell me you will manage property for nothing? If you are, I'd be happy to let you continue managing for me at the same price."

Managing property and tenants is not an easy job and whoever does it should receive compensation. I allow 10% on this line. However, that also includes legal and accounting, too. I do my own evictions when necessary. That's a bargain.

Line No. 8—Maintenance. I always allow at least 5% for maintenance expenses. It might be a bit less for newer properties, but it could go higher for older houses and apartments. Maintenance is the routine upkeep that's necessary to keep the property in good condition, so that it can continue to earn income. Maintenance does not necessarily improve the property. It merely keeps it running in proper order and at the same level.

Line No. 9—Repairs. When the doorknob falls off, you must put it back on. That's a repair. When the roof leaks and causes damage to the ceiling plasterboard, you must repair the roof and then the ceiling. It's important to remember that all properties will need repairs because things fall off and things break. Obviously, older properties will require more repairs. I always allow a very minimum of 5% for older houses, but 10% is not unreasonable.

Line No. 10—Utilities Paid by Owner. It will pay you to research and verify which utilities the owner pays. Sellers tend to state their expenses on the low side. Sometimes they'll produce receipts for heating bills in the summer months. Quite often they will group all their utility expenses and give you an estimate like $100 per month for everything. What you need to know is whether or not each house or apartment unit has its own separate meters for gas and electric service. Quite often apartments will have a separate owner's meter for the laundry room and exterior lighting for porches, hallways, and parking areas.

Utility companies will furnish printouts of electric, gas, and water usage. The owner of record is the only person who can obtain this information. My advice is to ask the seller to provide you printouts for the past 12 months of service so you can average out the costs for a full year. As a general rule, apartment owners must pay water, sewer, and garbage service.

The key here is to check everything out for yourself. You don't want any surprises after you purchase the property. Again, the most important thing to verify is if each house or apartment has its own separate meter, meaning that the tenants pay for their own utility services.

Line No. 11—Total Expenses. This line is the addition of lines 5 through 10. If the total of this line is more than 40% of line 1, reevaluate your purchase offer to make sure you are not overpaying for the property.

Line No. 12—Operating Income. This line is the amount of money that's left to pay the mortgage payments (debt service) after all operating expenses are paid.

Lines No. 13 and 13A—Mortgage Balances and Payments. Show each of the existing mortgages, monthly payments, and dates when each mortgage will be paid off (due dates). Total lines 13 and 13A—remember: these are totals for just the existing mortgages on the property, before you buy it.

Line No. 14—Monthly Cash Flow Available. Subtract line 13A from line 12. This is the amount of money you'll have left each month after paying all expenses and all existing mortgage payments. It's the cash flow available to pay the remaining balance of the seller's equity—in this example $29,600.

In this particular transaction, I propose to pay the seller a $20,000 down payment and assume both existing mortgages (a total of $145,400). The balance I will still owe the seller for his unpaid equity is $29,600. As you can see, on line 14, $66 is the amount of cash flow I'll have left each month to pay the seller's equity.

Proposed purchase price:	$195,000
Proposed cash down payment:	20,000
Mortgages (two) buyer assumes:	145,400
Balance of seller equity:	29,600
Total:	$195,000

Line No.	Income Data (Monthly)		Per Month
1	Total Gross Income (Present)		$2,500
2	Vacancy Allowance Min. 5% LN-1 (Attach copy of 1040 Schedule E or provide past 12 months income statement for verification)		$125
3	Uncollectable or Credit Losses (Rents due but not collected)		$125
4	Net Rental Income		$2,250
Expense Data (Monthly)			
5	Taxes, Real Property		$165
6	Fire and Liability Insurance		$150
7	Management, Allow Min. 5%		$250
8	Maintenance		$175
9	Repairs		$125
10	Utilities Paid by Owner (Monthly) Electricity Water Sewer Gas Garbage Cable TV Total	$0 $25 $0 $0 $51 $0 $76	$76
11	Total Expenses		$941
12	Operating Income (Line 4 – Line 11)		$1,309

Existing Mortgage Debt			Monthly Payment	Due Mo/Yr
	1st Bal. Due	$102,800	$806	Amortized (2011)
	2nd Bal. Due	$42,600	$437	Bal. Due (2005)
	3rd Bal. Due	0		
	4th Bal. Due	0		

Figure 9-1. Income property analysis form (Continued on the next page)

	5th Bal. Due	0		
13	Totals	$145,400 (13A)	$1,243	
14	Monthly Cash Flow Available (Ln 12 – 13A) (Positive or Negative)			$66

Note: Line 14 shows available funds to service new mortgage debt from operation of property.

Remarks: All lines must be completed for proper analysis. Enter the actual amount on each line or 0.

Figure 9-1. (Completed)

The Basis for Negotiating a Purchase

Armed with a properly filled out income property analysis form, your negotiations will be much more objective. That's because they will be based on accurate and reasonable projections.

All income should be verified by you and the seller. This can be done using current rent receipts or last year's tax return (1040 Schedule E). Either way, both parties can establish and agree on the figures.

The Most Controversial Expenses

Management, maintenance, and repairs are the expenses most frequently argued by sellers. Again, I ask for income tax records to substantiate the expenses. Two full years of 1040 Schedule E tax returns will do the job. I have never received tax returns that show the same numbers as given to me by the seller or his or her agent. In almost every case, the income figures shown on the tax returns are lower and, for some odd reason, the expenses are always much higher. I think it's something like the unexplained difference between the miles people drive, as stated on their automobile insurance forms, and the mileage they report for the very same period on their 1040 tax forms. Based on the auto insurance mileage, it would seem that many cars will never wear out; but for the purpose of tax deductions, they travel more miles than a Greyhound bus.

Always Get a Second Opinion

Doctors will often send their patients out for a second opinion, so why not get one for your real estate deals? My good friend and skilled investor, John Schaub, says, "The day you buy an investment property, you should be able to sit down with your wife/husband or someone and explain, in detail, exactly how you will make your profit from start to finish."

I find John's excellent advice is right on the money. I did not follow that same advice when I started investing and I always had problems making my houses' cash flow. My two biggest problems were overestimating net income and paying too much.

I've found that wives, husbands, and friends can always spot the things that are wrong with most plans. Write down your profit numbers and show them. Explain how much income you'll be taking in every month from rents. Then, using conservative appreciation numbers, estimate the profits you'll make when you sell 10 or 15 years from now. See if anyone else agrees with you. You don't have to make this exercise complicated. It's only a checkpoint, but it makes you prove your case—*it's very objective.* Outsiders—people other than you—are seldom as optimistic as you might be. This is especially true when you must explain to your spouse why you're investing the vacation money on rundown ugly houses instead of a family trip to Disneyland!

10

Negotiating Deals That Earn Big Profits

Real Profits Don't Come from Playing Games

Negotiating is sometimes nothing more than game playing. It's done by appliance dealers, horse traders, and real estate agents. It's most often like a ritual and sometimes it's not very effective.

Here's how it typically works. Let's say you ask your real estate agent the price for a particular property and he tells you the seller wants $100,000. You ask, "What do you think he'll take?" Your agent says, "Let's offer $85,000 and see how he responds." The seller counters with $95,000, to which you quickly bounce back with $92,500. The seller says, "OK, where do I sign?"

When it happens fast like this, you always think you paid too much. Did you? Negotiating isn't worth all the effort, unless you first know exactly what you need. Otherwise, it's only game-playing.

Develop the Right Approach

One of the best methods for negotiating is what I call the "Columbo

Technique." Lieutenant Columbo is the cigar-smoking detective on TV with the wrinkled raincoat. He doesn't appear smart enough to ever solve a homicide case, yet he always does.

If you get the opportunity, watch Columbo solve a mystery. Observe how he does it. Let me suggest things to watch for. First of all, you should observe that Columbo is never intimidating or threatening. He never appears to be competing with anyone, yet in his own special way he quietly and forcefully moves directly toward his goal, which of course, is solving the homicide.

Real estate investors can negotiate in a very similar fashion, with equally successful results. You'll notice that Columbo always has a specific reason for everything he does. His questions are always supported by clues or information he develops. His attitude is courteous and he often seems apologetic when he needs to ask the tough personal questions. In fact, most people even go out of their way to cooperate with him because he's courteous and seems genuinely concerned about their needs. Notice how Columbo steadily pressures villains into accepting surrender without putting up much of a fight. (I've never seen Columbo use a gun.) The reason is because he develops the facts and then confronts his suspect with hard, indisputable evidence, which makes a conclusion very obvious. He does it all without allowing his personal emotions to interfere.

His success in solving mysteries is in large part because he listens. Columbo asks short questions, then waits for long answers or explanations. That's a very effective method for learning about other people and it's just as true in real estate negotiating as it is solving homicide cases.

Practicing Columbo's Winning Ways Can Help You

So, what can you learn from Columbo about negotiating to buy real estate?

First, before you start arbitrarily changing or negotiating terms and/or conditions, make sure you can show the reasons why. If you can't, they're probably not valid; worst of all, proceeding without being able to show why can severely damage your credibility. You don't need that, believe me.

Second, it's very important to listen to the other side. You can answer yes or no if you train yourself, but listening to others will provide you a wealth of knowledge and information that will help you structure offers or counteroffers. People love to talk. If you're a good listener, you'll be very popular with most folks. Columbo is very good at this. In fact, suspects often tell him enough to hang themselves. This makes his job much easier, wouldn't you say?

Third, never get emotional. Don't be critical and, above all, never talk down to anyone. If you humiliate, embarrass, or ridicule, you'll lose all chances for negotiating a winning deal. Even sellers who are about to lose their shirts won't do business with someone who intimidates or tries to overpower them. Courtesy and understanding are two of the most powerful tools in your "negotiating kit." Use them generously; they'll pay big dividends. Once again, Columbo is a master at this.

Winning Over the Seller Leads to Winning Negotiations

Consider the following exchange between a seller (owner) and a potential buyer, who were previously strangers.

Seller: Mr. Buyer, why are you offering me 25% less than my asking price?

Buyer: Well, sir, the reason is that I know sellers always mark up their sale price because they expect offers to be lower! Obviously, you can still accept my offer because I think it's much closer to the real value of your property.

If you own a nice piece of property (your opinion) and you have worked very hard to fix it up and make it look attractive and then some buyer, a total stranger to you, tells you your property is worth 25% less than your asking price, what would you immediately think of him as a person? Chances are, your answer is not printable in this book. No one likes to be told their property is worth less than they think—even if it's the truth. That's human nature. You hurt their feelings and that hurts your negotiations.

Columbo never tells his suspects anything that would alienate them or stop the flow of information between them. He wins without shouting matches, embarrassing others, or making enemies along the way. These are excellent skills for any negotiator.

Don't Play Games if You Want Real Benefits

Arbitrarily cutting the asking price is *game-playing*, especially for the reason given above. Obviously, if the price is truly too high, it needs cutting. However, you should have a justifiable reason to cut it. If you have done your homework and if you can reasonably demonstrate why your lower purchase price offer has merit, fine. Otherwise, it probably does not.

When your offer is considerably less than the asking price and you can't explain why, it becomes very difficult to keep negotiations on a productive level. It's sort of like saying to the seller, "You really don't know what your property is worth, but I do!" If you mean it that way, you need to be in a position to tell the seller why.

I like to consider the terms I'm negotiating as if each one is a bullet in my gun and I have only so many shots. If I shoot at everything—that is, I attempt to change everything in the contract to suit myself, like asking for a lower selling price, smaller payments, a reduced interest rate, a longer mortgage term, less cash down, and even a different closing date—I should ask myself, "Am I shooting at the right targets or am I just wasting my shots, hoping to hit everything I can?"

Don't win the negotiations and lose the bargain. I've known buyers who have done quite well at persuading sellers to reduce their asking price, only to find out later that the price was still too high. If negotiating is to serve a valid purpose, that purpose must be to make the deal workable for everyone. It should not be a contest to determine who can have his or her way the most; otherwise, you'll end up like the little Boy Scout who cut the rope three times—and it was still too short.

The Three Most Important Buyer Objectives

Here's some advice you should pay particular attention to. It's worth big bucks to every small-time real estate investor. In fact, if you do this right, you can quickly move up the financial ladder from "small-time investor" to "big-time, cash-flow tycoon."

These are the three most important items you'll ever negotiate for:

- The purchase price
- The amount of debt service (monthly mortgage payment)

• The length of time to pay the debt

You can give everything else away if you have to, but you must get these three items within an acceptable range.

Obviously, financial circumstances for every buyer will be somewhat different, so there can be a little variation in the numbers. I'll show you how this variation might work for you as we discuss gathering income and expense data.

Your Chief Negotiating Tool

My chief negotiating tool is my *income property analysis form*. It's a simple form that develops a financial picture of the property I wish to purchase. It shows the financial situation of the property and approximately how much it will cost to operate the property. It also helps eliminate much of the emotion from negotiations. (The previous chapter explains this.)

Often, a seller will argue that he or she pays only $X each month for expenses. But, you're certain that the numbers are short or his or her memory is fuzzy, a common seller affliction. When the analysis form is filled out properly, with the seller's assistance, it's difficult to argue the facts. Generally, the form tends to jog a forgetful seller's memory.

It's Always Best to Let the Seller Participate

I always ask the seller to help me gather the information I need to fill in the blanks on my income property analysis form. After all, the seller should know better than anyone, since he or she operates the property and pays the bills.

The object of working closely (negotiating) with a seller, using a tool like my income property analysis form, is to develop hard evidence, the written proof of income and expense data. By assembling all the financial numbers on a single, one-page form, in an easy-to-read format, you have a very convincing tool for seriously negotiating the three most important buyer objectives—the right price, the right amount of debt service, and the right length of time to pay the debt.

Just as Columbo does, you must verify all information.

My experience has been that sellers will generally provide accurate information about the gross income, but beyond that they become forgetful. For example, when we reach line 2 of the form, "Vacancy Allowance," hardly any sellers will admit to having vacancies. When they do, they claim vacancies are rare. This usually changes after I ask to see their Tax Form 1040 (Schedule E) for the past year. Hardly any property owners give the IRS the same dollar numbers they give to me.

No One Reports Too Much Income to the IRS

It's quite common for investment property owners to be overly optimistic about their net rental income numbers. For example, the income property analysis form (Fixer Jay's Six Ugly Houses, which follows at the end of this chapter) shows a total gross income of $2,100 per month. If the seller's tax return, Schedule E, shows property rents of only $20,000 for the taxable year, my question is "What happened to the $5,200?" My guess is vacancies and credit losses (deadbeat tenants). Obviously, transitioning properties might have gone through rent increases since the last tax filing; however, that's fairly easy to determine.

The important point I'm making here is that investors should never allow less than 5% for vacancy loss or less than 5% for uncollected rents (deadbeats and skips). With rundown income properties, the percentages are often much higher.

Verify the Actual Expenses

I have found what works best is to have the seller provide proof of all expenses. The checkbook register or expense journals will generally provide this information. Expenses that need to be verified are costs for utilities, management fees (if managed by someone other than the owner), repairs, maintenance, and property insurance. I also want to see the county tax statements. In California, taxes are adjusted to approximately 1% of the sale price when a property is transferred (sold).

Expenses the Seller Is Likely to Argue

As I've mentioned in the last chapter, property sellers have told me there are no management fees or maintenance and repair expenses on this property.

"I do it all myself," they say. My typical response is "Will you continue doing it, for the same price, after I become the new owner?" I've never had a single taker yet.

Then I ask, "How much would you charge me to manage the property, if I buy it from you?" No one has ever told me less than 10%. Most won't take the job at any price. After a short discussion, they agree that my 5% management fee allowance is, indeed, very reasonable. After all, who will do it for less?

No one has ever developed a method for doing repairs and maintenance without spending money. When things break, it costs dollars to fix them. Painting, patching roof leaks, yard work, cleaning carpets, and patching walls are just a few of the maintenance and repair activities necessary to keep income properties doing what they're supposed to do—generating income. At the very least, you'll spend ten cents out of every rent dollar you collect for maintaining the property.

Don't include capital items like replacing carpets, coolers, and roofs, as that's not maintenance or repair. Repair expenses—things like fixing broken doorknobs, cracked toilets, and broken windows—will cost you approximately 5%.

Remember: these are the numbers I use on my income property analysis form. I consider these bare minimums. I rarely have any difficulty convincing sellers. Sometimes their own expense records, Tax Form 1040 Schedule E, will show higher numbers than my estimates.

Favorite Concessions for Buyers to Ask For

When homeowners become more motivated to sell because of problems with tenants or for personal reasons (see Chapter 5 for more on common reasons that motivate sellers), it's much easier for you to tighten up the deal. ("Tightening up" means asking for more concessions.) Owners will give maximum concessions to buyers who can both fix up junky, rundown properties and handle deadbeat tenants. Not everyone can, and even fewer are willing, so there's a strong demand for talented problem-solvers.

It's the same principle used by the famous oil well firefighter, Paul (Red) Adair. He requested and received astronomical sums of money for capping gas fire blowouts on oil wells, simply because he did it very well and because there were only a few others who even wanted the job.

You may recall it was Adair who was summoned to the North Sea to extinguish the raging fire and to plug leaks at the world's largest oil field disaster—the Piper Alpha Platform explosion that killed 166 men. It was also Adair who was hired to cap the flaming oil wells in Iraq, set purposely on fire by Saddam Hussein during the Gulf War. Do you suppose the folks asking for help were very concerned about Adair's fee schedule?

In the same way, many sellers with problem properties will be motivated to work out a good deal for someone who can relieve them of their problems. Here are several of my favorite *tighten-uppers*:

- Deferred mortgage payments until property is fixed up or until all deadbeat tenants are evicted (generally no mortgage payments for six months).
- Longer mortgage terms with less interest. Also, ask for delayed payments on owner carryback notes. Often you can get motivated owners to wait several years. This is a great way to improve operating cash flow when you acquire a property.
- Larger discounts on the purchase price, especially when deadbeat tenants occupy junker, rundown properties. Let the bikers help you buy cheap.

Typical Negotiations Work Like This

In my town, owners will expect to sell an older income property, like the Six Ugly Houses example in this chapter, for about seven times the gross income ($2,100 per month times 12 months equals $25,200, times seven for an estimated value of $176,400). Generally, they won't sell for a lower amount unless circumstances are unusual.

To find the actual dollar amount left each month to satisfy any new debt obligation for this example, take a look at line 14 of the income property analysis form. There are two existing mortgage payments totaling $795 per month (line 13A). The total mortgage balance is $100,000. Line 14 indicates that I would have $240 to pay any additional costs for the property.

Let's say I'm willing to give the seller a note or mortgage with payments of $240 per month (all that's left over); however, at 10% interest, the note could only be for $28,800 (10% times $28,800 equals $2,880, divided by 12 equals $240). If I agree to that and if the owner insists on a selling price of seven times gross ($176,400), I would need to come up with a $47,600 cash down payment ($100,000 existing mortgage debt, plus $28,800 new seller carryback note, plus $47,600 cash down equals $176,400).

A 10% down payment is generally the acceptable amount for older income properties. It's also about all I am willing to pay down for ugly fix-up properties. So, in this case, I might offer $175,000, with $20,000 cash down, and ask the seller to carry back a note for $55,000, payable at $250 per month (interest only) for a term of 10 years minimum. (I would try for 20 years.)

If the seller says $250 per month is not enough payment for his $55,000 note, I would ask him, "Where do you expect me to find the extra money? After all, I'll be paying you $10 more per month than the property is earning right now. Are you asking me to reach into my pocket every month to pay you more money than the property earns, when I've just paid you $20,000 cash for the privilege of owning the property?"

That's a hard question for sellers to answer. They look at the property analysis form, then they stare at the $240 on line 14. They might mumble something like "Maybe you won't have too many vacancies or credit losses. That would give you 10% more income" or "Perhaps you would consider giving up your 5% management fee. That's $105 per month" or maybe even "15% for maintenance and repairs? That really sounds too high."

The real value of my form is that when you and the seller have taken the extra time to agree on expenses and to fill out each line together as a joint effort, it's extremely difficult for the seller to go back and ask to undo the results. The seller doesn't like the low payments on his carryback financing, but he can accept them much more easily when the form shows that $240 is all that's available to pay him.

Don't talk about interest rates; discuss only how much money is available to pay him or her. Most sellers are willing to take back low interest notes (mortgages) as opposed to reducing their selling price. I've found that it's very difficult to get a lower sales price and offer only a 10% down payment. The risk of losing a good income property is much greater when cutting the price than when negotiating the seller into a "soggy note" or mortgage. ("Soggy" means a low interest rate or weak terms.)

Successful Negotiations Put Money in Your Pocket

If you are a do-it-yourself operator (you manage and do maintenance and repairs) and if you can negotiate a deal similar to what we've been discussing, you'll be in great shape. You'll own a property that has cash flow when you buy it or shortly thereafter.

Your profits will be enhanced by rent increases, and by minimizing vacancies and rent losses. Don't forget the monthly 15% maintenance and repair allowance ($315 total in our example): 30% of that ($95) will go for buying materials and 70% ($220) is labor—that's you! When and if you sell, the soggy seller carryback mortgage you've negotiated will allow you to sell for a premium price. Good financing is worth extra bucks because you can sell with good terms to the next person.

Line No.	Income Data (Monthly)	Per Month
1	Total Gross Income (Present)	$2,100
2	Vacancy Allowance Min. 5% LN-1 (Attach copy of 1040 Schedule E or provide past 12 months income statement for verification)	$105
3	Uncollectable or Credit Losses (Rents due but not collected)	$150
4	Net Rental Income	$1,890
	Expense Data (Monthly)	
5	Taxes, Real Property	$175
6	Fire and Liability Insurance	$100
7	Management, Allow Min. 5%	$105
8	Maintenance	$210

Figure 10-1. Income property analysis form (Continued on the next page)

9	Repairs			$105
10	Utilities Paid by Owner (Monthly)			$160
	Electricity		$25	
	Water		$80	
	Sewer		$0	
	Gas		$0	
	Garbage		$55	
	Cable TV		$0	
	Total		$160	
11	Total Expenses			$855
12	Operating Income (Line 4 − Line 11)			$1,035

Existing Mortgage Debt				
			Monthly Payment	Due Mo/Yr
	1st Bal. Due	$75,600	$600	Fully Amortized
	2nd Bal. Due	$24,400	$195	6.5 yrs, then all due
	3rd Bal. Due	0		
	4th Bal. Due	0		
	5th Bal. Due	0		
13	Totals	$100,000 (13A)	$795	
14	Monthly Cash Flow Available (Ln 12 − 13A) (Positive or Negative)			$240

Note: Line 14 shows available funds to service new mortgage debt from operation of property.
Remarks: All lines must be completed for proper analysis. Enter the actual amount on each line or 0.

Figure 10-1. (Completed)

11

Jay's Money-maker Foo-Foo Fix-Up Strategy: What to Fix and What to Leave Alone

Don't Fix Things That Don't Pay You Back

In order to be a successful fix-up investor (that means making money at it), you must fix only things that need fixing. Ask yourself, "Does it really need doing?" I believe most improvements should be justified on the basis of paying for themselves. I expect the payments to come from higher rents or bigger profits as my reward for doing the work. Your goal should be to get the largest return for each fix-up dollar you spend.

It's important to separate your "pet ideas" from proven moneymaking fix-up work! I'm not talking about repairs here; obviously, things that don't work must be fixed. I'm talking about things like moving walls around, adding rooms, making windows bigger, and ripping out and installing new kitchen cabinets. Remodelers do these things, but it's not cost-effective to do them in the fix-up business. The important thing to remember is that almost everything fix-up investors do should add cash value to the property, either for buyers or renters. Larger rooms and newer cabinets will seldom matter much when it comes to getting higher prices from your customer.

Remodelers Spend Too Much Money Fixing

Many fix-up investors haven't quite figured out the difference among three activities—*renovating*, *fixing*, and *remodeling*. Perhaps renovating and fixing are similar, like distant cousins; however, investors who remodel fixer-type properties can easily end up working their tails off for very little profits and sometimes even big losses. The problem is, remodelers change too many things that don't need to be changed. For some reason, remodelers have a fierce passion to make things better, from their personal point of view, with almost total disregard for what it costs. That's like saying, "I might as well spend my whole paycheck tonight and get it over with, so I don't have to worry about spending it later on."

Most Buyers and Renters Lack Vision

You must understand that most buyers and renters want clean, attractive houses and apartments to buy and/or live in. Most people aren't even remotely interested in hearing about what the property might be or could be in the future. They are concerned only with what it is right now. If you can grasp this concept, then my fix-up strategy will make perfect sense to you as we go along.

What You See Counts for Everything

When I was a small boy, my mother always told me that looks are not what really counts. "Beauty is only skin-deep," she would say. "It's what's on the inside that really counts." She was talking about people, of course. However, in the house-fixing business, that advice doesn't apply and will keep you broke forever. People will never ask to see the inside if the outside is ugly. Instead, the skin-deep fixing strategy works extremely well for house fixers. The fact is, attractive exterior paint is one of the top moneymakers when it comes to making big profits in the fix-up business.

It's easy to see why I always begin my fix-up projects in the front yard. I've seen professional appraisers value identical houses at as much as a $10,000 difference because of plain old filth and junk at one property. In other words, a clean house can be worth $10,000 more simply because the owner hauls away the trash and keeps the house looking nice. Think about that for a minute. That's a lot of money for ordinary clean-up skills. Suppose it takes a whole week (40 hours) to haul away garbage and clean up a property. That's $250 an hour—nearly as much as a brain surgeon earns on a day off.

Good looks are the key to making sales or renting properties to tenants. Houses and apartments are judged, like books, *by their cover*. Looks also have a great deal to do with who your customers will be. There's an old saying in the rental business, "The property attracts the tenant—*ugly houses will always attract ugly tenants.*" When you purchase as many rundown houses as I have, you'll discover this old saying is at least 95% true. That's why house fixers, like myself, will generally end up replacing most current tenants during the time when they're fixing up the property. Tenants I inherit when acquiring property are most likely not the kind I want to keep when I'm finished with the job.

My Two-Part Fix-Up Strategy

My fix-up strategy is designed to achieve two main objectives—both are equally important. The first is easier to understand, because it's what I call the "practical fix-up"—this is what must be done to rundown houses in order to make them habitable and, for the most part, it's just plain commonsense fix-up. Almost every investor, experienced or not, will concede that you must fix things that are broken, worn out, or missing—these are the basic necessities; they are not optional. Things like cracked windows, broken faucets, torn linoleum, holes in walls, leaky roofs, interior painting, running toilets, busted doorknobs, junk, and missing fixtures are, obviously, problems that everyone should understand must be fixed. Unfortunately, this part of fixing, while necessary, is not the part that attracts the big profits.

The second part of my fix-up strategy is to fix up the looks, which is just as important as fixing a toilet or the roof. The reason is simple—people rent and buy houses based, to a large extent, on how the property looks.

It's important to understand that potential customers make renting and buying decisions in a matter of seconds while driving by your property in their cars. It's that first look and their first impression that counts the most. If your property doesn't generate positive vibrations on that first drive-by, the new carpets and countertops inside don't count for anything.

What You See Is the Foo-Foo

Folks who attend my fixer camps and visit my rental houses are always fascinated by my foo-foo beautification techniques. "Foo-foo" is the term I use for cosmetic, gingerbread fix-up. The term originated under the big-top in the golden days of the circus. Paint and makeup worn by the clowns was known as "foo-foo." *Webster's Dictionary* defines "cosmetic" as *"correcting defects, making for beauty."* In some cases, my techniques might stretch Webster's definition a bit far, but most folks agree—my "foo-foo" techniques really do make ugly houses more pleasing to look at.

Let's be realistic here: if you decide to own and operate older houses, you will obviously need to compete with landlords who own bright and shiny new homes. You might be thinking to yourself, how in heaven's name can a fixer house operator be expected to compete with newer property owners? I'll tell you how—*you must accentuate the positive.*

Older houses and apartments may lack many of the up-to-date, push-button amenities found in newer properties, but there are more than enough positive values found in the oldies—things that many newer properties lack. Heading the list is what I often call "old-fashioned charm." Charm is worth big bucks to creative landlords and it can be developed inexpensively by skillful application of my foo-foo techniques. Charm is present, both inside and out; but outside is always the place to begin the fix-up task.

The Foo-Foo Cover-Up Strategy Exposed

Many older houses have ugly siding that detracts from their street appearance. One economical technique for more pleasing looks is to install new exterior wood siding panels (4 x 8 foot sheets) directly over the top of the existing siding. The new wood panels have a stylish design; once they're painted and new cedar wood trim is put around doors and windows, the house will take on an exciting new appearance. No need to do this treatment on all four sides. The street view is what's important here. You can patch up and paint the other three sides if possible.

I once fixed a small, cottage-type house that was listing badly to the "port side." (For my landlubber disciples, that means leaning to the left.) After many years, several of the foundation piers had actually sunk into the ground a bit, causing the house to tilt. I didn't have much money invested, but when the foundation contractor told me his fix-up bid was $6,000, I decided on an alternate plan—*you guessed it*—the siding technique.

I left the house leaning, but installed new siding panels in front, straight up and down (plumb) over the old exterior. Today the house appears nice and straight when you view it from the street. You realize it's crooked only if you spill a bag of marbles on the living-room floor and watch them race toward the sunken left wall. I might point out that not one tenant in this house has ever asked for a rent reduction because of living in a crooked house. My total fix-up cost to solve the looks problem was under $500.

Foo-Foo Means as Many Frills as They Can Pay For

A difficult lesson for many investors to learn is that it's not wise to provide too much house for the money. You'll soon go broke if you keep doing this. Let me explain what I mean. Many tenants can afford to pay $450 a month for rent, but that's their limit. It's my policy to give my tenants everything they can pay for with as many frills as I can. In other words, when I rent out my $450 houses, I want them to be the very best $450 houses available. Obviously, however, they won't be as good as my $600 houses—and they shouldn't be.

Sizzle Fix-Up Offers the Biggest Profits

When I talk about fixing for dollars, I'm primarily referring to what I call "sizzle" items—things like white picket fences, fresh paint, window coverings, ceiling fans, wallpaper, new counter tops (Formica), attractive floor coverings, planters, shower curtains, decorative porches or entrance doors, trees and shrubs, green lawns, new faucets, modern toilets, and new shower enclosures.

The reasons I call these "sizzle" items is because they are attractive as well as useful. Sizzle items seldom have anything to do with code problems.

For example, an old dingy carpet will pass a code inspection just the same as bright new carpets, and trees and shrubs or curtains or ceiling fans have nothing to do with codes or safety, but these items have a lot of customer appeal. Plus these fix-up jobs will pay for themselves very quickly.

Cleanup and Paint Change Looks and Image Quickly

General cleanup and fresh new paint are among the highest-ranking outdoor improvements because they can quickly and inexpensively change the looks and image of a property. They're also the most important jobs in terms of what new owner-investors should plan on doing first. The reason is quite simple. Most people associate value with looks. Therefore, an unattractive scumbag property always looks worthless.

For older houses with less than perfect exteriors, a light base color—such as off-white or beige—is recommended. Use a darker contrasting color for the wood trim, fascia boards, window surround, and porches. On stucco houses, use the base color and a darker trim color for the woodwork. Painting is a very effective foo-foo technique, because it covers up so many imperfections found in older properties. In terms of payback, a new paint job can add approximately 20% more value to a medium-price house and sometimes double the price of a cheap one.

Foo-foo creates the right look and adds the extra sizzle to help older, inexpensive houses compete with comparable-size, newer properties. When you consider that I generally pay about half the price that would be paid for newer, glossier houses, then rent them for approximately the same monthly rates as the new houses, you get some pretty good proof that my foo-foo techniques are working.

Lawns, Shade Trees, and Picket Fences Are Hot

Many older houses and smaller apartment buildings are just oozing with charm and homeyness. The problem is, you must educate yourself to spot these things while searching through many dumps. Identifying potential beauty in the rough can quickly move you ahead of the competition. Most buyers are frightened off by dirt and deadbeats.

Be especially tuned in when it comes to yards. Everyone loves a yard—and a nice yard can be especially appealing to potential renters. The combination of nice green lawns, shade trees, and a freshly painted white picket fence will keep your properties rented while others are left vacant.

Fix-up investors should always begin outside improvements before ever setting foot inside. The idea is to turn the property around (make it look better) as quickly as possible. Remember: people will judge the looks—and people make decisions outside, not inside. The very first thing I always do is trim trees and shrubs, cut the weeds (which I call grass), turn on the sprinklers, and revive dead yards. You should be watering at the same time you're fixing the houses. The goal here is to have an attractive yard to offer by the time the house is fixed up and ready to market (whether to rent or to sell).

Window Coverings Are Top Sizzle Items

Curtains, drapes, mini-blinds, and decorative shades will make any house or apartment look homier. Homeyness translates to about 10% more rent when you dress up your houses with window coverings. Also, attractive window coverings will make an empty house rent much faster than one with bare windows. These are good, sound economic reasons for installing them in all your rentals.

Anyone can hang curtains, right? *Wrong!* If you don't believe me, chances are you haven't watched tenants install them. One of my tenants installed curtain rods with nails so long they went all the way through the wall and came out the other side. I've seen four-foot drapes hanging on eight-foot windows, curtains that were at least a foot too short, and traverse rods that won't open. Take my advice here: do this job yourself, while the house is empty, before your tenants show up.

If you use drapes and traverse rods—which I like to use for most larger front-room windows—be sure you purchase them from a supplier who specializes in selling to apartment owners. You'll find their prices are much lower and it's easy, one-stop shopping, because they can supply drapes, rods and all the hardware to complete the job.

Houses with All the Right Things Wrong

Some folks say, "The real secret to making big money in the fix-up business is purchasing rundown properties with all the right things wrong." Indeed, there's a lot of truth to that; but seldom have I found exactly the kind of conditions I'd like to have. The truth is that the houses I find most profitable will generally require almost total reconditioning. Notice I didn't say "remodeling." The following is a list of fix-ups and repairs I find most common for properties I acquire.

1. Paint exterior. This includes siding or stucco repairs and anything else that looks bad. Exterior painting can make a tremendous difference in the looks of any property. I recommend medium-quality exterior latex paint. A two-color combination is very attractive. Use a light color for the main body of the house, with a darker trim color for doors, window surroundings, and the fascia or eave boards. With off-white or tan, almost any trim color goes well. Make this change and all outside improvements first and quickly so tenants, passersby, and potential customers get used to the new look.

2. Fix yards or landscaping. *Front yards.* The front street view is most important. Reseed lawn areas, plant inexpensive shrubs and trees for improved looks. (Pyracanthas are one of the best shrubs for front yards, because they grow fast, they're inexpensive, they're colorful, and they have thorns—which keep kids from pulling them up.) Repair, if possible, or rebuild existing fences. *Back yards.* Cut and water grass—and that's it.

3. Paint interior of houses. Do this after tenants move out, not while the unit is occupied. Use off-white semi-gloss latex paint.

4. Replace carpets and linoleum, only if required. If they can be salvaged and will look good afterward, repair and clean existing floor coverings. Do this after current tenants have moved out and before new ones move in.

5. Fix any plumbing that's not working properly—water valves, faucets, toilet assemblies (guts), shut-off valves, showers, tubs, and sinks. It is usually best to replace them if they are old and ugly or in poor condition.

6. Replace unattractive light fixtures with new, but inexpensive ones. All switches must work easily; otherwise, replace them.

7. Repair obvious problems like holes in walls, busted doors, malfunctioning door hardware, broken windows, etc. Exterior doors must have working lock sets—preferably with deadbolts. Rekey, as necessary, making sure to have a single key that works in all exterior doors; this way you won't have to make so many copies or carry so many keys on your key ring.

8. Replace old, ugly kitchen and bathroom countertops, if needed, with new ready-to-use plastic tops (Formica).

9. Cover the windows. Most houses should have full window treatments—plastic mini-blinds or drapes in living rooms, bedrooms, dining, or family rooms and inexpensive, colorful curtains in the kitchen and bathrooms. Always add shower curtains to make bathrooms look complete. Window coverings add that touch of class—and they hide minor flaws and imperfections found in older houses and apartments. If your money is running low, do the street side windows only. Let tenants dress up the back windows that no one can see from the street.

10. Make sure that heating units and coolers or air conditioners work properly. It should go without saying, but I'll say it anyway. In my town the temperature gets over 100 degrees in the summer. I use evaporative coolers (swamp coolers) in most of the lower-priced, economy houses and forced air heating with cooling in upper-scale houses. I furnish kitchen ranges—either good reconditioned or economy-priced new ones. I don't usually furnish refrigerators in lower-income rental properties, unless it's an upstairs apartment where it's difficult to move appliances in and out.

11. Repair or replace wooden window frames. If they're rotten and they can't be fixed, replace them. However, most can be repaired and re-puttied without much cost or labor. A little paint will fix most anything on a house that looks ugly.

12. Add frills judiciously. Frills are OK, if they're inexpensive. One of my favorites is ceiling fans. One or two ceiling fans add a lot of class to older houses and it's usually money well spent, because it attracts the attention of potential renters, who associate fans with higher-class rentals.

13. Make big-ticket repairs in stages. It may sometimes be justified to repair bad roofs, especially if they look ugly from the street, but you can do it in several stages. For example, on pitched roof houses, it seldom happens that both sides leak at once; generally the south side, or weather side, leaks first and the other side doesn't. In the first phase of your fix-up project, patch or repair only the half that leaks. The street side of roofs that are old, weathered, and ugly may not leak yet; however, ugly roofing equates to lower value because it distracts a great deal from the property looks. Replacing the street side is often justified for this reason. Do the back side later. Remember, however, that you can't get higher rents for new roofs. The function of a roof is simply to keep the water out—and that's it.

14. Install shutters. Extra sizzle items that cost very few fix-up dollars are exterior shutters on front street-side windows. You can get inexpensive plastic shutters for windows of various sizes in white, brown, and black from most do-it-yourself stores.

15. Put up a fence. I always recommend building a three-foot-high, white picket fence around front yard areas. White picket fences show off the property, to renters and potential buyers alike. They keep kids and dogs inside the property; thus, mothers like fences—and mothers make the decision to rent or buy. Need I say more? However, if money is tight, do front fences first, and save backyard fences until later.

16. Tend the lawn. Always carry a hose and sprinkler with you at all times; then, when you arrive at the job, you can set up your sprinkler and water dry areas of the front yard. Toss out some lawn seed anywhere you see bare ground. Lawn seed and weeds grow together to become a durable lawn when they're watered enough. The idea is to make all front yards green.

17. Save most inside fix-up work in multi-unit properties until the units become vacant. (This will happen when you raise rents.) As soon as the outside painting is done and the yards start looking nice, you should begin to raise the rents. The tenants will begin moving out, one by one, and you can replace them with tenants willing to pay more rent for a better-looking property. I call this process "tenant cycling." Multi-unit fix-up jobs will normally take a year to 18 months when you do them this way.

18. Fix up other structures. Old dilapidated garages, carports, and storage sheds can be made to look attractive by installing new, lightweight-metal, tilt-up garage doors and wood or Masonite exterior paneling. However, do this only on the front or whatever side shows. Old-style, heavy wooden garage doors, with those hard-to-adjust springs and bent hardware, should be replaced. The goal here is to fix up the building enough to have a nice exterior appearance. Tenants like garages—not for their cars, mind you, but because they love to store junk. Most renters are willing to pay $35-$40 more per month to have a garage. As a landlord, this is appealing for two reasons. First, it's more income, of course. Second, if they have a garage, you can usually convince tenants to keep their stuff hidden inside; otherwise, junk will end up all over the yard instead.

The big difference between successful fixers and the others who will crash and burn, financially speaking, is learning where and how to end a fixer project. Fixing older houses can cost you all the money you have today, plus every dime you might earn in the future. However, it doesn't have to be that way. Remember: it's not much fun fixing up junky houses and dealing with deadbeat tenants if you aren't getting paid well.

Be creative and work within the limits of your budget. It can be done, believe me. One of the best examples I can think of is the highway builders: they construct six-lane freeways, when every motorist can plainly see that 10 or 12 lanes are needed. They build what they have the funds to build—and that's it. When more money becomes available later, they'll add more lanes. That's exactly the same strategy house fixers must adopt to be profitable.

The Fix-Up Revolution—Made to Fit and Ready to Use

Newcomers might be slightly ahead of me on this stuff, but most old-timers will agree with me. Fixing houses today is a whole different ball game in terms of ready-made, easy-to-use materials and instructions on how to do things. Giant stores are in fierce competition for the do-it-yourself trade. They stock acres of every building product imaginable for doing home improvements or for fixing anything that's broken. The whole idea is to get the new generation hooked on doing things for themselves.

Don't read me wrong here: not every job is for do-it-yourself investors. As a general rule, I'd be very careful with jobs that concern safety—like gas piping and electrical upgrades. These jobs normally require building permits and, because of the added liability, you may wish to hire licensed contractors to do the work.

It's quite easy to learn exactly what you need to know about installing ready-made fixtures and doing minor repairs. Most salespeople in the do-it-yourself stores can show how your project should be done and explain what piece goes where if you get stuck or end up with parts left over. There are also several good illustrated books—like the Time Life series—that will show you every detail about any wiring job you may decide to undertake. Bob, a friend of mine who is very close to being a total klutz, recently rewired two add-on rooms in his house with just a little help from the clerk who sold him materials. Very knowledgeable, the clerk explained exactly how to install new wires and even drew a simple sketch showing my friend how to connect all the circuits together. The fact that Bob didn't burn down his house or electrocute himself sold me on the proposition that today's do-it-yourself movement has come a long way since the time I did my own plumbing work.

Hook 'Em Up and Glue 'Em Together

It seems like only yesterday that do-it-yourself owners had to learn some basic soldering skills if they intended to do their own plumbing chores. Today, unless you're messing around with copper supply lines, basic plumbing parts are all made from plastic. You simply cut them with a hacksaw and glue them together. All that maze of twisted pipes under the kitchen and bathroom sinks—it's all plastic now. And, the whole works comes in a packaged kit, with how-to pictures on the back. Drain lines are glued together and those hard-to-bend chrome supply lines under the sink can now be substituted. Flexible polyethylene lines of various lengths, with screw-on fittings at both ends, are the amateur plumber's dream come true.

Countertops—No Problem!

Not so long ago, installing plastic laminated countertops (Formica) could be a major undertaking. Plywood or pressboard panels and thin plastic sheeting had to be glued together, then held snugly in place with special wood clamps until it dried. Gobs of glue or air bubbles could make the job look like a third-grade ashtray project.

Today, you can buy countertops already made. They even come with

45-degree angle cuts so you can install professional looking corners. All you have to do is cut a hole for the sink and glue the counter top to the base cabinets and you've taken a giant step toward modernizing any ugly kitchen or bathroom.

Doors and Windows Just Plop In

With ready-made, pre-hung doors, all you need to do is install them in the wall and trim out both sides with standard molding. Most doors are already factory drilled for lock sets (doorknobs).

Steel pre-hung exterior doors are my favorite, because they don't crack, split, or swell up in wet weather like most wood doors. And, there's no drilling: all you do is nail the door and frame into place, install a key set and a deadbolt, and trim around the edges inside and out—and you've got a professional-looking door.

Windows are the same. Aluminum sliders, both single-glazed and double-insulated, are ready-made to fit the openings occupied by the old ones. Replacement windows come in every shape and size you'll ever need.

Easy-to-Install Electrical Fixtures

Modern electrical fixtures of all kinds are easy to install. Fans, blowers, and a large variety of light fixtures take up whole departments in the giant do-it-yourself stores. There's no longer any need to tear the walls apart when you add extra circuits. Decorative conduits can be installed to conceal the wiring along the baseboard without cutting into walls. Surface-mount boxes are available in various sizes for hooking up new fixtures. Do you remember the old rigid conduits that used to require an electrician with a pipe-bender? Forget that! Now there's flexible, aluminum conduit that goes around corners and anywhere else you wish to run new wiring. They even make it plastic-covered and weather-proof for outside uses. Electrical wires are not soldered and taped anymore. They're attached with plastic, threaded, screw-on connectors. As long as you remember to turn off the power at the main meter panel, you can tackle most of your basic electrical jobs.

But remember to turn off the main breaker switch or pull out the fuses before you start any electrical job. If you stick your fingers in a hot splice box and you hear a sizzling sound, stop immediately, pull your fingers back out and reread this paragraph.

You Won't Get High on Paint Fumes Today

Not so long ago, painting was a stinky job. Oil-base paint, in a small room or other closed area, brought tears to your eyes. Cleaning up the mess with solvents or thinner took almost as long as painting and it smelled worse. Water-base latex paint put an end to these problems. Plus, you don't need to keep cans of thinner around, because plain tap water cleans up the mess.

Painting is a major part of fixing up rundown properties and, fortunately, just about anyone can paint without much training or practice. Easy-to-use rollers, extension poles, and airless sprayers can help you look like a pro with a couple of simple lessons. Also—most physical therapists would agree—painting is one of the most complete body fitness exercises one can do. Almost all major muscle groups get an excellent workout when you paint. You might keep this in mind before you renew your membership at the local gym.

Cabinet-Makers Are Gone with the Blacksmith

Fixing kitchen cabinets with damaged drawers and missing parts was once an expensive fix-up chore that required specialized skills. Today, you can purchase most any size cabinets you need, already built and ready to install in kitchens or bathrooms. They're available with finished surfaces or you can finish them yourself. The best part is that almost anyone can install them with a few instructions.

Tub kits and one-piece shower enclosures, made from fiberglass and plastic sheets (skins), are available for any size bathroom. They are very easy to install if you simply follow the instructions that come in the box. I use plastic shower kits (plastic sheets) in my older houses where only a tub exists and I always convert tubs to a tub-shower combination. The only tools you need for installation are a tape measure, a straightedge marker, and a pair of scissors. The waterproof plastic sheets overlap one another and are easily glued to any wall surface. By replacing the tub faucet with a shower diverter faucet and installing a short riser (chrome pipe mounted up the wall) and a showerhead, you can have an inexpensive but efficient tub-shower combo.

Fixer Clinics

If you're interested in learning how to install floors, hang doors and windows, or do simple plumbing and wiring, then I'd recommend you attend clinics conducted free by big do-it-yourself stores.

The stores are after your business and nearly all are sponsoring evening or weekend clinics to show you how to use their materials. Taking advantage of one of these clinics, I recently learned some new tricks about finding and repairing leaks on my flat-roof houses. Naturally, in the process, I purchased several rolls of fiber tape and a couple buckets of high-priced goop to fix my problems. You simply can't learn enough about fixing leaks on flat-roof houses—short of just saying "No." to the next seller who offers you one.

How to Estimate What the Job Will Cost

Fix-up work has two parts that cost money. First and most expensive is the labor—on average labor costs 70¢ of each fix-up dollar; supplies and materials cost the remaining 30¢. Certainly, these numbers can vary slightly for some jobs, such as installing or overlaying exterior walls with new siding panels: the materials (4 x 8-foot sheets) are expensive and the labor involved is relatively quick and simple. However, a 70%-30% split is well within the ballpark for estimating most fix-up chores.

If you are able to purchase a fixer property for 30% under the estimated, fixed-up market value—for example, say a $70,000 market-value house for $49,000—and you estimate it will cost $10,000 to fix it up to its full market value, it will cost you somewhere around $3,000 for material and supplies. That means if you do all the labor yourself, you can expect to have an $18,000 equity in the property when the job is done. Doing fix-up ("adding value," as it's called) means you don't need to play the inflation game to make profits in this business.

My rule of thumb is to plan on spending 10% of the amount I pay for the property for fix-up. For example, if I purchase a house for $75,000, I'll plan on $7,500 worth of fix-up. It can, however, be as much 20% for the "real uglies."

Knowing What to Fix

Since almost everything that's a problem can be patched up, repaired, or replaced by skilled persons, it becomes necessary to further qualify fix-up work in terms of economics—"How much will it cost?" This information will help you decide how much work is too much and when it's best to simply pass over the deal and move along to the next one. The fix-up investor must be concerned with fixing for profits—not just fixing. This is a very important concept, one you must never forget. The two worst mistakes for beginning fix-up investors are *over-fixing* and *fixing the wrong things*.

In order to determine what to fix, you must first answer two simple financial questions.

1. What will it cost to complete the items you propose to fix or repair?
2. What will the fix-up value be after you complete the work?

Knowledge of cost and value is critical whether you intend to keep the property for rental income or to sell it quickly for turnaround profits.

Recovering Fix-Up Costs

When you spend fix-up dollars to upgrade a rental property, you should obviously get your money back in the form of higher rents. My goal is to recover most fix-up costs from increased rents over a period of one to three years. It takes longer to recover costs for items of more permanent value than for short-life repair items. For example, I often replace old, deteriorated wooden garage doors with new, lightweight metal doors. Although the lightweight metal doors will cost several hundred dollars installed, they add much to the looks and have a tendency to increase the overall property value. However, they require a longer recovery period in terms of payback from increased rental income. Perhaps a better way of explaining this would be to say that I'm satisfied to recover a certain portion of the total garage door costs from increased rents and the balance from extra profits on the permanent value when I sell or trade the property.

Remember: this example applies only to garage doors and similar replacements or repairs that have longer-term values. It does not apply to short-life repairs like painting and adding curtains. Dual-glaze window replacements are in the same category as metal garage doors. It takes much longer to get fix-up or replacement money back, but energy-efficient windows add much to the long-term value of any rental property.

Better Windows Means Lower Utilities and Higher Rents

There is another very important economic benefit that comes from installing modern insulated windows that helps shorten the long-term cost recovery period. The windows cut the cost of utility bills (heat and cooling), which creates an opportunity for owners to obtain higher rents immediately.

Here's how it works. Even though tenants are paying their own utilities through individual meters, most tenants try to budget a specific amount monthly for housing expenses. Tenants are concerned about their total monthly housing costs, not just the individual costs of rent, utilities, and upkeep. Thus, new insulated windows can provide the opportunity for higher net rent profits. Let's say you own two identical apartments, and the rent for each is $300 per month. The only difference between the two apartments is that one has old wooden, single-hung, single-glazed windows, with loads of charm—and lots of air leaks; the other has new, energy-efficient, double-glazed windows, without the charm—but no air leaks. Let's assume the winter heating bills in the apartment with leaky windows average $100 a month and the bills for the unit with energy-efficient windows average only $50 per month. You can charge a higher rent for the apartment with new windows.

New Windows Benefit Everyone

Let's say you are an apartment tenant who is accustomed to paying total housing expenses of $425 per month—$300 for rent, $100 for utilities, and $25 for upkeep. If you had an opportunity to reduce your expenses by $25 every month, would you do it? I'll assume the answer is "Yes" because all my tenants would. Also, would you be concerned over who gets what part of your total monthly housing budget, as long as you are saving $25 every month? Again, I'm sure I know your answer. Why should you care? After all, you're saving $25. Most tenants will agree to a $25 reduction with no questions asked. I think everyone is happy to save $25. The following chart shows the breakdown of expenses before and after installing new, airtight windows.

Old windows (with charm)		New windows (without leaks)	
Rent	$300	Rent	$325
Utilities	$100	Utilities	$50
Upkeep	$25	Upkeep	$25
Total	$425	Total	$400

Figure 11-1. Tenant's monthly housing costs

As you can see, new windows will provide worthwhile benefits for everyone. As the example shows, the landlord can get a $300 annual rent increase ($25 times 12 months), the tenant can save $300 annually, and the utility company will award you their prestigious "Blue Star" window sticker for energy conservation.

Before we leave this subject, let me just say that tenants today are very much aware of ever-increasing utility costs and they compare costs with their neighbors who live down the street. Your rental ads can read "*cheap utilities.*" Tenants know exactly what that means. As you acquire additional properties and rent to more tenants, at different locations, it becomes quite easy to develop a utility cost comparison chart showing the actual expense figures to back up your advertisement claims.

Garages: Another Quick-Return Cash Flow Generator

Another quick-return suggestion, which also features some extra rental income, is to look for properties with garages or carports. Even junker garages, with leaky roofs, are well worth their fix-up cost—within reason, of course. Why garages? Because most tenants want garages, often as on-site storage. They ask for them and are willing to pay higher rent for them.

I don't mean that you should consider building garages where none exist. All I'm suggesting is that you look for them when you are buying. Properties with garages and carports, either attached or freestanding, will always have more long-term value. They will also help the property rent much faster when you advertise them. Simply stated, as a landlord, I like garages because my customers like garages. It's strictly a bottom-line economic decision for me. Remember: higher rents make wealthier landlords.

Keep Your Eye on the Ball

When I write about this subject, I often compare fixing up houses to playing golf. In golf there's an old saying, "Drive for show, putt for dough." There are thousands of strong young players who can hit the ball a mile and look very good doing it. Precision is not critical as long as the ball stays in bounds and ends up on the fairway. However, to putt the ball those last few feet to the flagstick is very critical. It takes a lot of skill to sink the ball into a very small cup. It's impossible to play winning golf unless you learn to do both—drive and putt—equally well.

The same can be said for fix-up investors: you won't make any serious money by simply fixing up houses without a financial plan. So, to repeat myself, lots of folks can do fix-up quite well; however, you make the serious money when you learn how to purchase houses with the right things wrong, then limit your fix-up costs to those things that will generate returns or profits from your customers.

12

Where Do All the Profits Come From?

Buying real estate is easy. Becoming financially independent doing it is another story. To begin with, many investors simply don't understand where profits come from or what they must do to produce them. Many are of the opinion that proper timing is the most important ingredient in making real estate millionaires. Others think patience is more important for success: simply buy choice properties in an appreciating market and sit back and wait. "You can't go wrong," they say.

Playing the Appreciation Game

The biggest question for real estate investors who bet on appreciation is what happens if there is none? Worse yet, what happens if property values drop? Real estate is a cyclical business: prices and values go up and down. Betting on short-range appreciation is like shooting craps—you can sometimes double your money overnight, but you can also lose the ranch just as quickly.

Reaping the benefits of appreciation without having to worry about timing is a much safer strategy. Real estate will almost always increase in value over time. For example, consider a three-bedroom, single-bath house in Sacramento, California that cost $20,000 new in 1968. It reached a high value of $181,000 in 1992 and then dropped to $160,000 by the end of 1994. For short-term-profit investors, most of the '90s have been declining or stagnant years. However, over the long haul, that house in Sacramento has appreciated nearly $5,400 each year since it was built.

Appreciation Should Be the Bonus

Appreciation should be a plus for the wealth builder, not the whole plan. If you view it as a bonus, you don't have to worry about short-term up-and-down cycles. Instead, you can concentrate on how to make much bigger profits in the long-term.

To begin with, you need to understand that most wealthy real estate investors buy more properties than they sell. Selling properties, especially when you're just starting out, is like digging a deep hole and then filling it back in. The reason is because the minute you sell a property, your investment stops earning you money. Worse yet, any gains or profits you might make are immediately taxable. Obviously, paying taxes and building wealth don't go too well together.

Double the Value by Fixing 'Em Up

Let's say I've learned about the sale of 10 junky little rental houses on a half-acre lot near the edge of town, suffering from poor management and rundown conditions, which always means low rents and deadbeat tenants. Let's assume I offer to purchase the property at 5.5 times the gross rents of $325 each, or $3,250 per month totals, and the owner accepts my offer. That means I will buy the property for $214,500, or $21,400 per unit (12 times $3,250 per month equals $39,000 annually, times 5.5 GRM for $214,500).

Let's also assume that I can fix up the property and upgrade the tenants for about $3,000 per unit, including all the cleanup work and materials. I estimate it will take 12 to 18 months to do this job myself and to turn the property around. Property turnaround means getting a better class of tenants and establishing good property management policies.

It's not my intent here to discuss how much the down payment should be or where to find fix-up money. Rather, let me simply say with regard to both that down payments are substantially less and terms are substantially better with low GRM deals. Figure 12-1 will give you an idea of the terms and conditions you might expect for various 10-unit properties with GRMs ranging from 4.5 to 9.5. Now, imagine the profits when you make a two-point improvement in the GRM, which will yield significantly higher rents and an overall increase in the property value.

Rent Multiplier	Condition	Monthly	Annual Income	Estimated Selling Price	Probable Terms Required to Purchase Property
9.5 x gross	Excellent top grade	$500	$60,000	$570,000	$75,000 to $120,000 cash, no trades—firm price
8.5 x gross	Very clean, good shape	$475	$57,000	$484,500	$45,000 to $60,000 cash, trades probably not accepted
7.5 x gross	Medium	$440	$52,800	$396,000	$35,000 to $50,000 cash, possible trades for strong buyer
6.5 x gross	Dirty, needs some work	$375	$45,000	$292,500	$20,000 cash will work, trades acceptable (car OK)
5.5 x gross	Junky, ugly, filthy	$325	$39,000	$214,500	Low down $10,000, maybe less, trades (boats, cars, airplane-anything of value)
4.5 x gross	Falling down, pigsty	$285	$34,200	$153,900	$0 down is good possibility, best terms available

Figure 12-1. Probable terms and conditions for a 10-unit property

Do-it-yourself investors should keep in mind that labor amounts to approximately 70% of the total fix-up cost. In this example, we said fix-up costs would be $3,000 per house—or a total cost of $30,000 (10 x $3,000 = $30,000). That leaves material costs of $9,000, which must be paid as you do the work and purchase materials. I've found credit cards are ideal for spreading out the expenses. Just be sure, if you decide to use them, that you can pay the monthly bills.

Looking Good 18 Months from Now

Finally, when the job is done, everything looks spick-and-span, with nice green lawns (revived weeds) and white picket fences. The jacked-up cars are gone now and regular paying tenants occupy your units. Everyone agrees—the property looks great now. It's clean and the location is perfect for renters who need to be near shopping and schools. The nearby pizza parlor is an added bonus. With your GRM improved by 2 points, rents are $440 per month and worth every nickel. Your personal fix-up efforts have added value to make it happen.

The Magic of Compounding

Compounding real estate equities works the same way as your savings account, only better. That's because you can use something called *leverage* to speed up the moneymaking process. We'll talk more about leverage later, but first, I want you to fully grasp the power of compounding.

Compounding means earning interest on both the principal and the accruing interest. As it keeps growing over time, the results are simply astonishing. Most wealth builders are amazed when they discover how quickly money grows and multiplies. The following example serves to illustrate the power of compounding.

If you deposit $1,000 into your bank account every month for 20 years, never draw any money out, and earn 12% interest on all your deposits, plus the accumulating interest—that's enough to make you a millionaire (well, almost!). You will end up with $989,255 in your bank account at the end of 20 years.

Saving $1,000 a month might sound like a ton of money when you're just barely making ends meet. But $12,000 a year is not really a huge amount anymore. Many folks have mortgage payments twice that amount and vehicle expenses that equal it.

How can just 20 years of investing $12,000 a year make you a million-aire? After all, 20 years times $12,000 is only $240,000. Where does the rest of the money come from? It comes from the 12% interest compounding—and all you need to do is make your $1,000 deposits and leave the money in the bank. In 20 years, the interest alone adds up to $749,255. Compounding is very powerful—and it will do the same thing with $1,000 worth of real estate, only better.

Killing the Golden Goose

The magic of compounding comes from leaving your investment alone. In other words, if it's money in the bank, leave it there and don't touch it. If it's four rental houses, don't sell them for a short-term gain. I must warn you right now—the short-term profits you earn will never be enough to make up what you'll lose in the long run if you break up your compounding cycle.

Disturbing the cycle in the early years will cost you dearly. I'll show you why. At the end of the second year in our 20-year investment plan, the accumulated amount of principal and interest earnings would be approximately $27,000. If you withdrew $10,000 of that amount, it would result in a $230,000 loss by the end of the 20 years. Your accumulated total would only be $757,860, just because of that withdrawal of $10,000 in the second year of the plan.

In later years, as compounding builds and the dollar amounts get larger, withdrawing $10,000 slows down the earning power much less. For example, in the 17th year, the account balance would be $661,300 and will grow to $757,800 in the 18th year. If you were to borrow $10,000 at this point, it would hardly be missed, because the annual earnings would have reached nearly $100,000. During the 20th year, the account will earn $123,000, which is more than half the total amount you invested throughout the entire 20 years.

Buying properties to fix up and sell for quick turnover profits might seem like a great idea to some. But it doesn't help you build the lasting kind of wealth most investors are seeking. This is because selling does not allow long-term compounding to work at full strength. When you constantly buy and sell properties for short-term gains, you wind up losing a ton of money in the long run, as our example shows. Withdrawing $10,000 in the second year costs $230,000 in the long run.

Four Ingredients That Produce Profits

In order to maximize compounding, you've got to select the right vehicle to get there. Not just any properties will do. There are four basic ingredients that produce profits:

1. Cash flow earnings
2. Tax shelter benefits
3. Equity buildup
4. Appreciation or inflation

Keep each one in mind as you search for the right investment.

1. Cash Flow Earnings

Cash flow is the most important benefit for any investment. Without it, you'll eventually be forced to sell the property or, worse yet, you'll lose it. Cash flow gives you the freedom to keep your property through ups and downs in real estate cycles, without being forced to sell at the wrong time. Selling in a low cycle can easily cost you $30,000 on a $100,000 investment. Believe me, you don't want many sales like that.

As a general rule, when real estate is hot, at the top of a cycle, it's not at all difficult to sell property for 115% of the normal price. However, when the cycle hits bottom, 85% sales are more common. On a $100,000 deal, earning a 30% profit is certainly a worthwhile objective. Cash flow earnings of 12% are a very reasonable expectation for investors who buy run-down properties and add value to them. Don't forget what 12% compounding does for your bank account.

2. Tax Shelter Benefits

Depreciation is the magic expense item that causes your property to show a loss for tax purposes, but still generate positive cash flow. The reason for this is that the IRS allows investors to deduct—as an expense item—a certain percentage for things that wear out, like buildings, coolers, refrigerators, and carpets. This expense is really a "phantom" expense, because you don't need to write a check to pay it, like replacing the toilet.

The cash benefit comes from two sources. First, the depreciation expense will shelter the property income from taxes. For example, if the rental property generates $2,000 positive income, before deducting a $4,000 depreciation expense, the property will show a $2,000 loss for tax reporting purposes. Second, the same $2,000 loss against the property can be used to offset, or eliminate, taxes on $2,000 worth of income from the owner's salary or from another income source.

3. Equity Buildup

Equity buildup adds to your wealth monthly, each time you pay the mortgage. Although very small at first, a certain percentage of your mortgage payment goes to reduce the principal balance. With each principal reduction payment, you own a little bit more of the property as the bank owns less. Typically, on a 25-year mortgage, with an interest rate of 9% and a 20% cash down payment, equity buildup amounts to something like 3% or 4% annually.

As you can see, however, there are many variables. Obviously, in those cases where only interest is being paid, there's no mortgage pay down so there's no equity buildup occurring. In certain situations where you assume or take over a mortgage with only half of the original payments left before the mortgage is fully amortized, principal reductions will be substantially higher. But, regardless of whether mortgage payments are higher or lower, the important thing to keep in mind is that your tenants are paying off the property for you with their monthly rent checks. They buy the property and you own it. You can't beat that.

4. Appreciation or Inflation

Appreciation or inflation comes in two flavors.

First, there's the kind that comes from natural causes. Everyone gets a taste automatically if they happen to own properties in an area where appreciation or inflation is happening. Sometimes it's as little as 2% a year, but I've seen inflation jump to 25% or 30% for a short period of time. I've also watched properties nearly double in price in just two years. The problem with natural inflation is that there's no guarantee it will happen.

The second flavor of appreciation is forced appreciation—my specialty. I can count on it to work, because I have complete control. When I buy rundown houses and fix them up, I am forcing them to appreciate. The higher value comes from being able to attract better tenants, who are willing to pay higher rents. I upgrade the properties so I can provide a better product to my customers (renters). On several occasions, I've increased the property values by nearly 100% in just 18 months of ownership. You can do the same—and when 100% starts compounding, it won't take very long to add a couple extra zeros to your net worth. You'll also find that smiling at your tenants becomes a little easier.

Leverage Lets You Soar with the Eagles

High leverage can make you richer faster than any investment tool I know of. The idea is to safely borrow as much money as you can to put with your own down payment (if you have one) to purchase income properties.

For example, I can gain 90% leverage when I purchase a $100,000 apartment using $10,000 of my own cash for a down payment and sign a promissory note or mortgage for $90,000 back to the seller. If the property earns $10,000 in annual rents, that means the return on my cash down payment is 100%.

The problem is, that can be good or bad. If the expenses are $4,000 and the mortgage payments are $7,000, my 100% return doesn't mean much. I'll still be losing my shirt.

Leverage is a double-edged sword: you want leverage that's safe. In this example, if I can increase rents to $12,000 or negotiate a mortgage that would cost only $5,000 annually, I will then earn $1,000 on my $10,000 investment. A 10% cash flow, using 90% leverage is a very respectable return, especially for apprentice investors.

Not Everything Can Be Measured in Dollars

A rich man once said, "Money is not the most important thing in the world—but, it's still a long ways ahead of whatever's in second place." I certainly won't disagree that money is very important, but it's not the only measurement of an investor's success. There are many very attractive benefits that come with an investor's lifestyle. Most folks, however, never get to experience them, so let me share a few with you.

To start with, I don't need to operate my real estate business on a rigid time schedule, like most of my friends who work regular nine-to-five jobs. Since I've been there, I know the routine. My schedule is far more flexible. Try it—and I guarantee you'll like my way better. Also, I'm not stuck in a dead-end job going nowhere fast or working for a nitwit boss who should be my assistant. I'm also not part of that morning madness on the freeways, packed with hundreds of cars moving about half the speed I normally walk. That alone makes it worth dealing with my tenants—who generally act more civilized than early morning freeway drivers.

Brain Compounding Can Increase Your Wealth

When I started investing in fixer-upper houses, my simple plan was to buy them cheap (I had very limited funds), fix them up, and rent them out. Selling was never my first choice for making money. I always felt that having a continuous income from my investments was the best way to go. At that early stage, I was not yet aware of all the various strategies I could use to make extra money with my houses. As I went about fixing houses, I began reading all the books I could find about real estate investing. I soon learned new and different ideas about how to invest.

Reader's Digest (May 1973) published an article by Edwin Diamond entitled "Can Exercise Improve Your Brain Power?" In it, Diamond said that through selected mental exercise, like reading, you can actually increase the capacity of your brain to make it function better. Mental exercise, such as reading real estate investment books and learning at seminars, can actually cause your thoughts and ideas to compound, much like the compounding of money.

That's exactly what happened to me. New ideas and methods of acquiring real estate filled my thoughts. A good example was when I came up with the idea of *"lemonading"*—buying properties by using a combination of cash and personal property I no longer had any use for. It works extremely well when you find sellers who don't want their rundown real estate anymore and are willing to trade. This technique allows a small amount of cash to go much further, like hamburger helper. It can double or triple your buying power.

Before I began reading and educating myself (brain compounding), I had no idea I could present lemonade offers and get them accepted. I never realized I could buy back my own mortgages at big discounts. When I began fixing houses, these techniques simply never occurred to me. When I look back today, I realize *brain compounding* has been a major contributor to my accumulation of wealth.

Don't Walk Away from Your Gold Mine

I'm aware that most new investors tend to follow the same path I did. First, they learn how to acquire income-producing real estate, and, of course, that's a good start. However, most of them *don't* follow through and expand their moneymaking opportunities. Many small-time investors miss out on real profits, similar to inexperienced gold miners who, after easily finding shiny nuggets on the surface, leave the real fortune hidden by only a few inches of sand. Brain compounding happens when you continue to seek more knowledge. It will make your investment houses produce far greater yields than you can ever imagine.

Adding New Profit Bulbs on My Money Trees

I often refer to my investment houses as "money trees." I call each of my various profit-making strategies "profit bulbs." In the beginning, I had just my bare tree with two lonely bulbs—namely, profits from my rents and, occasionally, profits from a sale. That was back before I knew anything about *brain compounding,* when my knowledge was very limited, and before I started reading and attending seminars.

Over the years, I've managed to decorate my "money trees" with many more "profit bulbs." Obviously, the more bulbs I add to each tree, the more it glitters like gold. It's the same old tree (fixer houses) I started with, but now, with the addition of many new bulbs over the years, my gold mine has become much more productive.

My First Profit Bulb and Best Source of Continuous Income

My first "profit bulb" has always been my rental income. Although the IRS refers to rents as passive income, I don't—and neither will anyone else who manages tenants and collects the rents. Still, it's my best source of continuous income every month. Once you develop your landlording skills, you can easily net 5% to 10% of the gross rents, even with leveraged properties. I once owned 216 houses with average rents of $385 per month. You can see that monthly income adds up rather quickly, even with very modest rents. It's also important to remember that when you're doing this correctly, tenants are actually paying off your houses for you. Realizing this has always made me feel much better at the end of a hard day fixing toilets.

Fixer Jay's Favorite Profit Bulbs

Selling profits is certainly a bulb with a whole lot of glitter. However, as I said earlier, I still favor keeping most properties and allowing them to earn continuous monthly income for me. About the only time I'll consider plucking a rental bulb from my tree is when a buyer gets very motivated to purchase my property, regardless of the price. Naturally, I can deal with one fewer bulb on my money tree when there are serious profits involved. This will most likely happen during a hot seller's market or when I'm weeding out properties that I don't think will meet my long-range profit expectations.

Seller financing is a profit bulb that will earn you a lot of money. It's available when you sell properties and carry back the financing yourself. Interest income is *easy money* and takes very little effort, except walking down to the mailbox to pick up the check. You can design your carryback mortgages to be long-term when you're ready to travel around the world or retire. Also, when you're nervous about a buyer or the down payment is a little on the thin side, you should insist on additional collateral to protect yourself. (For details, see the final section in the following chapter, "Removing the Risk from a 'No-Down' Sale.")

Buying back your own mortgage debt is a very high-profit bulb. When

I first started buying rundown houses, I had no idea that property owners could do this. I was in shock (but happy) when I asked for and received a $29,000 discount for simply paying off my mortgage seven years earlier than I had originally promised. That's over $4,000 a year for doing nothing—you can't make money much more easily than buying back your own mortgages at steep discounts.

Half sales are another excellent profit bulb on my money tree. Rather than selling a good income-producing property—giving up all the depreciation and effectively selling the goose that lays golden eggs—why not just sell half the property? That's enough to substantially improve your cash flow. The basic strategy here is to purchase a rundown property with low rents for $100,000 and fix it up until it's worth $200,000, with higher rents to justify the increased value. Then, sell half the *fixed-up* property to a passive investor for little or no cash down payment. This makes a hard-to-refuse proposition.

By doing this, I'll wind up with a mortgage receivable for the half I sell. This means I have mortgage payments coming in every month. Also, I'll be able to increase my personal income by collecting a monthly management fee and payments for maintenance and repair labor on the half I don't own. This is one of the slickest strategies I know of for making negative cash flow properties produce positive income. It's an excellent strategy for investors who can do the kind of fix-up (adding value) we discussed in previous chapters. (You can read more about *half sales* in Chapter 16.)

Creating notes for down payments is a profit bulb that can make your money tree glitter even brighter when you own properties with equity, but lack sufficient cash to keep buying new ones. You can simply type up your own promissory note or mortgage—and use it for your down payment. Simple, huh?

This strategy allows you to select the note value, the amount of your monthly payments, and the length (term) of the mortgage. "How can I do that?" you're probably wondering. It's because you're preparing it and it's your typewriter—that's why.

Many times after fixing up rundown properties, I've increased the values from 50% to 100%. That means I've created borrowing equity. This new equity will be security for the promissory notes I create. For example, if I purchase a property for $50,000 and increase its value to $100,000, I created at least $30,000 of borrowing equity. I will still maintain a 20% loan-to-value safety margin, like the banks do. This technique works extremely well when combined with lemonading—where my offer includes some cash (the sugar) and something other than cash (the lemons). This combination is often irresistible to a motivated seller who can't find anyone else to purchase his or her ugly property.

Leasing houses with an option to purchase is another of my favorite profit bulbs. I use this technique to increase the monthly cash flow for my larger, more expensive houses. The smaller houses I own have excellent rent returns without offering leases or the rights to purchase. For example, I can rent smaller, two-bedroom houses, with 600 square feet, for about $425 a month—that's 70¢ per square foot. My nicer houses with three bedrooms, two baths, double garages, and approximately 1,300 square feet of living space will normally rent for $650. That's only 50¢ per square foot and not quite enough income for the exposure, in my opinion.

The lease option remedy allows me to collect higher monthly rents ($800 to $850 range) in exchange for giving potential buyers (optionees) a higher than normal rent credit back toward the purchase price if they exercise the option. My leases are for three-year terms and my selling prices are generally somewhat higher than appraisals. I have never yet met a house buyer who can tell whether the value is $95,000 or $105,000. I'm sure I don't need to tell you which price my option contract will specify.

Buying discounted notes or mortgages is another high-profit bulb on my money tree, one that I accidentally discovered along the way. Buying discounted notes or mortgages can be a potential double-barreled opportunity for hands-on fix-up investors like me. The reason is because I would always prefer to own *the property* that secures the note or mortgage rather than owning the mortgage. If I should take the property back for nonpayment, I'll also get the rental income and tax shelter, plus a 40% discount the day I take over. You couldn't possibly design a better purchase deal than that.

I have two questions I must answer for myself when I have an opportunity to buy a note or a mortgage:

Where Do All the Profits Come From?

1. Would I be happy to own the collateral, the property that secures the note?
2. Is there an adequate equity cushion, the difference between the property value and whatever is still owed against it (total mortgage debt)?

If my answer to both questions is "Yes," I'm always happy to move forward with the deal and purchase the note. Obviously, there's a good opportunity for me to earn even bigger profits should the note default and I end up foreclosing, as discussed above.

My debt limit rule for income-producing properties is 65% loan-to-value. That means that if there are three existing notes or mortgages on a $100,000 property and they add up to no more than $65,000, I'm generally willing to purchase any one of the notes at a reasonably discounted price. As you can see, buying discount notes or mortgages is really *two profit bulbs in one.* If everything goes well, I'll receive high-yield note payments; and if it doesn't go well, I'm more than happy to take over a $100,000 income-producing property for 65% or less of its full market value.

Every fix-up investor should explore this profit bulb opportunity very closely, so they can fully understand what I'm saying here. This bulb can truly add extra padding to a skinny bank account, believe me.

13

The Ingredients of a Super Deal: The Hillcrest Cottages

Creating Equity with Very Little Cash

For most start-out investors, cash is scarce. That was my situation when I started out: I had big ideas, but very little cash. I soon discovered that my big ideas would help me only if I rolled up my sleeves and went to work. When you don't have much money to invest, you must supply something else that will persuade sellers to accept your offers.

As you will learn, solving a distressed seller's problem can have as much value as a cash down payment, once you understand how it works. I decided to specialize in rundown fixer properties, because they would be easier to acquire with my limited resources—and I found that rundown properties quite often had owners who were in financial trouble. This combination is easy to find, because they often go together.

My investment strategy is to create equity quickly with the lowest cash down payment—sometimes none at all, as was the case with the Hillcrest cottages. My plan is simple: I purchase ugly, rundown properties from highly motivated sellers and turn them into beautiful profit makers.

Hillcrest Cottages—A Million-Dollar Problem

The Hillcrest cottage property was a perfect example of creating instant equity using personal skills rather than cash. Hillcrest was an ugly run-down property consisting of 21 cottage-type dwellings that was situated on a hillside lot in my hometown. No other property I've ever owned, before or after, has been uglier than Hillcrest and none have ever had so many things wrong. Even the sellers of Hillcrest were all messed up

The owners of Hillcrest, Pete and Mike (not real names), shared unequal ownership interests in the property. Pete—who owned 65% and lived on the property—had the most to say, because he had the majority ownership. This was a problem for both owners, because Pete was a very poor landlord: he simply could not handle tenants and ran them off faster than he could find new ones. The results showed and the rental income was not enough to pay the mortgage payments and expenses. Hillcrest was in serious financial trouble when I made the offer to buy it. Two lenders had already started foreclosure proceedings, even though neither really wanted the property back.

Knowing the Real Reason for Selling Is a Big Advantage

One of the most urgent reasons for selling investment property is when the income drops below the mortgage payments and expenses. The owner is faced with covering expenses out of his or her own pocket or allowing the lender to foreclose the mortgage and take it back. In the Hillcrest situation, Mike had a well-paying job, while Pete was living off the property. Mike was, naturally, unwilling to spend more of his hard-earned money to compensate for Pete's poor management.

Being aware of the financial problems of a seller is very important when you're trying to figure out his or her motivation level. I always do as much probing as I can before I write offers. Remember: the higher the motivation level, the less cash you're likely to need to buy the property.

Let me make a point here. If you can figure out the seller's urgency—like the property being in foreclosure, the seller in need of quick cash, job relocation, or pending divorce—and then time your offer to relieve the seller's problem at the very last moment, you'll get offers accepted that wouldn't normally stand a chance. My Hillcrest offer was a good example of perfect timing.

Another threat facing the owners was the City Abatement Committee. Pete had repeatedly told city building officials that he would repair numerous building code violations on the property, some of which were hazardous conditions. The city had inspected the units earlier, when several nonpaying tenants filed complaints in an attempt to avoid paying rents. The Abatement Committee red-tagged the property and had even scheduled it for demolition, if repairs were not completed by a specific date. Obviously, this created a very serious urgency for the owners.

Key Ingredients for a Super Deal

Let me pause for a moment so we can review why Hillcrest had the potential to be a "super money-maker" deal for me.

1. The property was run down and unattractive, thereby eliminating most competition as prospective buyers.
2. There was an abundance of fix-up work, which I could do myself—or knew how to have done.
3. I learned early on that the owners were in serious financial trouble.
4. It was an excellent opportunity to create immediate equity from fix-up rehab.
5. It was a partnership property where unequal partners were not in agreement. In fact, they were fighting.
6. Rent collections were low because of deadbeat tenants and poor management.
7. The mortgage payments were delinquent and property was in foreclosure.
8. There were problems with a government agency: the City Abatement Committee was demanding fix-up.
9. There were "red-tag" building code violations that had to be fixed in a short time, which created great urgency.
10. The property owners had a high level of motivation, without many options.

Seldom do you find so many things wrong with both the property and the owners as was the case at Hillcrest. I had a feeling that almost any purchase offer I made, within reason, of course, would receive serious consideration by both owners.

Hillcrest Purchase: Zero Cash Down

Remember what I told you earlier—I had big ideas but very little cash. I also said I was ready to roll up my sleeves and go to work. That's exactly what I meant. So I prepared the following offer to purchase Hillcrest.

I proposed, instead of a cash down payment, a property trade, using the equity in a three-bedroom house I owned. Naturally, the owners would have preferred cash; however, they didn't have a lot of time to negotiate, due to the pending foreclosure, and my offer was the only one they had. When you think the sellers are extremely motivated, you can adjust your trade equity upward until you're challenged. Don't forget: there is never any harm in asking for the moon.

The property I was offering in trade was an older three-bedroom house on a large commercially zoned lot in a major growth area. I had owned the property for a little more than a year and had it rented for about the same amount as the mortgage payment. I had originally planned to eventually convert the house to a small commercial venture, like an insurance agency or a real estate office; however, I had never gotten past the idea stage. I had purchased the property for $80,000, with a $20,000 cash down payment. (Sometimes at my seminars people ask, "Where did you get the $20,000 cash?" It came from a $50,000 refinance loan on another property.)

After a short negotiating session, Pete and Mike decided Hillcrest was worth no less than $234,000. Until I came along, they had been asking $295,000. But now, they needed a very quick sale, so they agreed to my property trade proposal. I had not yet told them what my property was worth. Here's how I determined my sale price.

The Hillcrest Cottages Transaction

I agreed to pay $234,000 for Hillcrest. I would assume three existing mortgages totaling $143,000. It wasn't hard to figure their equity was $91,000 ($234,000 minus $143,000 equals $91,000). Knowing the amount of their equity made it quite easy for me to come up with a fair market value for the property I was using to trade in lieu of a down payment. I simply added $91,000 to the existing mortgage balance of $58,000 and came up with a selling price of $149,000. See how easy appraisals can be.

Folks often ask me why the Hillcrest owners accepted my trade property at such a highly inflated price. They are quick to point out that buying a property for $80,000 and then selling it just 14 months later for $149,000 seems like a rather hefty markup. However, the $69,000 markup, hefty or not, was not even slightly challenged by either Pete or Mike. In fact, they were more anxious than I was to sign the deal.

The valuable lesson I learned from Hillcrest was that distressed sellers are not nearly as concerned about how much money I make as they are about getting relief from their problems. Solving problems and providing relief to sellers pays very big profits in the fix-up business. That's why I advise all beginners to become *problem solvers first* and deal makers second. As I mentioned in Chapter 1, I would eventually sell the Hillcrest cottage property, along with five small rental houses on Hamilton Avenue, as a package to one buyer. This sale alone would earn me over a million dollars in profits, because I was able to solve the seller's problems.

Fixing Up Hillcrest Cottages

Fixing up Hillcrest was quite a chore, but, because of my large down payment (the $91,000 house trade), I had enough equity to borrow all the fix-up money. A local real estate lender appraised the property and loaned me $51,000 to do the fix-up work. Since I did most of the fix-up myself, except for hiring an electrical contractor, I ended up with about $20,000 left over.

I worked for nearly two years getting Hillcrest fixed up and running smoothly. I filled in the ugly swimming pool and completely replaced most of the electrical wiring. I repaired sagging carports, built new floors, and replaced nearly half the plumbing fixtures. I also spent considerable time watering and restoring almost two acres of lawns, trees, and shrubs. Naturally, I painted the property inside and out. I built a white picket fence around the front lawn area.

Finally, the work was done and the property was beautiful. I had absolutely no trouble renting the cottages to good paying tenants. The fact is, I started keeping a waiting list. Needless to say, when I filled the place up, I had excellent monthly cash flow. Even with high interest payments on my fix-up loan, I was still making a nice profit every month.

Hillcrest was located along a major thoroughfare, where hundreds of cars passed by daily. People would slow down and stare at the property. I could see they were very impressed. Sometimes they would walk up to me and tell me what a wonderful job I had done. They couldn't believe how such a filthy, rundown property inhabited by winos and deadbeats could change so quickly. Of course, the answer was a bit more obvious to me. I spent at least three or four days every week working on the property. Later on, after I sold Hillcrest, I estimated that if I had worked 40 hours a week for two years, my earnings would have been something in the neighborhood of $300 an hour. I can tell you, I've worked at many jobs during my lifetime that paid a whole lot less.

Selling the Fixed-Up Hillcrest Cottages

Almost two years after I acquired Hillcrest, I sold the property to a local physician who was looking for investment real estate. He was also seeking a way to shelter his regular income from taxes. In order to create the right-size tax deduction, the doctor needed to acquire depreciable property worth about $600,000. He wanted to use maximum leverage, like a very small cash down payment. We put our heads together and I agreed to sell Hillcrest cottages, along with five small rental houses, to the doctor, all on a single contract, with no money down.

That was just what the doctor ordered. He agreed to my selling price of $594,000. You'll notice that my selling price closely resembles the amount of real estate the doctor told me he needed. I might point out, I've always prided myself on being able to accommodate a buyer's circumstances. This sale was one of several I designed to fit the special needs of my buyer. Obviously, it worked out very well for me, too.

Removing the Risk from a "No-Down" Sale

People often ask me, "Isn't it a bit risky to sell a property for no cash down payment?" The answer is "Yes, of course, unless you can offset the risk by using some other means." In this case, I asked for and received additional collateral.

I said, "Look, doctor, I normally insist on a minimum 10% cash down payment. However, I am willing to take a promissory note and deed of trust for $60,000 (approximately 10% of $594,000) on another property you own in lieu of a cash down payment. I'm not asking for any payments on the security and it won't cost you a dime as long as you make the $6,000 monthly payments on the $594,000 Hillcrest contract."

I also told him that after five years of payments (60 times $6,000, for a total of $360,000), I would release (reconvey) the $60,000 collateral note. This simple arrangement protected me and, at the same time, it allowed the buyer to use his existing equity to purchase more real estate without spending his cash.

Naturally, if he failed to make payments on the $594,000 contract, as promised, during the first five years, I would not only take back (foreclose) the Hillcrest property and five houses, but also the $60,000 worth of additional collateral property. I call this my *"two-for-one" contract*. I'll sell him one property, but, if he doesn't pay me as agreed, I'll take two properties back. After receiving payments for five years, I feel safe enough to release the additional security. By the end of 60 payments, a big percentage of the risk is gone. It's kind of like the first five years of marriage. Chances are, if you make it that far, you'll probably stick it out until the end.

PART 2

Creative
Financing

14

The Value of Seller Refinancing

Borrowing from the Bank Is Good for the Bank

Many investors spend too much time trying to figure out ways to borrow money from banks and other "hard money" lenders. The reason, they claim, is to purchase their next bargain property, then hold it for a while, and sell it for a big markup. Naturally, their intention is to pay off the lender and pocket a hefty profit for themselves. In theory, this sounds like a marvelous plan. However, consider several problems that are working directly against that goal.

To start with, bank borrowing costs lots of money, especially for inexperienced investors, without top-notch credit. It's even more expensive when you're buying property for nonowner occupancy (rental units). Normally, there will be points to pay, higher interest costs, and variable rate payment adjustments tied to indexes that are very sensitive to rising costs. Many bank loans are written with short-term call dates and very low loan-to-value restrictions. This means that larger cash down payments will be required. More often than not, there is personal liability included in bank loans—plus substantial prepayment penalties if you pay the loan off early or wish to refinance it.

Also required are document fees, appraisal costs, escrow charges, and, sometimes, expensive termite work. Sometimes deferred maintenance repair funds are held back and deducted right off the top, which reduces net dollars the borrower will receive. I may have missed several other hidden expenses.

So, let me ask you this question—Does borrowing money this way seem like a good idea? It probably does if you are a lender. Frankly, it sounds like a marvelous plan if your goal is to make your banker rich.

Borrowing money from commercial banks and moneylenders is more likely to make you poorer, rather than richer. Obviously, there's a much better way to borrow money for buying the kind of properties I recommend in this book. Seller financing should always be your first choice.

New Bank Loans Should Be an Investor's Last Choice

If you're someone who underlines important parts in books, then grab your pen and mark up these next couple paragraphs—they're important.

Always try very hard to borrow the bulk of your new mortgage money (the real estate debt) from the owner who sells you the investment property. Remember, bulk means "most"—and not in every situation. Sometimes, commercial borrowing is justified if the deal has positive cash flow. However, that's the exception, rather than the rule. It's OK to assume the existing commercial loans (mortgages) on a property when you buy it, but your goal should be seller-provided financing for the balance owing, after you pay the agreed-upon cash down payment.

For example, a common situation might be where you purchase a property for $100,000. You agree to pay $10,000 cash down and assume an existing $40,000 mortgage—*if it's assumable*. Next, you negotiate with the seller to have him carry back a note for the balance, which equals $50,000, in this case. With this type of real estate loan by the seller, you will generally end up with far superior financing than if you had borrowed new money from a bank or hard moneylender. Most sellers are much more generous with terms—especially when they're selling rundown properties.

With seller financing, there won't be any points to pay and it's quite likely you'll be able to negotiate an interest rate lower than what most banks would charge. You can also avoid a variable interest rate mortgage, unless you and the seller design your own to fit the transaction. The beauty of this kind of borrowing is that there are no set rules to follow. When there are no rules, the Golden Rule applies—*the party with the gold rules*. In most cases that can be you, if you're buying the kind of properties I suggest—the ones that look ugly at first glance, but get more beautiful with each dollar they earn.

Buyers of Ugly Properties Get the Best Terms

Sellers of old, ugly, or problem properties are not in a position to be very picky about who they sell to. They can't play hardball with the price and terms like owners of higher-quality, nicer-looking properties. The main reason is that the rundown and ugly conditions turn off 95% of all potential buyers. Consequently, lack of buyer competition will greatly limit the owner's ability to sell.

What this means is you can almost always buy these properties for much less cash up front (lower down payments). Also, it's likely the seller will be forced to accept much weaker terms. Lower equity payments and carryback notes are very common. Some of these deals can be 100% owner financing. Ugly, fixer-type properties are generally older properties. Many of them no longer have conventional mortgages (i.e., bank loans or savings and loan mortgages) to pay off. When they do, they are most likely low-balance loans with lower interest rates and nearly always assumable to new buyers. For beginning investors especially, let me say this loud and clear—owner financing is the kind you want. Owners are almost always more flexible than banks.

Property purchases where the owners will carry back low-interest financing are the kind of transactions that allow you to buy with minimum cash down payments and yet still be able to generate cash flow. Bank financing with higher interest rates and variable rate mortgages is not what you want. Bank financing will seldom be much of a problem when you buy older, rundown type properties like I recommend. The reason is that any original bank loans have long since been paid off—and most banks won't write new loans on older properties today.

Seller Financing Is the Cadillac of All Financing

Seller financing can't be beat when it comes to negotiating good terms like the following:

1. Long-term payoff (15-30 years)
2. Low interest rates, 6%-9% range in today's market
3. No "due-on-sale" clause in note or mortgage
4. No prepayment penalty in note or mortgage
5. No late fee in note, unless the seller insists on one
6. No other restrictive terms or conditions, such as buyer agreeing to repave common roadway when holes or ruts appear

Seller financing—when you structure it properly—is better than FHA loans, GI loans, or any other type of institutional financing. Naturally, fix-up property sales are perfect for this, because most banks simply won't write loans for this type of real estate. In many cases, sellers must finance the sale themselves or they can't sell. Motivated sellers who own properties that won't qualify for bank financing have no choice other than to carry back a mortgage or sell for cash (which is not too likely).

Financing That Fits the Needs of Both Parties

One reason I've had such good success with my fixer projects is that I've purchased older properties where sellers *could* and *would* provide the financing. Buyers and sellers can design creative terms that work to solve each other's problems. Banks and most institutional lenders simply cannot do business this way. Their rigid lending policies and strict bylaws will not permit the kind of creativity we often need to make these deals work.

Many good buys would have been lost for me if creative financing had not been an option. Always look for properties where owners can provide all, or most, of the financing. Quite often, new investors become totally baffled when they can't find a bank loan. I cannot overemphasize the importance of seller financing, especially for do-it-yourself investors who need to keep all their options open—like buying the note back at a discount price in the future (as mentioned in Chapter 12).

Buying Back Your Own Debt Is Worth Big Bucks

One of the most profitable opportunities you miss when seller financing is not a part of your investment strategy is the chance to buy back your own mortgage debt later on from the seller. During the course of 20 years or so, many things will change. For example, a seller who is only too happy at the time of the sale to receive monthly payments for the next 20 years may suddenly find himself in a cash bind several years down the road. Money shortages are quite commonplace for all of us. Things like death, divorce, college funds, lifestyle changes, and loss of employment or income can quickly create a serious need for immediate cash.

When you design your seller carryback mortgages with good terms for yourself, like I showed you above, they have much less market appeal to professional note buyers. Note buyers like to have a late payment clause, prepay penalty, high interest rates, and much shorter terms; they won't pay very much for mortgages without them. This means if they do make an offer to buy the note, the price they offer will generally be so low the seller will be insulted—and probably won't accept.

What this means is that the mortgage you purposely designed with very good terms for yourself is worth much less if it's sold before the payoff date. Now you can buy it back much cheaper, because the seller probably can't sell it to anyone who would pay as much as you will. This strategy is worth big bucks when you do it right. I purchased my own $77,000 note for $41,500, just three years after I signed it. You'll never get this opportunity when dealing with banks or hard moneylenders.

15

Investing with Others: Small Partnerships

Partnerships are like marriages—there are some good ones that last a lifetime and many that don't last as long as it takes to pay for them. Like marriages, partnerships stand a much better chance of working and lasting if the partners are selected for the right reasons.

Why Would Anyone Want a Partnership?

There is only one good reason I know of to take on an investment partner. It's that you don't have enough financial horsepower to do everything by yourself. In other words, you need some help, and most often, it's financial help. However, there might be other legitimate reasons for needing help. We'll discuss a couple of kinds of partnership as we go along. *Equity sharing* and *timeshare contracts* are two types of partnership investing. Both are designed for investors who don't have the finances to complete the whole purchase.

Developing partnerships to pool individual resources, knowledge, and experience can provide an excellent vehicle for acquiring wealth at a much quicker pace than investing by yourself. I've discovered that, in most successful partnerships, the partners will often have very little in common except a strong desire to make money. Sometimes, an accountant will team up with a carpenter or handyperson, a doctor might team up with a contractor or with a schoolteacher with extra hours and mechanical skills. Quite often a real estate agent who can manage property will make a very good partner.

However, the downside of partnership investing is that you might end up with someone who doesn't work out and it can be a serious setback for even the best of plans. You must be very careful when selecting a partner.

Always ask yourself if you really need a partner or do you just think you need one and if it is wise to split the profits. The answers should be very clear before you look for a partner.

Partnerships Must Be Based on Mutual Needs

Consider the wanna-be investor who knows just enough about real estate to be dangerous. He has loads of confidence, but very little cash. Most often, he will attempt to convince someone with money that simply by joining forces they can both end up rich. But, instead, they both nearly always end up broke. Stay away from people who have big ideas, but no money.

Joining with others to make money can and does work, if you can discipline yourself. You must be tolerant, understanding, and very patient. You and your partner must understand that your mutual success depends totally on both of you. You must stay focused on the idea that partnership investing takes full cooperation by all the parties involved—anything less will most likely cause failure.

The questions I ask myself when someone approaches me with a partnership proposition are these three:

- What's in the deal for me?
- What's the risk to me?
- What assurances do I have that a partner will do what he or she says?

One question you should always ask yourself is "What's the most I can lose if I do make this deal?" Naturally, I'd be very concerned that my partner and I shared equal risk.

Looking for Partners: The Selection Process

The process involved in selecting a partner is without a doubt the most important consideration for developing a lasting and profitable partnership. Individual needs, ability to contribute, and skills must all be considered and balanced effectively. The selection process deserves a great deal of thought. It's far too important for quick decisions or snap judgments. Get-rich schemes, given little thought or planning, are generally failures from the very start.

Contrary to a popular myth, investment partners don't need to be good friends to be successful partners. It might help when getting started, but it's simply not a requirement. Obviously, enjoying the same social activities has nothing to do with a profitable real estate partnership.

My number-one consideration for establishing a strong and lasting partnership is my own self-interest. Do I really care if my investment partner gets rich? I certainly do—because it means that I'll get rich too. If it sounds like greed provides the need, it's most likely true. Just concentrate on what I'm telling you and, later on, I think you'll understand why partnerships work best when there is self-interest or greed.

Partners Don't Need to Be Friends

Many small investment partnerships are created almost entirely on the basis of friendships between people who work together, attend the same clubs and churches, or perhaps enjoy the same social activities. Regardless of what mutual involvement brings folks together initially, partnerships founded solely on the basis of friendships are most likely doomed from the very start. No matter how compatible people might seem to be as friends and social acquaintances, they will almost always change when their personal money becomes involved.

This change often reminds me of the little old man in the driver education films. He's soft-spoken, shy, and well-mannered—until he gets behind the wheel. Then suddenly all that changes and he speeds down the freeway threatening anyone who dares to come near him. The point is that people don't always act like you'd expect. Perfect strangers are more likely to make better business partners than any of your friends.

How to Find a Money Partner

Many folks would like to create a profitable partnership venture, but don't know how to go about it. The first thing is that you must determine what you can provide to the partnership—investment capital, your time, or a specialized skill you possess. Include this when you advertise for a partner. There are many people looking for what you have to offer, but since they don't know you exist, they can't find you. You must let them know. One of the best ways to find investment partners with the particular qualifications you need is by advertising in the Help Wanted section of your local newspaper. Let everyone know exactly what you're looking for.

I can still remember my early classroom experiences, when I was a bit too shy to ask the teacher a simple question in front of my class. I was afraid the other kids would think my question was stupid and laugh at me. Then someone else would ask the same question and the teacher would praise him or her for asking such an intelligent question.

What I'm trying to say here is that there are many decent partners around, but you must do something to let them know you're looking for them. The worst that can happen is they'll turn you down—and, I assure you, that doesn't hurt. Just keep on trying until the right one finds you.

Benefits Must Be Totally Equal for All

The biggest problem I've observed about small investment partnerships is that they're almost always engineered or thought up by the person who doesn't have any money. This person has all sorts of wonderful ideas, but in order to make them work, he or she must find someone with money. The typical arrangement is where one partner is asked to put up hard cash and the other is supposed to contribute an equivalent share of personal services.

I don't know how you think, but I'm very skeptical about anyone who proposes a joint plan that uses my money and risks only personal services from the partner. The question I ask is aimed directly at the heart of the issue: "If your ideas are so good, then why is it I've got the money and you don't?" There may be several good answers—which I consider reasonable and acceptable—but unless the question gets answered to my satisfaction,

I will not consider going forward. If you ask that question and the answer doesn't satisfy you, then neither should you.

The Courting Period Requires Honesty

The biggest mistake *no-money partners* make in trying to entice a person with money is to oversell and overstate the benefits the money partner will receive. If I actually received all the profits I've been promised, I would need to rent the Bank of America headquarters building to store my money. Fortunately—or unfortunately, whichever way you view it—I did not invest my money in most of these proposals, so I'll never really know for sure. But, I can tell you this much: a very high percentage of the deals went bust.

Since I have a lot of experience on both sides of partnership investing, as both the person who's broke and the person with money, I feel I'm qualified to pass on a few tips to help you structure a partnership that will hopefully survive the high fatality rate. Because there are many more wanna-be investors who don't have money, I'll concentrate on helping you find someone willing to put up the money.

Jay's 60/40 Rule for Investing with a Money Partner

My "no-compromise" rule for investing with a money partner is the same rule as I use for landlording. I call it my *60/40* rule. What it means is that I'm prepared to give more than I receive—60% to be exact. Here's the way I apply it to partnership investing.

I've always felt that investors with no money should be willing to give up at least 60% of the partnership benefits in order to attract the money. What this means is, if I'm the broke partner, I must be content with 40% of the deal.

You should ask yourself this question about the partnership: Who is more likely to make it alone—*the person with the money or the one without?* Without overanalyzing this question, I think you can get my point. The person with the money will always have a much better chance than the one with no money. Don't you agree?

Money opens many doors. Therefore, let's simply concede that the most valuable person in a small partnership is the one who furnishes cash—a.k.a., *the money partner*. If you develop your plans accordingly, it will help you structure a partnership or co-investment with the best possible chance for success.

A Plan to End Your Money Problems

When I first decided to invest with someone else, I had no question about how I would fit in or what my role would be. Since I didn't have any money, I would be the worker partner and I was perfectly willing to give up 60% in return for my 40%. I was more than willing to do whatever it took. I already knew that, as the working partner, I'd be responsible for making the property pay off for the partnership.

If you're successful at doing this—that is, your partnership makes money—and if you're the partner who is performing the personal (work) services, you'll never need to worry about finding money to invest again. That's because there is no shortage of investors willing to invest their money with a winner. What is in short supply are partners who can turn the money into handsome profits.

Let's discuss a plan that works very well for a small investment partnership. You might call this plan a "partnership proving ground."

A Simple A-B Partnership Plan

Partner A has money to invest. Partner B has the time and skills to operate a real estate investment. Let's suppose I'm Partner B and I'm looking for someone to put up $25,000 for a down payment on some apartments. I find a person with money who would like to invest, but he will first need some assurance that I can operate the property and, eventually, turn a profit. I will need to satisfactorily answer the four basic questions that any investor with money (Partner A) will want to know about the investment and me. Here are the questions.

1. What's in the deal for me?
2. What is my risk if I invest?
3. What assurances will I have that Partner B can manage the property?
4. What will Partner B lose (risk) if he or she can't manage the property?

Like I told you earlier, the benefits must be equal before I apply my 60/40 rule. I always insist my 60/40 rule is what makes a deal work.

I want you to underline this next sentence and read it often: you must never forget it. *The better you can become at solving problems for others, the more success you will enjoy for yourself.* This applies to everything you touch in real estate, but it's especially true when you're a broke partner looking for someone with money. Now let's explore the answers to the previous questions.

Question 1: What's in the Deal for Me?

I'll set up some hypothetical numbers to illustrate my partnership proposal.

$100,000	purchase price of the Good Deal Apartments
−25,000	cash down by Partner A
$75,000	mortgage balance with payments of $650 per month

Rents (income) estimated to be $1,100 per month ($13,200 annually).

I've already advised my partner that there will be little or no cash flow for partnership distribution to start with. I propose to set up the partnership agreement for a seven-year term. (Five to 10 years is the normal range.) My basic plan is to rent out the property for seven years, then sell it and close out the partnership. We'll then split the profits 50/50.

$150,000	estimated property value seven years from now
−25,000	return of capital (down payment) to Partner A
$125,000	balance
−70,000	unpaid mortgage balance
$ 55,000	profits to split between partners

Cash distribution: Partner A and Partner B get $27,500 each.

The partnership will agree to pay $100 per month management fee to Partner B. All cash flow from rents (projected for years three through seven) will be divided 90% to Partner A and 10% to Partner B. Average 5% annual rent increases will raise rents by approximately $5,000 during the seven-year term. Cash flow distributions to partners will most likely occur starting after three years of operations.

Profits and losses from operations (*tax benefits*) will be allocated to partners in the same ratio as rents—90% to Partner A and 10% to Partner

B. This can be a money-making benefit for Partner A, depending on his tax bracket and gross income from regular wages or other ordinary income.

In summary, this plan will allow Partner A to net out very handsome profits during the seven-year partnership term. First, the $25,000 investment will return a $27,500 profit. Second, there will be income tax savings from his ordinary income (tax shelter). Finally, cash flow from rents will accumulate, beginning at year three and going through year seven of the partnership term.

Partner B, who invests no money, will benefit from the $27,500 profit after seven years, plus the $100 monthly management fee for 84 months ($8,400).

This is not an unusual partnership arrangement. In fact, it's quite common. As you can see, there are excellent benefits with earnings that far exceed other types of investing. Imagine if you're the broke investor (Partner B) and you're successful at putting together a few of these partnership deals. It's truly an excellent opportunity to build wealth starting with no money at all. You can use your skills in lieu of investing money.

There are many other opportunities that become available as you gain experience and expand your creative skills. For example, if you happen to be handy, you can do all repairs and maintenance yourself and bill the partnership for your labor. You'll do fine even if your billing rate is half of what licensed tradespeople charge. The partnership saves money on expenses and, obviously, you earn more money. If the rental income doesn't cover your expenses in some months, keep a running log and collect it later. Your flexibility helps the partnership as well as building wealth for yourself.

Question 2: What Is My Risk if I Invest?

Obviously, the money partner will be very concerned, especially if Partner B doesn't have a proven track record. He needs to feel safe and you must be able to assure him. There are a couple of methods to do so.

First, you can purchase a property as *tenants in common* with undivided and unequal ownership interest, such as 90% for Partner A and 10% for Partner B. This arrangement (*ownership percentage*) should be specified in a co-owner agreement. More about that later.

The problem with this arrangement, from the money partner's viewpoint, is that all the money invested is his or hers. Partner B has no money at risk. If Partner B can't or, for some reason, won't perform his or her duties, then Partner A has a couple of serious problems. First, he or she has no day-to-day manager or anyone to handle the apartment operation. (Remember: Partner A is a passive investor and can't handle daily operations.) Second, he or she could have a tough time trying to get Partner B's name off the property. It is possible to avoid this problem by having Partner B sign a quitclaim deed in advance, to be recorded in the event that something goes wrong. Still, there is a good possibility for a lawsuit, with attorney fees involved.

If this first arrangement is not satisfactory to a money partner, perhaps my second method might offer a better solution.

Question 3: What Assurances Will I Have That Partner B Can Manage Property?

With the option arrangement above, Partner A can quickly get rid of Partner B if he or she does not meet the terms of the *co-owner agreement*. This plan is generally quite favorable with money investors, because it represents less liability to them if something goes wrong. The worst that could happen is that Partner A would be the sole owner of a rental property without anyone to help manage. That's not so bad, as he or she can easily hire a professional manager.

If I were Partner B in this hypothetical case, I would have no problems with this arrangement. After all, I'm the partner who must prove myself since I have no cash to invest. Again, don't forget my 60/40 rule. You must be willing to give more—and it will make you very wealthy in the end, believe me.

Question 4: What Will Partner B Lose (Risk) if He or She Can't Manage the Property?

If I'm the money partner, I'm naturally concerned about my own risk. However, I'm also concerned about what my partner stands to gain or lose on the deal. Obviously, it's not cash, since he or she has none invested initially. However, in our hypothetical transaction, Partner B stands to earn $6,400 annually. Naturally, he will lose that much if he blows the deal.

Quite frankly, $6,400 is a very respectable incentive when you're broke.

Here's how I figure Partner B's gain or earnings.

$27,500	profits at the end of seven years (termination or sale)
8,400	management ($100 per month for 84 months)
8,400	labor billed to partnership ($100/month average for 7 years)
500	10% share of cash flow, years four through seven
$44,800	

$44,800 divided by seven years equals $6,400 per year, for terms of partnership.

A partner without money who can earn $533 per month for seven years has a lot to gain. Even though he has no up-front money invested, chances are very good that he or she will consider a profit of $44,800 worth the effort. I always want my partner to make big profits, because in doing so he'll automatically earn big profits for me, too.

Alternate Partnership Plan: Option to Purchase

Here's another possibility. Partner A could be the sole owner. That is, purchase the property in his or her name only. Partner B can protect his or her interest with an option to purchase the property at the end of the partnership term.

Let's say the option to purchase says that after seven years Partner B has the right to purchase 50% interest in the property for the initial purchase price of $100,000. He can do this by putting up an equal cash down payment of $25,000, just as Partner A did to acquire the property. In reality, Partner B won't put up a dime. It's done in the form of a credit. The net results will be the same, as shown below.

$150,000	selling price (value)
−25,000	return of initial down payment to Partner A
$125,000	left over
−25,000	Partner B's cash down payment (exercise option-to-purchase)
$150,000	balance
−25,000	return of cash down payment to Partner B
$125,000	left over
−70,000	mortgage balance
$55,000	balance to split between partners

As you can see, the bottom line or profit remains the same. Each partner still receives $27,500 as his share. However, with this arrangement, Partner B is not on the title until he exercises his option. The right to exercise the option can be tied to specific performance. If performance is not achieved, then Partner B cannot exercise the option and Partner A does not have the problem of trying to clean up the title. He is already the sole owner of the property.

A Tenants-in-Common Partnership

Co-ownership investing can be an excellent way for a couple of individuals to acquire real estate together. Often two investment-minded people will get together and decide it would be a great idea to pool their resources and buy rental houses. They figure they can sell them later and split the profits. With this sort of informal plan, the best way to acquire property and take title is as *tenants in common*. Don't confuse this with being a renter—called a *tenant*—or with *joint tenancy*—which is generally how husbands and wives take title to jointly owned properties.

Formal partnerships have several disadvantages for smaller, mom-and-pop investors. First, it can be more expensive to set up the bookkeeping. A formal partnership is like a separate taxpayer in terms of income tax reporting. Federal taxes are prepared on a special form (Form 1065), with a Schedule K-1 for each partner. Aside from being more formal and expensive, they can be a pain because 1065s are excellent sources for government tax audits. Also, partnership statements and fictitious business name documents must be filed in each county where partnership property is owned. That means you'll always need copies and updates for bank loans or refinancing.

Perhaps the most serious reason to stay away from formal partnerships is because you cannot exchange partnership interests using tax code Section 1031. For this reason alone, you should give serious thought to keeping your association informal, because tenants in common investors can benefit from 1031 exchanges.

Most banks or institutional lenders will not make direct loans to small partnerships. Individuals generally have a much easier time borrowing money. Having information on file will most likely require you to purchase a local business license to operate rental properties.

Tax reporting is done by each partner on his or her individual tax form (1040) for Federal taxes. There are no additional tax forms requiring information about the partners. As a tenant in common, each partner can own any percentage of the property agreed upon—50/50, 20/80, 90/10, or any other combination. Whatever it is, however, it should be specified on the property deed when the ownership is recorded. If a tenant in common dies, his or her share of ownership in the property is passed to his or her heirs. That's different from joint tenancy, where the surviving joint tenant gets the share of the deceased tenant.

A Partnership Design Is Negotiable

The hypothetical partnership we have been discussing is only to show you how it could work. There are dozens of ways to structure a small partnership to meet the needs of the parties involved. There are absolutely no limits to how creative you can be.

The terms of the partnership—who gets the cash flow, how profits and losses are allocated to the partners, who does what work, and how to divide the profits at the end—are negotiable and strictly up to the individuals who set up the partnership. What is most important for the success of any partnership, no matter how it's structured, is that everyone gets at least what he or she is promised. I cannot over-emphasize this point. That's why my 60/40 rule works so well.

When I'm involved with a money partner, I work extremely hard to make sure my partner gets all of his or her benefits before I even consider mine. If you follow my advice, you'll never have to worry about down payment money again. Investors with money will start calling you after a while.

Sound Advice with a Harsh Bite

With partnership investing, you definitely need a partnership agreement, but it doesn't have to be expensive. I will show you exactly what kind of agreement you need to keep you and your money partners on the right track. You do not need to be formal partners to invest together. There's a simpler way, as I shall explain. First, however, allow me to offer a few suggestions and some personal philosophy, since I've been a participant in many small, informal investment groups.

This advice may sound somewhat harsh; however, I received it years ago from a friend and it has worked very well for me. The advice was from a marriage counselor who told a young couple contemplating their wedding, "Before you get married, consider what you plan to do when you get divorced."

I'm not sure how long the counselor lasted in the counseling business or how many couples sought his advice, but from a purely objective standpoint, his advice makes a lot of sense. In fact, it's exactly the same advice I pass along to anyone who is thinking about buying real estate with another party. The best way to guard against failure is to be prepared for it and then do everything you can to prevent it.

The Partnership Promise: A Co-Ownership Agreement

Once negotiated, everything the partners agree to must be formalized. That means you need a written document—the *co-ownership agreement*. Do not run your business on verbal promises. You'll end up on the short end of the stick if you do.

The co-ownership agreement doesn't need to be very long, especially for small, two-party associations. You must, however, spell out your investment plan. For example, how will you purchase the property? How much money will it cost? Who pays for what and when? You'll also need a statement about the purpose of the partnership (what you're doing).

Important Terms to Include in the Agreement

Next, you need to write up the rules of the co-ownership agreement. These are the important terms the partners must live by. I will list the important terms you must make sure to address in the co-ownership agreement.

1. Names of partners, place of business, dates
2. Form of business (e.g., general partnership, corporation, or limited association)
3. Capital contribution—Who puts up the money, when, and how?
4. Sharing income, expenses, profits—How will they be divided?
5. Who is in charge of daily management of property?

6. Who can sell, encumber, transfer, or purchase new property?
7. What to do about disagreements?
8. Who will keep books and records and do taxes?
9. Death of a partner—What will the surviving partner(s) do?
10. Indemnification of each partner against debts of the other(s)
11. Violation of terms of agreement—What will you do?
12. Restrictions of the partners (e.g., don't allow borrowing or pledge the property)
13. Termination—When, how, for what reason? Is extension OK?
14. Withdrawal partner—How to split assets and in what manner?

These are your primary considerations. When you agree to invest your skills and money, take the time to write down the rules you'll conduct business by—it pays. You'll find an example of the co-ownership agreement at the end of this chapter.

Never Invest Without a Written Agreement

The agreement to buy real estate and deciding how to conduct business and pay taxes are the easiest part of partnership investing. Not unlike new marriages, the real test always comes after the initial promises.

The biggest mistake any two partners can make is to begin buying properties without a written agreement. You must decide who is responsible for what, who does what, how the money is allocated, and—last, but perhaps most important—how to terminate the investment, in case things don't work out.

This contract is not meant to be exactly the same for every transaction. But, it is typical of the kind you might use for co-investing. The contract is what you write up to formalize and document the terms you agree to when you make a deal. Remember the important terms we've already discussed when you write up your own contract. Never forget that, when investing in real estate, if it isn't in writing, it just ain't so.

A hypothetical co-ownership agreement between Fixer Jay and Sam Moneybags is shown at the end of this chapter. It outlines the terms agreed to by both investors. The agreement can be recorded at the local county recorder's office. I always prefer to record a memorandum of the transaction instead, without specifying the terms on public documents.

Memorandums are my choice, because I don't like telling the general public about my business affairs.

Finding Money When You Don't Have Any

One plan that has worked very well for me is another variation of having a partner or co-ownership arrangement.

Let's say you are like many other short-of-cash investors trying to get your investment plan off the ground. You have that big dream, plenty of personal drive, a willingness to work hard, but your bank account is empty.

We'll say you've already found a good income property, but the seller wants the normal 20% cash down. Let's assume that, even though you have a regular 40-hour-per-week job, you've made up your mind you are willing to work evenings and weekends to build real estate wealth. You don't have much money, but you're willing to do whatever it takes to get your investment plan in motion. To put it another way, you're ready to contribute yourself—you're willing to substitute your time and energy in lieu of the cash down payment.

No Money Is No Problem—Once You Prove Yourself

What you need now is someone who has money—a partner who is ready, willing, and able to put up the cash down payment. As I said, you've already found a good solid investment property with great potential, but you need the down payment money fast.

Let me ease your mind by telling you that lots of people are willing to invest their money in these kinds of transactions: they are more plentiful than you might ever imagine. However, there is a catch—they can be very difficult to find when you're starting out. The problem is that all investors like safe bets. They like to deal with winners. The ones I know are always eager to invest their money, but only if they think you can make them more money.

You Must Develop a Good Record

Hands-on working investors—who develop the ability to find rundown properties, fix them up, and make healthy profits for their cash-investing partners—soon develop good reputations. The problem for new investors is obvious: they have no track record yet. So when you're new, there is no evidence that you know how to invest money and earn a profit. That's the biggest obstacle you must overcome. It's not an easy task. However, many others have done it, with less ability than you. So you can do it, too.

A Sample Co-Ownership Agreement

The following is a sample of the kind of agreement you should prepare in setting up a co-ownership agreement. It assures that all parties are on the same page and spells out the terms of your understanding. Any such document should be notarized by a certified notary public as well.

1234 Easy Street, Golden City, California

THIS AGREEMENT is made effective as of the first day of April, 2002, between Fixer Jay and Sam Moneybags.

1. Transaction: Fixer Jay (Jay) and Sam Moneybags (Sam) will join together as co-owners for the purpose of owning and operating that certain real estate located at 1234 Easy Street, Golden City, California (the Property), for the mutual benefit and profit of each. Each party agrees to perform fully under this Agreement for the success of both parties herein.

2. Acquisition of Property: Sam and Jay have purchased the Property for a purchase price of Seventy-Five Thousand Dollars ($75,000). The cash down payment of Twenty Thousand, Five Hundred Dollars ($20,500) was paid by Sam. Both parties will take title subject to the existing mortgage lien in the amount of Thirty-One Thousand, Five Hundred Dollars and 00/100 ($31,500). The seller of the Property has agreed to finance the balance of the purchase price, approximately Twenty-Three Thousand Dollars and 00/100 ($23,000), with installment payments of Two Hundred Dollars and 00/100 ($200) or more per month, including seven percent (7%) interest until the entire principal is paid in full.

3. Cash Distributions from Rental: All excess cash derived from rental of the Property, after payment of all expenses and debt service,

---

shall be divided eighty percent (80%) to Sam and twenty percent (20%) to Jay.

4. Cash Proceeds from Sale or Refinancing of the Property: Net cash proceeds derived from the sale or refinancing of the Property shall be shared as follows:

First, Sam shall receive back all of his capital invested in the Property by way of the initial down payment, fix-up expenditures, and operating expenses made pursuant to Paragraphs 2, 11, and 12 hereof. Thereafter, all remaining proceeds derived from the sale or refinancing shall be shared eighty percent (80%) to Sam and twenty percent (20%) to Jay.

5. Management: All decisions regarding the management of the Property shall be made upon the joint approval of both Sam and Jay provided, however, it is agreed that Jay will have primary responsibility for the day-to-day management operations, such as rent-up, property maintenance, repairs, cleaning and the like, in order to conduct an efficient rental business. (Rent-up is the time it takes for newly constructed or renovated rental properties to be fully occupied.) Jay shall receive a 6% management fee per month (fee based on income) for managing the property. In addition, Jay shall be reimbursed for his actual out-of-pocket costs and expenses incurred in connection with such management.

6. Books and Records: All books and records will be kept at the office of Jay. A statement of operations will be provided to Sam on a monthly basis. This statement will be prepared by Jay as part of his management duties.

7. Bank Accounts: Jay shall maintain a commercial checking account at Gold Street Bank, 2930 Silver Lane, Golden City, California, or at such other banking institution that shall be approved by Sam, for the purpose of operating the Property.

8. Indemnification: Each party shall indemnify and hold harmless the other party and the Property from and against all separate debts, claims, actions, and demands of said party.

9. Termination: This Agreement shall terminate upon the sale of the Property or by mutual consent of Sam and Jay. Sam shall have the sole right to determine when the Property is to be sold, provided, however, that Sam shall first offer Jay the right to purchase the Property for the same amount and upon the same terms and conditions as Sam is willing to sell the Property pursuant to a bona fide offer received from any third party. Jay shall exercise said right of first refusal within ten (10) days after the receipt of notification from Sam of his intention to accept said third party offer. Jay shall consummate the transaction within sixty (60) days after the exercise of his right of first refusal.

10. Death of Parties: Upon the death of Sam, Jay shall have the right to either purchase Sam's interest in the Property in the manner described in Paragraph 9 hereof, based upon a bona fide offer received by Sam's estate or, in absence of such an offer, Jay shall have the right to cause the Property to be sold and the proceeds divided in accordance with Paragraph 4 of this Agreement. In the event liquidation is elected, Jay shall proceed with reasonable diligence to liquidate the Property within twelve (12) months after Sam's death.

11. Initial Fix-Up Expenditures: Initial fix-up funds for rehabilitation of the Property will be contributed by Sam. All work will be performed by employees of Jay. Employee time sheets and material invoices shall be part of Jay's record keeping.

12. Operating Funds: All expenses for repairs, improvements, taxes, insurance, maintenance, and other operating expenses deemed necessary for the operation of the Property shall be paid first from rental income derived from the Property and, thereafter, from additional funds to be contributed by Sam.

13. Business Address: The official management office for the Property will be Jay's One-Stop Rental Company, located at 2020 End of the Trail Drive, Golden City, CA 96001. The mailing address is c/o Fixer Jay, P.O. Box 492029, Redding, CA 96049-3039.

14. No Partnership or Joint Venture: The relationship between Jay and Sam under this Agreement shall be solely that of co-owners of real estate and under no circumstances shall said relationship constitute a partnership or joint venture.

IN WITNESS WHEREOF, the Parties have executed this Agreement as of the day and year first above written.

_____

Sam Moneybags

_____

Fixer Jay

16

Sell Half the Property to Increase Your Income

There are some very worthwhile advantages to fixing up real estate first, then finding an investment partner to help bail you out of debt. One advantage is that you can sell your "sweat equity" for a premium price or a very high markup. The following is an actual case I became involved with. The names have been changed.

Allen, a student of mine, recently came to Redding for counseling and a tour of my fixer houses. He wanted to see for himself exactly what kind of properties I recommend for most investors. He also wanted advice about how to generate more cash flow without selling the properties he'd worked so hard to develop.

Over the past several years, Allen has managed to acquire several properties with low down payments. Today, he owns two single-family houses, a five-unit "leper property" (a property no one else wanted to touch), and a seven-unit apartment building. He's done very well with low down payments; however, he suffers from the affliction common to most all *low-cash-down* buyers—elephant-size mortgage payments every month.

Allen has managed to fix up the properties himself as he goes along, but he's in a cash bind now, because his fix-up expenses have basically been paid from his personal bank account, which is running on fumes. Nothing stops a good investment plan faster than running out of money. Allen has reached the point where he fully understands the flip side of no-down- or small-down-payment buying. It generally means no cash flow or very little.

The Best Computer in the World Doesn't Help Broke Investors

Allen came to Redding well prepared to discuss his financial dilemma. He brought along six sets of computer spreadsheets to show me why he was losing money every month. None, however, offered a solution for how he might stop losing money. Allen saved that problem for me to solve.

My seminar students understand I'm not a computer person when it comes to earning money. I use a rather simple technique—what I call the "MLO (money left over) formula." It works like this.

Every month I deposit all my rents and other income from carryback notes in my bank account. During the month I write checks to pay my employees, property expenses, and mortgage payments. Finally, when the last day rolls around, I check the balance in my account. If there's something left for me, that's MLO! See how simple accounting can be? I might add, there's an extra $10,000 in my account today, which I've saved over the years by not buying a computer to figure out whether I'm making money or not.

50% Sales Can Greatly Improve Cash Flow

One of my favorite methods for generating income quickly, which of course is what Allen wanted to hear about, is to purchase a rundown property with good upgrade potential—fix it up, then sell 50% of the ownership to a passive investor. You might be wondering, Why sell only 50%? Why not sell the whole property?

First of all, if I can relieve my cash flow problem by selling only 50%, I'm more than happy to keep the other half for myself. As you shall soon learn, there's extra money to be made by the 50% owner who manages the property in addition to the profits from the sale itself. Let me show you how a typical transaction might look. We'll call this property "El Dumpo Villa."

El Dumpo Villa—Two Duplexes and Three Single-Family Houses

Seven rental units on a large city lot (older, shabby, and rundown):

Financial Data

Monthly income ($375 rent per unit x seven units)	$2,625
Annual income ($2,625 x 12 months)	$31,500
Purchase price (offer) (6.5 x gross rents) ($31,500)	$204,750
Purchase price (accepted)	$205,000

Terms

$15,000 cash down. (6% to 10% is average for rundown properties.)

$190,000 unpaid balance. Seller agrees to carry back the mortgage at 9% interest amortized over 20 years.

Monthly payments (principal and interest) are $1,709.49.

Typical Property Income and Expense Setup at Beginning

Monthly Income

Gross income (rents)	$2,625.00	100%
Vacancy and credit losses (uncollectibles)	$ 265.00	10%
Gross operating income	$2,360.00	

Monthly Expenses (owner is the manager)

Taxes	$180.00	7%
Management	0	10%
Insurance	105.00	4%
Repairs	265.00	10%
Maintenance	130.00	5%
Advertising and accounting	50.00	2%
Utilities	105.00	4%
Total expenses	$835.00	
Net operating income	$1,525.00	
Mortgage payment	$1,709.49	
Cash flow (positive or negative)	($ 184.51)	

The Task Is to Quickly Fix Up the Property and Add Value

Let's assume the fix-up costs (labor and material) will be 10% of the purchase price, or $20,000. On average, the cost breakdown between labor and material, as mentioned earlier in this book, is 70% for labor ($14,000) and 30% for material ($6,000). The buyer will provide the labor for this project. Therefore, the buyer's out-of-pocket costs for material will be $6,000.

Depending on how fast the buyer can accomplish the fix-up task (I always estimate 12 to 18 months), he'll probably lose a few tenants who don't see any need for improvements. They also see the handwriting on the wall, which tells them that in the very near future, when things are cleaned up, rents will likely increase. Tenants of junky properties who are paying under-market rents understand the reason rents are low—and they know very well that rents won't stay low for long once the property gets fixed up.

Rents and Gross Multipliers Go up Together

Finally, the big day arrives and the property is all fixed up and looks great. Along the way, we had some tenants come and go. The new ones moving in should naturally be paying higher rents. A fixer property of this size, purchased at 6.5 times gross rents, with $20,000 worth of fix-up work completed, should easily command 25% higher rents. That means total rents of $2,625 per month can be increased to $3,285 when the fix-up work is done. A 25% increase is very modest, in my experience. More often, I'm able to achieve 40% to 60% or even higher increases, especially if my fix-up job takes longer than a year. New tenants will see the big improvement and are willing to pay higher rents.

With new looks and a higher income, the property is now worth much more than the lowly 6.5 GRM. For example, in my area, a 6.5 GRM is what you will most likely pay for ugly, rundown properties. After they've been fixed up, however, they will generally sell for about 8 times the gross rents.

How to Market a Fixed-Up, Fixer Property

The secret to selling 50% ownership in a fixed-up property for the highest price is to make an offer the buyer can't refuse. My suggestion is to offer a *no-down deal* to a qualified buyer. Naturally, if you need to retrieve your fix-up costs in order to keep buying groceries, a *no-down* sale may not work for you. However, folks with good jobs (the kind of buyer you want) are always eager to purchase investment real estate for no down payment, especially if you'll manage it, and they are happy to pay you monthly installments. Most of them will not even question your selling price. From a personal income tax standpoint, most buyers can generally offset a good portion of their monthly payments with tax write-offs (savings) from their regular wages or salary.

No, I haven't forgotten about the $21,000 cash that's tied up in this deal ($15,000 down payment, plus $6,000 materials). However, the income we can generate from a 50% sale will quickly pay that back. Let's take a look at a marketing strategy for the fixed-up property. You should understand that no-down buyers are willing to pay top retail prices in exchange for an easy buy-in (no cash). In this example, selling for 8.5 times gross rents should work. Here's how the numbers would look:

New annual rents: $3,285 per month x 12 months	$39,420
Selling price: 8.5 x gross rents (rounded)	$335,000
Existing mortgage balance:	$189,000
Total equity:	$146,000

Notice that the selling price of $335,000 represents more than a 63% markup, which is pretty good when you're calculating profits.

Obviously, a 50% buyer will be entitled to half of the income. He or she will also assume half the existing debt and share expenses 50-50. The buyer will be paying you for 50% of the equity with monthly installments. In this case, his share is $73,000 (50% of $146,000). I generally draw up a promissory note amortized over 10 years at 10% interest. That works out to 120 monthly payments of $964.71. Certainly, 15 years would be acceptable to me if my buyer insisted on smaller payments.

The sale gets reported like this for setting up the buyer's 50% purchase:

Total sale price:	$167,500
Buyer to assume existing mortgage:	$94,500
Buyer to execute new promissory note in favor of seller:	$73,000

The transaction can be done with a *deed* transferring title or a *land contract* without a title change, which is often done with no-down transactions. Either way it's OK, strictly a choice.

When the 50% sale is completed, here's how the new operating numbers will look. They show who gets what and who pays for what.

Income and Expense Setup—After 50% Sale

	Seller 50%	Investor 50%
Monthly Income		
Total monthly income:	$1,642.50	$1,642.50
Vacancy and credit losses		
(deadbeat tenants):	-164.50	-164.50
Gross operating income:	$1,478.00	$1,478.00
Monthly Expenses		
Taxes:	$177.00	$177.00
Management (your share free):	0	165.00
Insurance:	66.00	66.00
Repairs:	164.00	164.00
Maintenance:	82.00	82.00
Advertising and accounting:	33.00	33.00
Utilities:	66.00	66.00
Total expenses:	$588.00	$753.00
Net operating income:	890.00	725.00
Mortgage payments:	854.74	854.74
Cash flow (positive or negative):	$35.26	($129.74)

Converting Negative Cash Flow into Positive

As you can see from the after-sale setup, the seller's negative cash flow—originally -$184.51—has been eliminated. Instead, the seller now has a $35.26 positive cash flow. That's not much, but we're just beginning. Each month for the next 10 years, the seller will receive $964.71 from the buyer until the $73,000 equity purchase is paid off.

It's starting to get more interesting, wouldn't you say? So far the seller is earning $35.26 positive cash flow from operations and $964.71 from his note receivable. That increases the seller's monthly income to $999.97. But we're still not done yet. You'll notice the $165 management fee on the investor's side of the after-sale setup. The law says that owners can't pay themselves a fee for managing properties they own, but they certainly can receive management fees for the portion they don't own. If the co-owner is managing the 50% he doesn't own, then he is entitled to the $165 management fee. Now, his monthly earnings are up to $1,164.97. It's getting better, wouldn't you say?

Do you recall the 70%-30% labor/material cost breakdown? Once again, if the co-owner performs labor on the 50% share of the property he doesn't own, he's entitled to earn the labor fees. In this case, the investor's setup shows $164 for repairs and $82 for maintenance—a total of $246. 70% of $246 equals $172, which goes to pay the co-owner for the labor associated with repairs and maintenance.

Now, let's review exactly what we've accomplished in terms of improving our cash flow. When the El Dumpo Villa property was acquired, the income and expense setup showed a bottom line loss of $184.51 per month. Now, after selling 50% of the property, you'll see the seller's monthly cash flow has improved dramatically. Take a look at what the co-owner will now receive each month if he manages the property and does repairs and maintenance.

Cash flow from operations:	$35.26
Mortgage payment from investor:	964.71
Management fee from investor:	165.00
Payment (repairs and maintenance) from investor:	172.00
Total MLO (money left over), after expenses:	$1,336.97

You'll notice the seller's cash flow is a whole lot better after selling 50% of the property. Two millennia ago, Julius Caesar said, "Divisa et impera"—"If you can divide them, you can conquer them." That same strategy works just as well dividing real estate as it did for the ancient Romans.

17

Jay's 90/10 Money Partner Plan for Cash-Poor Investors

My 90/10 money partner plan is a shared ownership arrangement, an ideal two-party investment vehicle for the active investor, with the ability to fix up and manage the property, and for the passive investor, who can supply most of the cash that's needed.

It means that my partner and I will both invest in a property. The partner will contribute 90% of the cash down payment—making him or her the money partner—and I will pay the remaining 10%. For this plan to work, the down payment should be at least 20% to 25% of the purchase price. I prefer not to scrimp on the cash down payment. The reason is that when the mortgage debt exceeds 80% of the purchase price, there is great danger of having negative cash flow while operating the property. The down payment should always be large enough to reduce the principal balance so that the income generated from the property will cover both the mortgage payment and operating costs.

When you locate a property that seems promising, keep in mind that you will need to thoroughly check out the income and expenses. You don't want any hidden costs of operation to show up after you close the deal. It can be very awkward explaining to your partner that, because you under-estimated operating costs, he or she must now come up with additional money every month. It's also not very good for the track record you're try-ing to establish.

How the 90/10 Plan Works

The 90/10 plan works like this. I find a money partner who will put up 90% of the cash down payment after I locate a good solid money-maker prop-erty and agree to do the daily management. The money partner is basical-ly a hands-off investor. I will be the field manager and operate the proper-ty. I agree to do the renting, cleaning, fixing, advertising, and whatever else is needed to make our joint investment profitable for both of us.

To illustrate how my 90/10 plan works, let's go through some num-bers. Assume we locate a $90,000 rental house that we can purchase for $80,000. That shouldn't be too difficult to do when we can pay $20,000 cash down. The money partner in this case puts up $18,000 (90%), of the down payment cash and becomes a 90% owner. I contribute $2,000 (10%) and get 10% ownership in the property. Remember, I'm only talking about the down payment here. I continue to contribute my services throughout our ownership period, which is normally set up for a period of 10 years on my agreement.

By the way, don't make these deals without a co-ownership agree-ment. Investment partners should always decide up front how long they wish to be partners. I personally like to state a firm termination date, then provide for extending it if we should choose to continue. The agreement doesn't need to be long and complicated; however, it must cover the important terms, as with any co-investment venture. See the previous chapter for an example of how to use my co-ownership agreement.

For Just 10% Cash, I Receive 50% Profit

Although I'm only a 10% cash investor, I will earn 50% of the profits at the end, plus there's an excellent chance I'll make a few dollars from cash flow along the way. At the end (the date is specified in our contract), the profits are split like this. First, the 90% investor and I will both get our down payments back ($18,000 for the 90% investor and $2,000 for me). After that, the balance is split 50-50, after subtracting what we still owe on the mortgage. For example, let's say the $90,000 property we buy now for $80,000 sells for double that amount 10 years from now—$180,000—and the original $60,000 mortgage debt is paid down to $50,000. Here's how the numbers would look:

Original purchase price:	$80,000
Cash down payment:	-20,000
Mortgage balance to start:	$60,000
Selling price after 10 years:	$180,000
Mortgage balance after 10 years:	-50,000
Gross profit:	$130,000
Original cash down payment (returned to investors):	-20,000
Net profit to split 50-50:	$110,000

I realize there will be selling expenses (escrow fees) and, perhaps, real estate commissions to pay. However, as you can see, there's still a sizable profit.

Depending on how long the contract agreement is and how much the property appreciates in my particular investment area, I expect to earn a substantial return on my 10% portion of the down payment. Naturally, I'll get my $2,000 back, too.

High Returns and Buying Power Are Keys to Plan

The reason I like the 90/10 plan so well is that I get a maximum for my money. High-percentage returns and leverage are the big wealth builders in real estate.

This plan allows a skilled investor, with a very small amount of up-front cash, to generate the same "horsepower" as a much larger, traditional down payment. A $2,000 down payment would not be enough cash, in most cases, to bargain with sellers about their price. Most would not be willing to sell for such a small down payment.

This is the kind of deal that works very well for folks who don't have much money to invest, but who are willing to invest their time and professional skills. I always view single ownership (me only) as the best kind. However, lack of cash makes this plan an attractive alternative, until you have more money. Real estate investors need to be creative. This plan creates big opportunities for ambitious folks who are temporarily short of money.

Contributions Are Equal for Both Investors

The 90/10 plan provides for clean accounting of the transaction. The money partner who contributes 90% of the cash down payment also gets 90% of everything else. That includes income, expenses, depreciation, and tax credits. He or she is also responsible for 90% of additional contributions, if needed, for upgrading or repairs. The 10% partner (field manager) is responsible for the remaining 10% of everything, including any shortages during operations of the property. He or she also receives 10% of the cash flow.

How does this deal stack up in terms of equality? What are the values of each contributing partner? Obviously $18,000 and $2,000 are not equal cash contributions. To determine the noncash values, let's make several assumptions. First, we'll say the property we decide to purchase will rent for $800 per month, or $9,600 annually, to start out. We'll also say our co-ownership agreement specifies a term of 10 years and that the working partner will be allowed a 10% management fee.

The 10 years of management fees will be calculated at 120 months times 10% of the $800 for a total of $9,600. Also, rents are estimated to increase at least 3% each year during the 10-year term, which amounts to roughly $400 in additional management fees. After 10 full years, my contribution will be the $2,000 cash down payment, plus $10,000 worth of management fees, for a total of $12,000.

OK, that's much closer to the money partner's contribution, but still less. However, the money partner gets some tax benefits. Assume the $80,000 property will have $60,000 worth of depreciation. For this purpose, let's consider only the 27.5-year depreciation schedule ($60,000 divided by 27.5 years equals approximately $2,200 annually). The value of a 90% share of depreciation to a 28% tax payer, who qualifies for the deduction under current tax rules, is $554 annually, or $5,540 for 10 years.

Now, you see how the contributions of both partners are starting to balance out. The money partner's net contribution after taxes is $18,000 less $5,540 for a total of $12,460. The 10% remaining depreciation is worth about $600 to the working partner if he has adequate income to use it. Also to be considered is the distribution of cash flow, particularly in the later years of ownership. The cash investor will be entitled to 90% of all rental income, over and above expenses. This rent money will reduce his net cash invested even more before the partnership ends. Basically, the contributions end up about equal for both investors.

Never Forget the Golden Rule of Investing

When you're first getting started, a money partner will always be the most important member of your investment team. I call my 90% money partner the "golden partner," and with all golden partners, the Golden Rule applies—*He who has the gold, rules!* Look at the situation this way—no matter how important you value your personal skills or how much money you think you might earn for the partnership, it isn't worth a hill of beans unless you can first acquire the property to apply those skills. If you don't have the money to purchase property, nothing else matters much. I hope this point is clear. That's why a money partner is truly a "golden partner."

The Main Street Apartments: An Ideal 90/10 Partnership

First Main Street was a 92-unit studio apartment built in 1927. After many years of neglect and of being rented to the wrong kind of occupants, the three-story building was badly in need of some TLC—or *tender loving care.*

Structurally, the building was very solid, but many pipes were leaking, the paint was peeling, and the carpets smelled like a thousand cats were locked inside. The seller had great ideas when he purchased the property, but renting it out was his downfall. He had no screening requirements for tenants, other than that they had to pay the first month's rent. To get a key required no applications and no interviews and there obviously were no rules for living in the building. It was a perfect plan for disaster and, of course, that's exactly what happened. After four years, he ended up in bankruptcy and was forced to sell the property.

I negotiated with the seller for almost a year, making offers that would have been very beneficial to me—if he had accepted them. However, since he didn't accept any of them, I was forced to make my offers a bit more realistic. The seller was broke, but he wasn't stupid. The building had a lot of potential—we both knew it—even though it would take a lot of money to get the apartments fixed up and rented out to decent tenants. I estimated the studio apartments, once fixed up, would rent for at least $250 a month. That's potentially $23,000 per month—more than a quarter of a million dollars annually.

In Search of Investor Cash

The big problem for me was finding the immediate cash I needed to fix a building of that size. I had never attempted to fix up so many apartments at one time and I knew I would need some financial help to get the job done. I decided to schedule an appointment with a local physician who had purchased several properties from me over the past several years. When I told him about the potential income and the very generous depreciation allowance for partially furnished units, he was ready to write me a check. We agreed to set the deal up using my 90/10 investment plan.

Here's how it worked. The doctor would put up 90% of the required cash, which would include the down payment and all the fix-up costs. Naturally, the fix-up money would not be required all at one time, since the bills would be paid as we went along. I estimated the job would take about three years from start to finish. It was my plan to improve the cash flow and use the extra rent money to help pay for some of the fix-up work. I also knew that many of the tenants we inherited would most likely not survive too long under our much stricter renting policy.

The building had only 53 tenants on the day escrow closed and I expected to lose some of those as fix-up progressed and I began systematically weeding out undesirable renters. By fixing up vacant apartments first, we could bring in new tenants at a higher rental rate.

Selecting the Right Partner Is Critical

I cannot overemphasize the importance of a good investor match-up if this plan is to help you create wealth. In my view, the only time partnership investing makes good sense is when each investor needs what the other possesses or can immediately provide. It will work only if both are made stronger by joining together. Quite often you will see investors of equal means attempting to work as partners; however, they are seldom successful because they are no stronger together than as individuals.

First Main Street required my fix-up expertise and the doctor's money in about the same proportion. To put it another way, without a lot of money, all my fix-up skills could not earn me one thin dime and the doctor could do absolutely nothing to take advantage of a high-profit opportunity without my fix-up skills and ability to manage the building and the tenants. This is what I mean when I say that both investors are stronger together.

Separation of Duties Is Essential for Success

Although it is clearly spelled out in a 90/10 plan agreement who is responsible for what, it's extremely important that each co-investor be allowed to perform his or her specified task with the least interference from the other. Obviously, a fairly high level of trust is necessary to get the job done. For example, the doctor didn't try to give me fix-up advice, unless I asked his opinion, nor did I have to beg him for money when the big invoices started rolling in for payment. This kind of understanding is absolutely necessary before any joint project is started.

Co-Investors Are Tenants in Common

My basic agreement for First Main Street was quite simple, as agreements should be. Both investors will take title as tenants in common. (I have, generally, found it best to conduct business as co-investors or tenants in common, rather than create a separate tax reporting partnership.) The 90% investor (money partner) will receive 90% of the total benefits, including rents, credits, and depreciation, during the period of fixing up the property. The 10% investor (operator)—that's me—will receive 10% of the benefits, plus a management fee equal to 5% of the gross monthly rents until the property is sold or traded.

The co-investor agreement should specify a future date when a sale is planned. Naturally, there should be enough flexibility in the written agreement to allow for selling whenever you can take best advantage of a good seller's market. When the property is sold, each investor will be fully reimbursed for his or her total cash contribution first. The net sale proceeds will then be split on a 50/50 basis.

By the way, co-investing doesn't mean you should be sloppy about written rules or agreements, merely because it's not a formal partnership. In fact, let me once again emphasize that you should never invest with anyone without first preparing and executing a written agreement detailing exactly who does what and when. Refer to the example of my co-ownership agreement in the previous chapter. You can rearrange the terms of the agreement to suit your particular transaction.

Fix the Building, Then Up the Income

We acquired the building for approximately $450,000, which was an excellent price, even though it was a mess. It would require several years of fix-up work and enough time to rid the place of its flophouse reputation. As I had planned, the monthly cash flow paid for much of the fix-up work. I initiated tenant cycling and raised the rents almost immediately and new tenants moving into the upgraded apartments had no objections to our $60 per month rent increases. Painting and cleaning made a tremendous improvement to the looks. Most tenants had nothing but praise for our fix-up efforts.

Dividing Up the Money at the End

After three years of fix-up and tenant cycling, the First Main Street Studio Apartments were like new again. They were easy to rent, even though the larger units were renting for $125 more than when we acquired the building. Speaking for the operator/manager side, I was quite proud of what we had accomplished—and, because we were able to attract 35 more renters along the way, our cash contributions for fix-up were much less than we had anticipated at the start.

When we were ready to sell the First Main Street apartments, my total cash contribution added up to $16,000 and the doctor had invested $145,000 as 90% co-investor. However, an opportunity to sell didn't come up for another year and a half. Finally, we sold the apartments for $300,000, over and above the total amount of money we had invested.

When escrow closed, the doctor's check was $295,000, more than double what he had invested. He had also enjoyed substantial tax write-offs in the first three years of ownership. That benefit sheltered lots of doctoring income.

I chose to carry back a promissory note for $150,000, secured by the First Main Street property. The terms provided monthly payments of $1,500 (12% interest only), with the principal all due in 10 years. My total compensation for the use of my fix-up skills and property management was very pleasing to me, as the following numbers show.

52 months of management fees:	$40,820
120 months at 12% interest payments:	180,000
Principle amount from note receivable (end of 10 years):	150,000
Total earnings:	$370,820

Leverage is about investing a very small amount of your own money in order to earn a very large amount from someone else. First Main Street is a perfect example of how maximum leverage can help your bank account.

I've estimated that I spent somewhere near 2,500 hours on the job while I owned the apartment. Some days, the work required 10 or 12 hours, but many days it was only a few minutes. According to my calculations, that gave me hourly earnings of almost $150 for this project. You can easily see that personal skills are worth a great deal more than having a regular job down at the sawmill, as we discussed back in Chapter 1.

Give More of Yourself Than You Expect in Return

I have had many experiences working with well-heeled partners. Their buying power and ability to obtain quick credit has allowed me to build personal wealth much faster than I could have ever done alone.

Again, I will repeat my personal philosophy about working with others, because it has much to do with being successful. It also has everything to do with repeat business—investors who will keep reinvesting with you because you make money for them. Always give more than you expect to receive (Jay's 60/40 rule). If you set up a 50-50 partnership arrangement or a 90/10 investor plan, don't be content merely to contribute your portion. Instead, do a little more. When the word gets out, you'll find more cash investors than you can find deals to include them in. Just a small 10% extra will buy you lots of super deals and much faster wealth, believe me.

18

100% Financing with Seller Subordination

Frequently folks tell me, "I've tried to purchase properties the way you suggest, but my bank always says 'No.' What should I do now?" My answer is to keep on trying. If one particular technique doesn't work, just hang on and don't give up. There are lots of other ways that will work. Right now, however, let me tell you about a subordination technique that works particularly well, if you have a decent job and a good credit rating.

Subordination means the owner/seller will allow the bank to make a new loan against the property in front of or senior to the seller carryback mortgage. This means that, if the property should ever be foreclosed, the seller could lose his or her equity or part of it because senior priority mortgages would be paid off first from the foreclosure sale proceeds. However, without seller subordination, the bank could not fund the loan that's required to make this particular type of sale work.

Seller Subordination: A No-Money Technique That Works

In case you're wondering if this method really works, let me assure you I've made about a dozen of these deals. I've purchased $1.5 million worth of houses using a combination of subordination and owner financing. I call it my "30-30 plan." Let me show you how it works.

First, you must find a seller who truly wants to sell—not just a luke-warm seller who has little or no motivation. I have found this method works best with sellers who have average, medium-grade rental properties. You don't want trashed-out junkers and you don't want pride-of-owner-ship properties. You want a property that can stand a few improvements, but not one that is seriously run down, because most lenders won't loan money on junky-looking investment properties.

The typical lenders in my area are thrifts like Beneficial Finance, AVCO Thrift, Chrysler First, and Fireside Thrift. These are the old personal property (chattel) lenders with an add-on license to do real estate loans. Many folks call them "godfather loans," because their interest rates are general-ly higher. However, unless you've done business with these lenders lately, you may not be aware of all the changes that have taken place over the past few years. Today these lenders make real estate equity loans combined with chattel mortgages. Their licensing allows them to write loans secur-ing both real estate and personal property. The extra personal property security allows them to be more liberal with borrowers than regular banks, so it's generally easier to qualify for their loans.

Loan Terms Are More Important Than Interest Cost

It's true, these thrifts do charge higher interest rates; however, not as high as you might think. More often than not, their equity loans have fixed interest rates and are generally amortized over a 15-year term. Another very important consideration with these lenders is that they're seldom concerned about junior priority loans on the secured property—that is, loans that are recorded behind or after their own. Banks quite often pro-hibit additional loans on the secured property, even though the security is junior to their own loan.

Remember this about financing: it's much more important for investors to borrow money from lenders that will give flexible terms than to borrow strictly on the basis of the lowest interest rate—within reason, of course. Flexible terms will add value to your properties when it's time to sell, because you can pass along the good terms to your buyer.

The Attraction of the Southside Property

My Southside property consisted of four rental houses located on a large city lot. The property was in average condition. The sellers had owned the houses for many years and had done extensive upgrading, like blacktopping the driveways and building privacy fences. They had also added carports and installed several new roofs. Generally speaking, the property looked in pretty good condition when I bought it. On a scale of one to 10, I'd call it about a seven. It's important to remember that lenders like properties that look good.

The sellers' motivation was a strong desire to retire. The owners had operated a small travel agency for many years and now wanted to close shop and travel themselves. Like most owners who decide to sell their average-looking properties with a large amount of equity, they wanted a rather substantial cash down payment from the buyer. At least 20% to 25% was the amount they would take, according to their real estate agent.

The property looked good and, of course, the competition is always much keener when a property shows well. Looking back now, I must admit that the good looks impressed me, too. I paid a bit too much for the looks, so Southside turned out to be less profitable than most of my other deals—but that's another story. We're talking financing now. We'll look at bigger profits another time.

An Ideal Candidate for My 30-30 Seller Subordination Plan

The Southside property was an ideal candidate for my *no-money-down* 30-30 subordination plan. First the seller must agree to finance (carry back) at least 30% of the purchase price. Second, the existing financing on the property should not exceed much more than 30% of the total purchase price. It must also be assumable.

Here's how the numbers looked when I made the offer to purchase Southside:

Asking price = $115,000 (reasonable for rental income and condition of the property.)

$105,000: My offer to purchase (accepted)

$ 34,650: Existing mortgage (assumable)

$ 70,350: Sellers' equity

The sellers agreed to accept my offer of $105,000 and allowed me to place a new second mortgage (loan) on the property for $37,500. The loan funds were disbursed as follows: $32,500 went to the seller, $1,500 went to pay escrow closing costs, and $3,500 came back to me at closing. I not only accomplished a no-cash down purchase, but also got money back on the deal.

Where Does All the Money End Up?

Ideally, an existing mortgage on the property you're buying should be approximately $30,000 to $35,000 (30%). The seller must agree to subordinate to a new loan (mortgage) for about the same amount (30%). And finally, the seller must agree to carry back a third mortgage for the balance (30% to 35% range).

The obvious question you are probably asking yourself is "Why on earth would a seller surrender his or her equity by allowing a new loan to be recorded on the property ahead of his or her interest?" The answer becomes clearer when you follow where the money goes—and understand the benefits to the seller.

The seller gets the money, at least most of it. That's what makes this deal work. Some investors try to play games with this type of financing, by attempting to pocket a large share of the new loan proceeds. This tactic is very poor business, because it grossly over-finances the property. It also increases the monthly debt service, which in turn adds far greater risk to all lenders involved. A buyer can be quickly overcome by negative cash flow, caused by high payments to service too much mortgage debt.

I have found this financing arrangement works best when you give all the borrowed money, except expenses, to the seller. Here's an example, using a $100,000 deal. Let's say you can assume a $30,000 existing mortgage. The seller has agreed to carry back a $35,000 third mortgage and will subordinate to a new bank loan for the balance. Obviously, an appraisal must substantiate the property value; however, most lenders would be willing to loan up to 70% of the appraisal. In this example, a 70% loan means the lender would be willing to loan $70,000 on this property. Since there is an existing first mortgage for $30,000 against the property, it means any additional borrowing cannot exceed $40,000 ($30,000 plus $40,000 = $70,000).

In this example, I've tried to use very reasonable numbers. In other words, my ratios and loan percentages are well within limits for most lenders. With a decent job and good credit rating, an applicant could reasonably expect to receive loan approval without too much difficulty. Obviously, you'll need an appraisal and, of course, the standard financial information all lenders require from investors.

How Does a Seller Benefit?

The big advantage for a seller with this arrangement is he or she gets $35,000 cash up front. That's an extra-large down payment for rental houses. Typically, sellers are accustomed to receiving only 10% to 20% cash down payments for average rental properties. As you can plainly see, this plan will net the seller far more cash at the closing table.

There's also another big benefit for sellers who have owned their rental properties for a long time and have large equities or profits build up. (By the way, this 30-30 plan is more or less geared for long-term owners, because the numbers work better.) Quite often, the extra-large down payment (30% to 35%) will allow the seller to get all or nearly all of his or her original cash investment back. In other words, the large down payment will totally cash the seller out of the property, leaving none of his or her own money in the deal.

It's a bit easier to finance or carry back a mortgage for the appreciation or growth because you're only financing the profits you've earned. It's always riskier for sellers when their own money is still left in the deal. Most investors are reluctant to carry a mortgage without first getting all of their hard dollars back out of the property. If they can do that, they're generally a lot more agreeable to seller financing for the balance of the sale.

I personally don't object to financing my profits, because I like the additional interest income it earns. It's a marvelous recipe for making bonus profits. On the other hand, I need my down payment dollars back when I sell, so I'll have the funds for my next investment.

Advantages to the Buyer

The major advantage is that you can acquire real estate with *no money down*—that is, none of your personal money! What this means is that lack of cash doesn't need to stop you from buying income properties. However, as I told you earlier, you must have a decent job and a good credit rating to qualify with commercial lenders. If you do, then my 30-30 plan can work very well to help you acquire investment properties that you might otherwise have to pass up.

To avoid negative cash flow problems with this plan, you must be very careful not to take on mortgage payments in excess of what the property can support! This is where my *income property analysis form* (Chapter 5) can be an extremely helpful tool. Basically, you'll need to carefully calculate all the expenses necessary to operate the property, then subtract them from the gross income. The remainder is what you'll have left to pay the combined mortgage payments.

The most serious problem with no-money-down deals is that the total purchase price must be financed—unless, of course, other trading is also involved. You must carefully negotiate the mortgage payments so they don't exceed whatever amount of income the property is capable of earning. Effective use of the 30-30 plan requires special planning and skillful negotiating to avoid negative cash flow.

Lenders Want Clean, Sweet-Smelling Properties

Lenders are like 98% of the population: whatever they do is generally based on how things look! They will gladly lend money if your project looks good, but they don't want anything to do with the "ugly duckling" properties. Believe me, looks count for everything—loans included! It will serve you well if you understand this basic human characteristic, because it's exactly how lenders think! If your property is reasonably clean with no visible signs of a problem, chances are quite good that most mortgage lenders will finance up to 70% or more of the purchase price or the appraised value, whichever is less.

In our hypothetical case, the seller is willing to carry back a $35,000 mortgage and will subordinate to a second mortgage to be placed on the property. The buyer agrees to assume the first mortgage that exists on the property at the time of purchase. Right about now is where we (the buyer) must ask the seller to cut us a little extra slack. It should be obvious by now that three loans on this property will cost more than the property can afford to pay back under normal circumstances. To illustrate what I mean, let's review the numbers once again in our hypothetical transaction.

Full Purchase Price	Mortgages on Property	Monthly Mortgage Payments
$100,000	$30,000 Buyer to assume (existing)	$242.66
	35,000 Subordinated loan (new borrowing)	$420.06
	35,000 Seller carryback mortgage	(Continue reading for explanation of amount)
	$100,000 Total financing	

The scheduled income for this property is $350 per unit, or $1,400 per month in gross rents. For the purpose of planning, let's assume it will cost 40% of the income each month for expenses to operate the property. That's $560 per month. The debt service (two mortgage payments) will cost $662.72. The total cost for expenses and mortgage payments is $1,222.72 per month. Obviously, there's little money available to pay another monthly payment on the seller's carryback mortgage. Therefore, I propose asking the seller for some special consideration for the payback of his note. I would tell him that $175 to $200 is all the property can afford to pay him.

Paying Back the Sellers' Note

Back to my Southside houses .... They presented a similar problem for me at the time. Here's how I explained things to the sellers.

> Look, Mr. and Ms. Seller, I'm more than willing to place a new loan on the property in my name. No risk to you because the loan won't be in your name. Also, I'll give you all money from the new loan except closing costs and the $3,500 for repairs that you've already agreed to do. It's much easier for you to deduct the repairs from loan funds than spend your own cash out of pocket.

> I'm sure you realize that my 35% down payment is more cash than most investors are willing to pay. Also, most buyers would certainly want you to finance (carry back) a much larger share of the sale. I'm more than happy to use my good credit to get you the most money, but I do need a favor from you.

> I'm willing to work at the property and do the repairs and manage the tenants, without taking any money from the property for myself. However, as you can see from the income and expense information (income property analysis form), I'm not going to have enough rent money coming in at first to pay you the monthly mortgage payments. I need you to give me a little extra time 'til I can raise the income a bit.

Special Terms Required: Deferred Payments

I told the sellers I'd pay 10% interest on their note in five annual payments. That's $250 per month (10% of $30,000 is $3,000, divided by 12 months equals $250). That way I'd have the first 12 months without any mortgage payments. It would give me breathing room and some time to get the rents up a little.

Also, I'd have the opportunity to gain one full year's worth of tax deductions. Assuming an 80% improvement ratio and $12,000 worth of depreciable personal property, an investor in the 31% tax bracket would realize a $1,600 annual savings. That makes up more than half the $250 deficit. A $30 rent increase would take care of the difference.

In addition, don't forget when I figured out the expenses (40% in this case), approximately $110 per month was allocated for maintenance, repairs, and management—that's my job! Obviously, owners can't pay themselves, but saving those expenses amounts to the same thing as getting paid for it. It's still my money, because it's my property.

Getting a Stake in the Game

Right about now you might be thinking to yourself, "Have I missed something here? I can't possibly see how I'm going to get very rich with this deal! This program is tighter than a banjo string. If I lose one month's rent or a toilet breaks down, I'll end up paying money out of my pocket. There's no safety margin!"

Let's be realistic here. I'm not telling you how to get rich. I'm telling you how to get a free stake in the game. If you agree with me that owning income-producing real estate is the right way to go and, further, that rental properties continue to become more valuable, year after year, I would ask, "How can you go wrong?"

You've got a winning hand. First, your name is on the deed: you are the owner and that's good for you! Second, as almost everyone agrees, income real estate appreciates: rents continually go up, therefore, so does the value of the property producing them. Third, your return on a no-down investment can be phenomenal: everything you take out of the deal is pure profit! That's because you have nothing in the property to begin with. You could lose the property, but never any money! In terms of risk, I'm sure you would agree, the odds will never get better.

I might just mention that Southside was purchased for $105,000, with none of my own money down. Today it's worth $205,000 and rents are $2,300 per month. Counting appreciation and rents, I've earned a profit of $9,400 for every year of my ownership. It also shoots down the theory that it takes money to make money. In the case of Southside, good credit and a decent job was all I needed.

No Limit to Creativity in Real Estate

Subordination by the seller, as we're discussing here, is not a new idea. Folks who sell empty building lots do it all the time. They sell the lot with an agreement that they will record their mortgage (seller financing) behind a new first mortgage on the property to serve as collateral for the bank's construction loan. That's how a new building gets financed.

Ray Kroc, founder of McDonald's, was moving along at a snail's pace trying to franchise his hamburger chain until he met up with Harry Sonneborn, a real estate wizard who understood the power of subordination. Prior to meeting Sonneborn, Kroc's expansion dream was bogged down for a lack of construction funds. Sonneborn did the same thing for Kroc as I'm telling you about here. He asked lot sellers to subordinate to McDonald's lenders in order to get construction loans to build hamburger stands. Obviously, it worked quite well.

Variable Rate Mortgages Offer Another Option

Another transaction, similar to Southside, came to me several years back. The seller insisted on receiving monthly payments. However, he agreed to my variable payment plan. This allowed me to start with reduced payments and gave me some extra time to build up my rental income as the mortgage payments went up. The owner carryback mortgage loan was $42,000, payable in 9% interest-only payments, and all due in 13 years. Interest-only payments at 9% amounted to $315 per month. However, we structured the note to start with payments of $210 per month (6% interest) and ended up in the 12th year at $420 per month (12%).

This arrangement worked for both of us. The seller got a 9% average interest rate and I had low payments—$210 at first, which was about all I could manage when I took over the property.

I've had other transactions where I've secured the seller's carryback note to other properties I own. Obviously, you must have multiple assets to make this arrangement work.

As I said in another chapter, you won't need 100 ways to buy real estate. Half a dozen good techniques will most likely do the trick. I also told you that good credit will be one of the most valuable tools in your investor kit. Naturally, all banks and commercial lenders will approve or deny credit based on the kind of records you develop. If you've paid your bills in a timely fashion over the years, no doubt you have a good track record established. If not, you'll need to begin the necessary repairs to get it fixed. Fortunately, that can be accomplished over time.

Investor's Success Requires Borrowed Money

Stated another way, investors who cannot borrow money for financing and fix-up with a little left over for groceries will quickly find their investment plan won't get very far. Borrowing money is the only way most of us can ever achieve our financial goals in a reasonable time.

Money borrowing rules are changing almost daily. It doesn't take a rocket scientist to understand that finding money to do ugly fix-up projects can be difficult, especially for investors who are just starting out and plan to do most of the work themselves. Still, it can be done. So keep on reading—you'll see.

Making Yourself a Better Borrower

There are several self-help measures to ease borrowing difficulties. The first, obviously, is to protect your credit rating if you have a good one. If you don't, I'll show you a few things you can do to make it better.

You'll also need to keep your personal financial and accounting records up to date and on-line. You should do this at least annually, so you develop a good history. Sometimes more often is better and will generally be required if you are an active buyer/borrower. I will discuss the financial records (tools) you need for every lender, both private and institutional. Having good financial tools is just as important for the do-it-yourself investor as having good plumbing tools and a sharp saw.

Bankers Like Homeowners with Steady Jobs

When I worked at the telephone company years ago, I had an excellent credit rating. Banks were willing to loan me money even when I didn't need it. The first two questions bankers would always ask me were "Where do you work?" and "For how long?" When I answered, "At the telephone company" and "20 years," the loan manager relaxed into his easy chair and said, "How much do you want and when do you need the check?"

I began buying rundown houses long before I quit my telephone job. The first time my banker drove out to see my fixer houses, I thought he was going to throw up.

Still, he remained impressed with my 20 years of telephone employment. But he also gave me some personal advice about buying any more junky properties. He even hinted about not making any more loans. Soon afterwards, Beneficial Finance became my fix-up property lender. They didn't mind junky houses quite so much, as long as I was still employed at the phone company. Quite a number of these early 18% to 20% interest loans got paid back over the years, which made the folks at Beneficial smile from ear to ear.

Banker Enemy Number One: An Unemployed Loan Applicant

If there's anything a loan officer hates worse than an unemployed deadbeat, it's an unemployed house fixer who wants to borrow money. The news that I had quit my telephone company job turned every lender against me. If I had been playing monopoly with my banker, he'd have sent me directly to jail without passing go. One thing you need to understand is that bankers don't like loan applicants who can't produce a copy of a W-2 form. It's their only evidence that someone else thinks you're worth spending money on.

I never realized how important a regular job is to bankers. Before I quit my job at the telephone company, my Beneficial mortgage payments alone were about three times more than my monthly paycheck. Still, Beneficial seemed totally unconcerned—until the day I quit the phone company. My 20-year, squeaky-clean credit record didn't mean anything toward getting additional loans with them. When the paycheck stops, it's like starting all over again. We must somehow prove to lenders that we still have the ability to pay them back. Bankers can visualize only two kinds of customers—*low-risk employed folks* and *unemployed deadbeats*.

How to Build Your Financial Integrity

Borrowing money is much easier when you can show lenders good financial records for yourself and your real estate business. It's very important to demonstrate that you know exactly where you stand financially. Lenders admire organized applicants. They don't like borrowers who show up asking for money, but can't explain exactly how much they need and, even worse, how they'll pay it back. These problems can be partially overcome with good sound financial records.

Jay's Five Basic Financial Documents for Borrowing

Financial records are the same whether you own one property or 50. Obviously, if you start while your investments are few, you'll need less paper. However, the documents themselves will always remain the same. I think every investor should prepare his or her own records and keep them updated annually—more often, if necessary, for loan activity.

I will briefly describe each of the five financial documents and, I hope, give you enough information so you can develop your own records. Remember: nothing is magic or sacred about these forms. You can simply draw them up yourself on plain white paper or obtain financial statement forms from a bank or the local stationery store.

Another important benefit you get from preparing these forms is it gives you an excellent financial picture of yourself. Many investors don't have the slightest idea about their net worth. Some are afraid to find out.

Following is a description of the basic financial tools I suggest you prepare and start using. I promise they'll help you a great deal next time you're ready to borrow money from the bank or you need evidence to show a seller who is contemplating a carryback mortgage for you.

1. Schedule of Real Estate Owned (Form Setup)

This form should be typed up on plain white paper with headings as follows:

Property location	Type units	Market value	Mortgage liens	Lender/ bank	Mortgage payment	Taxes ins.	Gross income	Misc. repairs	Net income

Almost every conventional loan application form requires this information, in the same order. Therefore, when you keep this form updated, it can simply be made part of any loan application package you plan to submit. Standard 8½ x 14 paper (horizontal) is best to use because it matches the size of most bank application forms.

2. Schedule of Real Estate and Notes Owned (Form Setup)

This form is very similar to the previous one. However, it contains some additional information. I have found it very helpful, especially when private lenders (sellers who agree to carry back financing) ask for financial data to consider financing a sale to me. This form also contains the information you will need to fill out the *asset/liability* section of any financial statement you prepare. The following headings are used to prepare this document. It should be typed horizontally on plain white, 8½ x 11 paper.

Location description	Market value	Your equity	Mortgage balances	To whom payable	Address lender	Scheduled rents/ note income

3. A Personal Financial Statement (Blank Forms Available)

This form can be standard stationery store copy or a form obtained from your local banker. Often, the various lending institutions have their own special forms with their names printed on them. Sometimes their forms have special or unusual questions that they want answered—for example, "How do you plan to make your payments in case you die?"

All financial statements are pretty much the same. You list all your assets on one side and liabilities on the other. The difference equals your personal net wealth. You might be surprised when you find out what you're really worth.

4. Profit and Loss Statement (Form Setup)

This form should show your total income at the top. Then you will list all operating expenses. After that, list mortgage payments and depreciation. The bottom line will show a profit or loss for the period.

I always prepare a profit and loss statement annually. However, you may need to do so more often if you are aggressively shopping for loans. You can type this information on plain white 8½ x 11 paper.

Income should include all sources, such as rents, deposits (if you mix them with rents), coin laundries, notes receivable, and management fees (if applicable). Expenses are all your operating costs, which generally include payroll, licenses, insurance, maintenance, repairs, supplies, utilities, advertising, telephone, taxes, legal fees, and accounting. Remember: owner draws are not to be mixed in with employee payroll. Draws can be a separate item if you choose.

Net operating income is what's left over after you subtract the operating costs from total gross income. Mortgage payments should then be subtracted from the net operating income to determine positive or negative cash flow (profit or loss). Depreciation can also be shown as an expense item. However, I like to keep it separate from my regular expenses, because it's really only a paper expense. (You don't write a check to pay it.) Lenders will often ask what your profit or loss is before depreciation. You'll really impress them when you know the difference and have the correct numbers.

Good impressions, along with good records, will often make the difference between loan approval and loan denial.

5. Business Financial Statement (Form Setup)

A financial statement about your real estate business is almost exactly like a personal financial statement about yourself. If you're just starting out in business, chances are your personal statement is all you need. However, if you have several properties already, or perhaps a real estate partnership interest, I would suggest you prepare a business statement to better demonstrate your financial capacity.

In my real estate business, the management division—One Stop Home Rental Company—owns trucks, special tools, and furniture, which are not included on my personal financial statement. As you expand your real estate activity, you may find it's better to have several separate business entities. Each should have its own financial statement.

19

Free Fix-Up Money from Uncle HUD

More Than One Way to Profit

The message I have for investors is that nothing is going to happen for you unless you make it happen. It's always been that way and always will be. Because real estate investing offers such a wide variety of profit-making opportunities beyond simply buying and selling properties, investors should never find themselves bogged down in a position where they can't do something to improve their net worth.

For example, I don't concentrate on selling when it's a buyer's market, when buyers have all the advantage. There are too many properties available for too few buyers who want to purchase them. When the situation reverses, I start to think about selling. Obviously, fewer properties and more buyers means a higher selling price for me. Meanwhile, I can work on other ways to improve my real estate wealth. One of my favorites is the HUD grant-funded, rental-housing program, sometimes called the *matching funds program*.

Uncle Sam Provides Money for Fixing Affordable Houses

Quite often when normal real estate activity has slowed down, smart investors can still find high-profit investment opportunities. One such opportunity is government-assisted *low-income rental-housing rehabilitation*. The program is available nationwide in various formats.

The purpose of this program is to financially assist owners of rental properties in expanding the availability of safe, affordable housing for the benefit of low- and moderate-income persons living in the community. Often, the program targets specific areas within a city or a community to prevent slum conditions or reduce blight and further deterioration of a neighborhood. Each city or community uses federal block grant funding, along with state housing monies and sometimes special assessment district funds to improve the supply and quality of housing within its boundaries.

Grant funding is the most active program the government uses to help landlords fix up substandard rental properties, making them available to lower-income and subsidized tenants. What makes this program so attractive to property owners is that grant funds are *free money*. That's a huge difference from loan funds, which must be paid back. Free money is the government's "dangling carrot" to attract property owners to participate. If you learn the ropes and do this right, I will assure you it's well worth the time and effort it takes working your way through the so-called government "red tape."

Fix Up Your Rental Properties for Half the Normal Price

If I told how to get your rental properties fixed up for half the normal price, would you be interested? You should be. It's a very good deal and you can do it with funds from community development block grants. Funds are administered by local city and county housing departments. In my town it's called the Public Housing Authority (PHA). If your rental house needs $10,000 worth of allowable fix-up work, here's how you can do it for half price, or for only a cost of $5,000 to you.

First, visit your local city or county housing department, where you must fill out an application and several other forms with information about your property and the tenants. After the housing department receives your application, it will inspect the property and make a thorough fix-up and repair list of the work that needs to be done. All code violations—plus worn-out or damaged items, such as roofs, paint, floors, appliances, windows, doors, etc.—must be fixed. The house must be brought up to an acceptable condition where everything is safe and works properly.

After you and the housing representative agree on what work needs to be accomplished, a cost estimate is developed and bid specifications are drawn up by the housing department. There is generally a cost per unit limit—such as $10,000 for a three-bedroom house. If the estimate is $10,000 for the rehab work, you will be required to pay $5,000. The housing department will give you the other $5,000 to do the work. Remember, this is not a loan. There is no payback involved. It's a free grant from the government to you for participating in the housing program. It kind of makes you feel better about having to spend so much money on repairs.

In addition, once the rehab work is completed, a Section 8 subsidy can be given to the first family to occupy the unit under HUD low-income guidelines. This can be the current tenant who is living there during the rehab, if he or she qualifies for HUD assistance. Subsequent vacancies—after the original tenant of the rehabilitated unit has left—must be filled by open market renting.

Avoid Vacancies–HUD Tenants Stay Longer

Before I get too specific, let me say something about keeping your units rented—no vacancies. In areas where housing is scarce, keeping your units rented is seldom a problem. However, apartment construction goes in cycles. During easy-money times—when loans are available—it tends to accelerate, causing vacancy rates to rise as well. Many tenants move to the newer units, if they can. This is where city housing and subsidized rents can really help landlords who have older properties.

I've found HUD tenants stay much longer; they don't move around as much as non-HUD tenants. Therefore, I'm a lot better protected against high vacancies. Owners of newer units can't stand too many vacancies; otherwise, they won't be able to pay their mortgage payments. HUD programs can work quite well if cash flow is your chief concern.

I don't recommend that all your rental properties be occupied by HUD tenants. However, guaranteed rents can be a real lifesaver if you're just starting out. About 20% of my current renters are HUD tenants. The city and/or county pays about 75%, on average, of their monthly rent directly to me. I must also point out that it's never late. HUD checks are very dependable: I can always count on the money on the first of each month, no matter what else might happen.

Housing Authority Needs Landlords to Participate

Even free money is not without a price. Many property owners will have nothing whatsoever to do with city/county housing programs, because of the seemingly endless "red tape" and regulations that are associated with the bureaucracy. It's true, you must put up with some nitpicking; however, I've found that it is more than offset by the benefits I receive.

After many years and a good number of projects, I'm financially better off from participating with the local housing authority. It's greatly helped me toward my long-range profit goals. I've done moderate rehabilitation conversions and grant-funding projects and I continually participate in the rental certificate and voucher programs. I highly recommend that all landlord/owners learn about the various programs in their own communities and use them.

Another important point I must mention here is that with all local HUD programs—including the annual rental assistance contracts—the city or county folks will always do their best to see that you achieve cash flow. They want you to make a profit. It's in their best interest to have you profitable. They thoroughly understand the value of your staying in business. Remember, they need you, too. Knowing that they will help you keep your rental units full is very satisfying, particularly if you're just getting started in this business and lack of cash flow is one of your biggest problems.

City Hall Must Allocate Its Funds or Else Lose Them

Just as price and terms will be different depending on whether you're buying or selling, so it is with the housing folks at city hall. Certainly they have rules and regulations to follow, but in the final analysis, housing departments are both judged and funded on how much housing they provide. For example, let's say my city has been allocated funds (block grants) to rehabilitate 50 houses during the next fiscal year, but, for various reasons, they complete only 25 houses.

What happens? They lose the money. Normally, the funds are transferred to another city that has a faster, more efficient housing department. Also, it's quite likely that next year my city won't get funding for 50 houses. Instead, it'll get enough for only 25. I don't think I need to tell you that giving back unspent tax money is the worst thing that can happen to any government-funded agency.

Local housing politics can often benefit you financially if you make it your business to know what the city wants, particularly if you own or plan to acquire property in the middle of your city's hottest target area. The reason is that, quite often, the city government wants rehabilitation work done even more than the property owner does. This is particularly true in cases where local agencies (city and county) have made promises to the federal government to clean up specific areas as a condition for receiving large federal block grants.

How to Get Started from Scratch

The first step is to visit your local city or county housing department, often called the "housing authority" or "housing assistance office." Incorporated cities generally have their own housing department under the direction of the public works official. In rural communities, the county performs the same function.

In my area (Shasta County, California)—with a county population of approximately 165,000, and a city population of approximately 70,000—I deal with the city primarily because most of my properties are within the city limits. Outside the city limits it is county jurisdiction. Quite often there are big differences between the two government agencies, even though their funding sources are the same.

One significant difference is worth mentioning here. Within the city limits, property owners are not allowed to perform grant-funded rehab (fix-up) work on their own properties, unless they're licensed contractors and are approved to bid on city housing projects. In the county jurisdiction, the rules are not nearly as strict. I am allowed to do all rehab work on my houses, as long as I can convince the county housing authority that I am responsible and that I have the necessary know-how to complete the work. The county is also much more liberal when it comes to obtaining building permits associated with low-income housing projects. Only extensive work would require a permit for HUD rehab jobs.

The main reason I'm passing this information along is to make you aware that local housing departments differ a great deal in their methods of administering housing rehab funds. It will be to your advantage to search out all the pertinent information and rules concerning your own particular area, before you formulate a plan of action. In summary, first visit the housing authority and ask for all information about grant rehab funding for landlords, to find out how it works. Then, get a map of the area where the city or county wants to apply its funding. I've found it's usually in the older, rundown sections of town. That's where rehab is needed the most.

Dealing with the Local Housing Authority

Often times, city housing won't give nonowners the time of day. The housing department considers it a waste of time to discuss rules and regulations with anyone who cannot participate. Local real estate agents are responsible for this, as many agents have a tendency to badger the city housing staff in an attempt to secure loan information or rehab commitments for their listed properties. Obviously, available funds would make properties easier to market. In my town, the very first question city housing will ask is "Do you own the property?" That's the first requirement.

Your initial visit to city housing can be a bit awkward. At best, you'll come away with mixed feelings: you won't know whether to thank them or resent them. Milling around public agencies can be a particularly frustrating experience for those who think of wasted time as wasted dollars.

There's a standard clause in real estate contracts that says, "Time is of the essence." That clause has little meaning at city housing. You'll see what I mean after a few visits there. Housing folks are a very patient bunch. They view the world as always having many more tomorrows. The only exception I've ever experienced was with a project where I was asked to convert my two-bedroom houses into three-bedrooms. The housing department needed six three-bedroom houses to maintain its spending level—and thus preserve its annual budget.

You can benefit a great deal by knowing this kind of information. I suggest you make friends or develop a good contact within your local housing department. It pays big profits in the long run—as you will learn later on in this chapter.

The Extra "Red Tape" Is Grossly Overstated

All government operations use more paper than they should. That's especially true when HUD is involved. However, most of the paper goes in files, never to be seen again after you sign it. Your application for a city HUD loan or grant funds won't be much different from any bank application. Financial information is about the same for all borrowing, even though the forms may vary slightly.

For every housing loan I've obtained, my standard personal financial records are all I've ever needed to satisfy city or county agencies. Financial information is common to all borrowing. You need five basic forms or documents to provide an adequate picture of your credit and financial capacity to housing lenders. (See the previous chapter for a detailed explanation of the five basic financial tools I use.) Just prepare the forms yourself and you're ready to go.

No-Money-Down Deals Are Very Possible

Some cities and/or counties have more money than others to spend on housing. Some also have "pet projects" and will offer more incentives, such as loans, for these particular projects. This too is valuable information. It's another reason why you need a contact in the housing department.

I've found that the financial climate is always changing, especially when it comes to federal block grants. Some days you can't find any money and on the very next visit they seem to throw money at everyone. However, unless you stay in close contact, you'll never know exactly when you have an advantage.

On the day I first noticed the "un-yellowed" squares on the bulletin board, I had no idea that I'd stumbled onto a gold mine. I found out by asking questions, which most housing folks were happy to answer. They generally give you lots of information if you just keep asking—and that's all I did when I saw the "un-yellowed" squares. (More about these in a few pages.)

I had no idea they would loan me city and California housing funds, until they told me it was available. They explained that city housing had an emergency fund for special uses and that they would seek approval to use it for converting my two-bedroom houses to three-bedrooms. On that particular project it cost me only 20¢ out of each fix-up dollar to completely upgrade six houses. The balance was funded with low-cost housing loans.

Since that time, I've done a variety of jobs (with matching grant funds) for which the city or county housing departments have paid for everything (total costs). First, they gave me 50% free grant money. Then they loaned me the balance for my 50% owner contribution. The bottom line is that my units got completely upgraded and I was not required to come up with any out-of-pocket money. Was that a great deal or not? I certainly thought so.

Selecting the Right Property

If you already own rental property in an area where city housing wants to commit rehab monies, that's good. You're ready to submit an application and get started. If you don't own a suitable rehab candidate yet, then it makes good sense to visit your local housing office and discuss where they are doing grant-funding jobs with landlords. Better yet, get a map of the area, if they have one. Then start looking for deals.

Each city and/or county will set maximum dollar limits for its matching fund projects. Limits are similar in most towns. The maximum amount of a grant is based on the unit size. Generally it is tied to the number of bedrooms and it applies to both apartments and detached houses.

Dollar Limits for Maximum Grants in My Area

Studio units	$5,000 grant maximum
One-bedroom unit	$6,500 grant maximum
Two-bedroom unit	$7,500 grant maximum
Three-bedroom or more	$8,500 grant maximum

Matching grants can only be used for serious work, not cosmetic stuff. Eligible repairs or rehab means basic housing improvements.

Swimming pools or servant quarters will not qualify under this program. Eligible items include roofing, plumbing, electrical upgrading, painting, floor coverings, fencing, and most anything having to do with energy conservation—such as double-pane windows, new doors, weather stripping, and better insulation.

Multi-Units Earn You More Profit for Each Dollar Spent

Let's suppose you own a single-family, three-bedroom house you would like to rehab. Under the matching grant program (50-50 split), applying the maximum grant fund limits described above, you would have to get the work done for $17,000—$8,500 free grant money, plus your $8,500 cash contribution. From experience, I can tell you that $17,000 gets used up very quickly. Let's say the housing authority estimates the total job (based on whatever rehab it determines must be done) will cost $25,000. Now, the math works against you. The city still contributes $8,500; however, your share jumps to $16,500. It's no longer a 50-50 deal because it exceeds the maximum grant allowed.

For this reason, it works much better with multiple units or several houses clustered together on a single property (lot). It gives you more free grant dollars to work with. With multiple units, chances are that every unit will not require the maximum grant allowance. That means that if some exceed the unit limit and some cost less, there's a good possibility that overall you'll stay within the grant limits for the project.

Watch Out for the Hidden Costs

In addition to basic housing fix-ups, cities and/or counties often include their pet projects with grant-funding approvals. Some local agencies will insist on the construction of sidewalks and gutters, storm drain extensions, sewer and water hookups to municipal utilities, and the resurfacing of parking lots and driveways. These items can be very expensive.

You may assume these things won't cost you; I assure you they will. While it's true these items improve your property in the long term, making it more valuable, it must always boil down to present economics. For example, how much more rent can you collect from a low-income tenant who has 65 feet of new storm drain and a new sidewalk along the side of his two-bedroom apartment? If your answer is "none," you're right. What about selling the property sometime in the future? Your property may be more valuable because of the additional sidewalk and drain pipe, but I doubt it. It's really just a wild guess at best, I think.

The purpose of this discussion is to make you stop and think. Sure, grant money is free, but the matching funds are not. That's your money. If sidewalks and drainpipes add $12,000 to the cost of the project, then $6,000 of that amount must be paid by you. So, you need to figure out how much more rent you'll receive and how long it will take to recover your cash outlay, to make sure it's worth doing.

HUD Assistance with My Viola Cottages

Several years ago, I completed a matching funds project on an 11-unit property called Viola Cottages. Each unit had one bedroom. At that time, the maximum grant allowed for one-bedroom units was $5,000. Because there were 11 cottages involved, the maximum amount of free grant funding available to me was $55,000. As it turned out, the project actually cost $90,000. I received $45,000 of free grant money and, of course, was required to contribute an equal amount of matching funds. Two of the cottages cost more than $10,000 each to rehab. However, the cost of the other units was much less than the $5,000 limit.

In these situations, it's not the least bit uncommon for cities to go beyond simply approving your 50% grant fund application. In addition, they will often loan you your share of the matching funds, assuming, of course, you don't have the money to contribute yourself. Most of us don't. Wouldn't you agree?

Why would the city give you free grant money, then loan you an equal amount without requiring you to put up any money at all? They want to see the job get done, so they're willing to provide additional assistance. What owner could ever say no to a rehab project that costs him or her nothing? That was exactly the situation with my Viola Cottages project. The local housing department wanted to see the project done even more than I did, so they loaned me the money to make sure it happened.

City Loans Work in Tandem with Grant Funds

You are most likely to receive city HUD loans by going the extra mile. That means owning property and being willing to participate with your local HUD housing in special target areas where the city is highly motivated to clean up older, rundown neighborhoods. Also, single-bedroom units in locations where there's a shortage of affordable senior housing will cause the housing folks to push a little harder. Often, that translates to making easy loans. We've already discussed proper timing, which is always important when negotiating with HUD representatives or, for that matter, anyone else.

City loans are the very best kind of loans, because they are generally designed to fit a particular need or situation. For example, city housing will always insist that you make a profit—generally about 8% or so, but it varies. Let's say the city gives you 50% grant funding and then agrees to loan you the other 50% (which is your 50% contribution). The loan will be designed with a special interest rate and terms so you'll be able to make loan payments and still make a profit. The city does this by lowering the interest rate to fit the deal, based on projected income. They also set the rents you can charge, so they know exactly what income and expenses should be. Most loans are amortized over 10 to 15 years and sometimes they even forgive payments if you will rent to special hardship tenants who are on the HUD waiting lists.

The Flip Side: Other Requirements by the City

It's important for me to point out here that when cities and/or counties design easy-pay loans for you and guarantee that you can make your monthly profits for doing rehab projects with them, there's a flip side— they will require periodic inspections of the property and they will expect you to manage the units well and keep them in good condition. Remember: the sole purpose of giveaway grants and low-interest loans is to provide incentive to owners and investors to create safe, affordable housing for lower-income citizens who might otherwise be left out in the cold.

The City Is a Flexible Lender

The federal government often bails out large banks and businesses to prevent them from going broke when they are characterized as "too big to fail." It's only fair that this same courtesy be extended to landlords who own smaller properties occupied by low-income HUD tenants. I have known investors who have had their housing loans forgiven or the payments reduced when the reasons were justified.

City housing is not your typical "hardball" lender. They are flexible like owners who finance their properties with carryback loans. Cities never want to own the rental properties; therefore, it's comforting to know—when you're working with city HUD and the economy falters—that you won't be foreclosed or you won't lose your investment property. It's more likely that city housing will adjust your mortgage debt to fit whatever amount of income you have. Safety nets like this are very valuable, especially for landlords who are concerned about cash flow.

The Easiest Loan in Town

It goes without saying, you should have your financial tools updated on a continuing basis. That way, when an opportunity presents itself, you are ready to respond.

HUD-assisted loans made by housing agencies are quite easy to obtain. For example, in my area, the city will loan up to 90% of the property value. Banks that write loans (mortgages) in second or third position for rental properties normally require at least a 30% safety margin of owner equity. Also, your personal credit is seldom any major issue for housing loans. Don't forget: these agencies want to give you a loan if it fits their own goals. They generally assume your credit is good if you already own rental property. To summarize, housing agencies will require you to submit all the financial forms we've mentioned. However, they are not likely to scrutinize them with a fine-tooth comb, because they want you to qualify.

The key to getting the most help is that you must own or acquire properties in target areas. You will get this information by asking your housing department. My approach to the grant-funding program is the same as I use in all my real estate activities: determine the needs of others, then "tailor-make" your project or plan to fit that special need. By doing this, you'll make more profits than all your competitors, I'll guarantee it.

The Application Process: Steps to Take with Properties You Own

The application process—"red tape," as some will call it—is really not that difficult to complete. The housing department will give you its standard application forms and you can simply fill in the blanks. You will need to provide each tenant's name, rent amount, size of family, and estimate of tenant's income (information from the tenant's rental application you have on file). You will also need to provide information about the property, such as location, size, number of bedrooms, upstairs, types of heating and cooling, and utilities servicing the property. I always provide a sketch of the property (prepared by me at the time of purchase). You can fill in the required information with different colored pencils. Sketches are very useful. Refer to the example of Jay's typical property sketch in the Appendix.

Housing agencies will want to know financial information, such as your personal estimate of value, number of mortgages, balance owing, and the monthly payments (debt service). You must provide proof of insurance and a copy of your latest property tax bill. If you owe back taxes, you can sometimes get them paid up to date with grant funds. Always ask first. After you complete the paperwork, submit it to the agency. They, in turn, will review your request and visit the property to determine what needs to be done. Next, they will call you to set up a feasibility meeting to discuss their findings and to inform you whether or not the property fits under their program guidelines.

At the feasibility meeting, they will answer all of your questions. For example, you might be wondering if you can do the rehab work yourself. Now is the time to ask. The agency will inform you if your current tenants qualify for rent subsidies. (More about this later.) In short, the feasibility meeting is the time for all parties to ask anything and everything they'd like to know about the proposal before moving forward.

If everything gets satisfactorily resolved and you receive approval, you will need to provide a termite report (not over two years old). If you don't have one, you will need to get one, at your own expense. However, the cost of any recommended work will become part of the rehabilitation project.

Once the termite report is completed and submitted to the housing agency, they will inspect the property thoroughly and proceed to write up a complete itemized repair list (bid list), along with cost estimates and specifications for doing the work. After costs are established, most housing agencies are required to submit their plans to a loan committee or housing review board whose members will make a decision on the agency's recommendations. Assuming all goes well and the project gets approved, the next step is the tough one. Once approved, the owner must put up his or her share of the total cost—as I said earlier, normally 50%.

It Pays to Learn What Makes City Housing Tick

I've done several very profitable rehab projects (fix-up jobs) on my houses, obtaining easy-to-pay, low-interest city loans, because I took the time to learn exactly what buttons to push and when to push them. Timing has everything to do with getting your jobs approved and making the highest dollar returns at your local housing department.

Before my city housing department used computers, the staff kept track of all rehab jobs on a large cardboard poster mounted on the wall. Houses that were funded for rehab were represented by squares drawn on the poster. Some squares were for two-bedroom houses, others were for three-bedrooms, and so forth. As the budget year progressed and as the various houses were rehabbed and completed, the housing folks would "yellow in" the squares with a felt-tip pen. Obviously, those squares not yellowed meant the houses were not yet scheduled for rehab.

Several years ago, late in the housing budget year, on a routine visit to city hall, I discovered an entire row of un-yellowed squares—each representing a single three-bedroom house that was funded, but for which fix-up work had not yet been contracted or even scheduled. For some reason landlord/owners with three-bedroom, fix-up houses were not responding to the program in the numbers the city had expected. Less than 90 days remained for the housing department to contract and rehabilitate these nine three-bedroom houses or face the loss of grant funds to a faster-spending agency.

City housing did not wish to lose funding, no matter what, and I clearly sensed an urgency on the edge of panic. So, I proposed converting my two-bedroom houses to three-bedrooms by making the garages into third bedrooms and adding a carport. Normally, the city won't do this, because it's much too expensive per unit. At the time, the cost limits were $7,500 per house and I would be required to furnish $3,750 (my 50% share) plus everything over the $7,500 limit for each house. The bid estimates were $12,000 per house and I advised the city I could not come up with $8,250 for each house.

Quickly the city became very creative. They said, "OK, Jay. How much money can you provide?" I said, "$2,500 per house is my limit." They didn't like it, but they didn't say "No."

What finally happened was that they made me a city loan at 5% interest for 15 years of amortized payments, combined with a California housing loan at 3% for 15 years with deferred monthly payments (that means none). They also provided 15 years of housing subsidies with rents 20% higher than normal for each of my converted three-bedroom houses. I now have cash flow and guaranteed rents for 15 years, even when the houses are temporarily vacant. It's a very good deal for me because they always provide positive cash flow.

You Help Yourself Most When You're Helping Others

The moral to this story is simple. Find out what city housing needs, then deliver it in a timely fashion. Think not what city housing can do for you, but rather what you can do for city housing. You'll find, as I have, it pays big dividends.

I recommend that all landlords pay a visit to city and/or county housing departments. Find out exactly how these programs work in your own area. Each agency uses various combinations of federal block grant funding along with local loans. I have found that each city has its own specific goals for upgrading community housing. It also has particular sections of town (generally older) that it targets for major fix-up funding grants. Often this information can be extremely helpful when you're considering where to purchase your next property.

You'll find it's good business to learn all you can about local HUD programs in your area. It will give you insider knowledge about where you might consider investing. Plus you'll be able to find out how much rehab money you might expect to receive if you acquire fix-up properties within the city's special rehab target areas. Over the years, my work with city housing has been very profitable for me—and it can work the same way for you.

20

Buying Back Mortgage Debt for Bonus Profits

When I first began buying real estate, I had no idea that I could buy back my own debt, let alone how to make it happen. The very first time I made money doing it was completely unexpected! The mortgage holder asked if I'd be willing to pay off my mortgage, immediately, if he reduced the amount I owed him. I said, "Yes." He knocked off $16,500—and I was never so pleasantly surprised in all my life. What an easy way to earn $16,500, I thought!

Quite by accident, I had stumbled into my first discount buying experience. I quickly realized I was onto something big! I remember thinking to myself, "If I can make $16,500 on just one medium-size mortgage, how much could I make if I had a hundred mortgages to work with?" That's when I began to realize that the more private notes or mortgages I could assume when I acquire the property, the greater the odds of buying some of them back for a discount.

Strategies that go far beyond the simple wisdom of acquiring properties below market values can double and triple your profits, even after you already own the property. If this sounds too good to be true, believe me, it's not!

We've already discussed wraparound financing and the opportunities to buy back underlying mortgages at substantial discounts. However, buying mortgage debt is not limited just to wraparound mortgages when you sell. It can work anytime when you own properties and are making mortgage payments to private parties. Let me show you how this is done.

Setting the Stage for Discount Profits

If you want to make big bucks buying your own debt, you must locate and acquire the kind of mortgage debt that creates an opportunity for discount buying. The more common institutional financing—the kind of mortgages that banks and savings and loan lenders make on properties—is not what you're looking for here. Newer properties (non-fixers) are almost always financed by institutional lenders, rather than by sellers who carry back a mortgage. Therefore, if you insist on acquiring newer real estate, chances are this lucrative opportunity will not be an option for you.

Older properties are where you'll find the private notes or mortgages. Since many banks will have nothing to do with financing older properties, especially nonconforming, multi-unit rentals, it means sellers of these types of properties are forced to carry back the financing themselves, in order to sell them. Quite often these properties will sell every few years, with each seller, in turn, creating a new mortgage or promissory note for a portion of his or her equity. I have personally bought properties with as many as seven personal notes secured by a property. Three or four seller carryback notes are not the least bit uncommon with older rental properties like we're discussing here.

Look for Property with Private Mortgages

Your first step is to buy the right kind of property, one with the potential for adding value like I was able to do at Hillcrest and with other properties. It must be securing one or more private mortgages or promissory notes.

To illustrate, let's say we locate an older rundown apartment building and discover it's had three owners during the past few years. Further research reveals that with each of these sales new owner carryback mortgages were created to facilitate the transactions. These mortgages, commonly called *owner financing* or *purchase money notes*, are long-term and they are assumable to a new buyer.

The seller is asking $300,000 for the building, a price that seems reasonable based upon the income. The seller will take $30,000 cash down payment (10%) and allow the buyer to assume the three existing mortgages with remaining balances of $85,000, $50,000, and $35,000. To complete the transaction, the seller is willing to carry back another mortgage for the balance of the sale price. The new purchase money mortgage will be for $100,000, secured by the apartment for a term of 20 years.

These are excellent terms for a buyer. Obviously, the seller must be fairly motivated to make this deal. In most cases, the properties I find with these kinds of terms have been "milked"—that is, allowed to run down because the owner is not willing to spend any rent money for routine upkeep. High expenses and management problems are top motivators for selling, I've found.

I realize I haven't presented a complete picture of this apartment building—things like deferred maintenance, bad tenants, and the location. However, I've told you the rents are reasonable for the asking price. That's really all you need to know to move forward. Don't negotiate too much over the asking price, if it's reasonable.

Here's where you need to spend your time and efforts. First, ask for copies of all three existing notes (mortgages).

One of the things you'll want to find out about each of the notes or mortgages is the face amount, the amount when it was originated. For example, let's say the note with the current $50,000 balance started out at $57,500. That means $7,500 of the principal amount has been paid so far. Having copies of each note will also give you the names of the buyers and sellers, the exact amount of the payments, interest rates, remaining time until payoff, and any special provisions you should know about. Private party notes can have a wide variety of provisions. Always read them very carefully.

I once had a note that stated, "The Beneficiary may increase the interest rate from 9% to 11% beginning January 1986, if the duplexes are not properly maintained." I seriously doubt if it's enforceable, but it's still one of the terms stated in the note. The only way I would ever know it's there is to see the note for myself. Notes drawn up between private parties often contain very unusual terms. My advice is to get copies and read them several times! The term you don't want to see is a *due-on-sale* clause, meaning you would have to pay the note or mortgage off if you sold the property.

Let's continue with the apartment example. It's the right kind of property, because it's property that's been around for many years, long enough to have been sold multiple times. So, it has multiple notes (mortgages) secured by it. Newer buildings are less likely to have accumulated these notes from multiple sales.

Let me clarify. I'm not talking about notes or mortgages where cash money was borrowed against the property. Those are often called *hard-money* loans—and you can forget about discounting them.

Purchase money notes are the kind we're looking for. These are notes where no money was actually given to anyone. They're a form of credit extended to the buyer to facilitate the sale. These are the kinds of notes or mortgages that can earn you big money! And, this is where having knowledge about the players (beneficiaries) can earn bonus profits for savvy investors. The more you can learn about the folks who receive the payments, the better your chances for plotting a strategy that will hit pay dirt!

Most Sellers Would Rather Have Cash

Let's say, for example, Mr. Jones is receiving monthly mortgage payments from the sale of his apartment building. Jones sold the apartments several years back, because the tenants were about to drive him completely bonkers. In a moment of weakness, Jones rented to a rock band that played loud music all night, slept all day, and paid rents only when Jones stayed up late enough to catch them! Jones is now 67 years old and retired. He sold the apartments and carried back a note for $90,000, which now has an unpaid balance of $85,000. Jones is scheduled to receive payments of $780 per month for 25 more years.

Jones would have preferred a cash sale for his apartment building. He wasn't keen on financing the deal himself. However, because he got behind on the maintenance and suffered rent collection problems with the band, there was only one buyer who showed any interest in purchasing his property. So he pretty much had to take the offer or forget the sale. Jones took a small cash down payment and carried back the balance of his equity on a note for $90,000. It's the only way he could get anywhere near the price he was asking!

When and How to Talk about Discounting the Mortgage

Life expectancy for Jones is 73 years. That's only six years from now and his note will still have 19 more years of payments. If you're trying to purchase the property, the time to talk to Jones about discounting is after you already own the apartment and have assumed the note. If you attempt to discount the note during negotiations, Jones is quite likely to insist on more cash, because he feels he has more bargaining power! Waiting until after you own the property before asking about discounts will generally get you better results.

I always like to meet with most mortgage holders at their homes. You can learn a great deal about people by seeing how they live. For example, you'll be able to answer questions like "What kind of cars do they own?" Are they old junkers?" and "What's the condition of their furniture? Is it expensive?" and "Do they have college-age children who cost extra money?" This information helps me determine their needs. If I can learn what they might need or want, then figure out a way to give it to them, I will nearly always come away with a sizable discount. This personal information can be very valuable, believe me!

Jay's Red Mustang Strategy

I always like to tell the story about my red Mustang transaction! It illustrates the importance of understanding human nature and how it can be used to make big money in this business.

Susan and her boyfriend unexpectedly inherited my mortgage when Susan's mother passed away. The balance was $48,000 and my payments were $441 per month. The note had 11 years to go before the balance would finally be paid. I learned of the mother's death when I received an address change for mailing the payments. Shortly after that, I contacted Susan with an offer to buy the note.

I explained that I could refinance my property, but would only be able to net out about $25,000 after expenses. So, that's what I offered. Susan's boyfriend was a typical deadbeat who always needed cash, but, surprisingly, he didn't like my offer. Reducing my debt by $23,000 was a little more than he could stand to see me get; otherwise, I think Susan would have gone for the $25,000 cash. However, they stuck together and refused my offer.

If at First You Don't Succeed, Try Harder

Quite often your first offer won't be accepted. Don't give up—just try a little harder! The day I drove by Susan's apartment and saw her boyfriend's junky Subaru sitting on wooden blocks with the engine missing, I knew how to redo my offer. Human nature being what it is, I knew that young people living in a tiny one-bedroom apartment with no transportation will soon self-destruct! When I saw them again, they were a lot more motivated and willing to talk about selling the note. They were on the couch watching TV when I drove up in a shiny new red Mustang convertible.

My credit union had already agreed to loan me $20,000 so I could pay cash for the Mustang. It was a beauty! My loan payments would be $381 per month. The dealer also gave me a trade-in allowance for my 21-year-old pickup. Had I purchased the car on a regular installment contract from the dealer, the total cost would have been around $25,000, including the $2,000 credit for my pickup.

I left the motor running when I went to the door and knocked. When it opened, they both saw the car at the same time. It was love at first sight. They both immediately fell in love with my shiny new red Mustang convertible.

I let Susan drive around the block a couple of times and squeal the tires. When she got back, she wouldn't get out! It was as if she were glued to the seat. "Anyone can own a new Mustang convertible," I told her. "All you need is $25,000 and they'll deliver it to your door."

As we talked, I was watching the boyfriend. Several times he glanced over at his jacked-up Subaru, then back to Susan, who showed no signs of getting out of my car. I could tell by now, the boyfriend was hooked! "Can we both take a ride?" he asked. I agreed, but only around the block—one time!

Reeling in the Big Ones

Marketing folks call it "the hook." Others use the term "setup." But the name doesn't matter. I will tell you this much—*if* you can figure out how to structure your proposals in a manner that will fit the wants or desires of a particular client, you can "hook" clients with a remarkable rate of success!

Susan and her boyfriend needed a new convertible like they needed a hole in the head. But once they saw the car, they wanted it very badly! Seeing it in their own driveway, holding the keys, and then finally driving around the block was a bit more temptation than either of them could stand.

In less than 24 hours the deal was done! They had traded the note to me for much less cash than my original offer. You recall my offer was $25,000 cash. The deal they finally accepted was this new convertible and $3,000 cash. To me this deal was much more attractive than my original cash offer, because there were no appraisals, no points, and no new deeds on my property. I paid $20,000 cash to the car dealer with money borrowed from my credit union, so the only out-of-pocket cash I needed was $3,000 to close the deal.

Here's the bottom line. My $48,000 debt is gone, along with the $441 monthly payments scheduled for the next 11 years. Instead, I now have $381 monthly payments for only six years. If you forget the payments for a moment and just consider the trade itself, it cost just $25,000 ($20,000 borrowed funds, $2,000 trade-in, and $3,000 cash) to buy back $48,000 worth of long-term mortgage debt.

Where Your Negotiating Skills Will Earn the Biggest Profit

I'm sure you can see for yourself that buying the right kind of properties— like the kind we're discussing here, with private party notes attached—can offer some exciting high-profit opportunities, once you get the hang of using this technique!

I recall being a part of one particularly long and drawn-out negotiating battle where the sellers and I exchanged four or five counteroffers back and forth. We argued for weeks over a $4,000 difference in the selling price! My offer was $146,000. The seller wouldn't budge below $150,000.

Let's suppose this property had three $25,000 private notes attached, all of which could be assumed. Say we finally purchase the property and eventually are able to buy back the debt, with something on the order of my Mustang deal (about 50¢ on the dollar). That means three $25,000 notes (mortgages) discounted by 50% would be $37,000 worth of discounts.

When you match this kind of potential profit against the small $4,000 difference in the seller's asking price, you can begin to see where your negotiating skills will earn the biggest profits.

Again, let me emphasize—*you must buy the right kind of property*. You obviously won't be able to do what I'm suggesting here if you purchase property with the normal 20% cash down and finance the balance with a bank loan. There's simply no room for this kind of creativity in deals like that!

Timing Is Critical: Buy Back the Mortgage *After* Purchasing the Property

We've discussed buying the right kind of properties—the ones with good assumable debt. I've also told you that you can best use this strategy after you become the new owner. Quite often I'm asked, "Why not buy the existing notes (mortgages) at the same time you buy the property? For example, during the escrow period, couldn't we simply negotiate with each mortgage holder, asking if they would be willing to sell their notes for a cash discount? It seems reasonable that if the note holders would agree to sell while the property is in escrow, we could wrap everything up in one glorious transaction! We could buy the property, obtain our discounts, and close the escrow all at one time! That would save a lot of time!"

Remember what I told you earlier about human nature? Real estate knowledge is not what makes this idea work. It's much simpler than that. It's the human nature factor inside all of us!

I well remember trying to do everything in one glorious transaction, as stated in the question above, and it turned out a horrible mess! I told the seller I had just enough money to pay 10% cash down for his property. I then contacted both private note holders who had mortgages on the property totaling $78,000 and got their approval to sell me both notes for $53,000 cash. My plan was to refinance the property to get the payoff money. Everything was moving along fine until the seller got wind of my $53,000 cash offer. He demanded a bigger down payment—plus he told me, "Since you plan on refinancing my property anyway, I'd rather not carry back any mortgage myself."

I've never made that mistake again! The lesson I learned was to nail down first things first, then move on to the next step. Remember: there are many sellers out there who are perfectly content to accept your 10% cash down offers. They're willing to carry back all of the financing as well—unless they get the idea you're holding back on them. If that happens, greed takes over and you may lose the entire deal!

Factors That Motivate Sellers to Give Discounts

I keep a file on every private note holder I'm making payments to. I can't tell you exactly what this information is worth, but a modest guess would be about $50,000 a year. In other words, that's the amount of profit I expect to earn annually from buying back my own debt. My files contain information on every beneficiary (the folks who get my payments) including number and ages of family members and when children will be ready to start college, so I'll know when to start sending them letters pitching my $35,000 cash tuition plan!

One of the best opportunities occurs when note holders pass away. My Mustang deal is perhaps the best example. Through my beneficiary files, I had been tracking Susan since she was only 13. You saw the results! Most people who inherit valuables, like mortgage notes, tend to lust for cash instead. Keep a good eye on the obituaries. I always cut out the notice when one of my beneficiaries dies. Then I make it my business to find out who will inherit my payments.

Joint note holders who divorce are naturals for substantial discounts. Keep good track of them too. Divorced folks seldom want payments. Most often they need cash—and quickly!

It's also good business to send note holders a Christmas card around November 30. Lots of good discount deals pop up when people are in the mood to buy gifts or take a winter cruise. Of course, you must spell it out—*paint them a picture* when you send out your cards. Let them know you have cash available, usually about half of what you owe!

I hope you've got the picture by now. Next time you're negotiating to purchase a property, take a good hard look at the various ways you might profit from the deal. You never want to miss the opportunity to deliver a Mustang. The experience can be quite exhilarating, believe me!

The Top Reasons Why Mortgage Holders Sell for Discounts

Why in heaven's name would anyone sell their mortgage for less than the unpaid balance? Why would the former property owner be willing to accept a lot less money now than he or she previously would take when selling the property? Obviously, there is no end to the list of answers, but here are some of the most common reasons I've found.

1. Note (mortgage) holders want cash instead of monthly payments, for many reasons. Perhaps they wish to ...
    a. Purchase a car, boat, or recreational vehicle.
    b. Take a vacation.
    c. Buy something that requires a lot of cash.
    d. Start up a business venture.
    e. Send the kids to college or help them buy a new home.

2. Partners break up and separate or divorce.
    a. Partners need to split the money and go their own ways.
    b. Divorce often creates a need for immediate cash.

3. Investors who sell rundown properties often carry back the mortgage to facilitate the sale, but they would rather have received cash.

4. Lifestyles change—health or death of beneficiary.
    a. Older mortgage holders may want cash for "one last fling."
    b. The mortgage holder suddenly needs cash for the hospital or a retirement home.

c. Younger relatives who inherit mortgages often want cash immediately, instead of payments over time. Many folks are impatient
just like Susan and her boyfriend.

Finding the Right Mortgages Is Well Worth the Search

If I could pick an ideal property to purchase, it would be one that has at
least four private-party purchase money mortgages that I could assume.
Purchase money mortgages are the kind that result from sales where the
seller carries back the financing. They're different from mortgages where
cash is loaned against the property. As I mentioned earlier, they're an
extension of credit. No cash is dispersed.

Here's a typical example. An owner sells his $100,000 property on
terms. Both parties agree to a $10,000 cash down payment and a seller
carryback mortgage or promissory note for $90,000 at 10% interest,
with monthly payments of $800 (interest and principal), until the bal-
ance is paid.

The $90,000 mortgage or promissory note is a *purchase money mort-
gage*—the kind of mortgage you should be looking for. First of all, it's a
long-term note: it will take about 28 years to pay it off, which means you
will have many opportunities along the way to contact the holder (or his
or her heirs) about selling the note back to you for less than the balance
owed, more commonly referred to as a *discount*.

Naturally, the mortgage should not contain a due-on-sale clause in the
terms! However, most seller carryback notes do not have due-on-sale
clauses. They don't have prepay penalties or late fee charges, either. This
makes them weak in terms of their value as commercial paper. Mortgage
brokers and professional note buyers want these kinds of terms when they
purchase notes for cash.

A $90,000 note with 25 years of payments remaining, no due-on-sale
clause, and just three years old with only a 10% down payment is almost
unmarketable. The cash amount anyone would likely pay for such a note
(soggy paper) would not make the note holder very happy. In reality, the
person most likely to pay the highest price for this weak note is the mort-
gagor, the property owner who is making the payments on it.

Don't Throw the Gold Away with the Sand

New investors have told me they won't buy properties with more than two mortgages on them! If there are more than two, they insist that the mortgages be consolidated (paid off), leaving only a single loan or mortgage when escrow closes. They claim that having just one mortgage payment simplifies everything, as there's only one payment and one lender to worry about. It makes a nice, clean manageable transaction, they say.

Well, I must tell you that having clean and manageable transactions should never mean tossing your money or profit potential out the window! If it does, you're in for big trouble as an investor! Never lose sight of the target or you'll be passing right over some hefty profits that could easily be yours for the asking. It's much like having big gold nuggets in your pan, then throwing them out with the sand because you fail to recognize them!

Note-Buying Strategy Requires Detective Work

My note-buying strategy is based more on events and circumstances in the lives of my payees than on the yield charts. For example, when I locate a property I'm interested in buying, I always make it my business to see copies of the promissory notes to determine if they are good candidates for my future buy-back strategy. Notes are not public information like recorded deeds, so you must ask the sellers to produce them.

After I determine that the terms are acceptable, I try to dig out information about each of the beneficiaries, using my "Detective Columbo" techniques. I want to know if they're rich or poor, young or old and, if they have kids, how many and their ages, especially if they're about the right age for college. To do this right, you must force yourself to be a little "snoopy," but it will pay off over time, believe me!

Jay's Christmas Letter Generates Profits Year-Round

Let's imagine that I discover that a note holder is an average family man, with a 10-year-old car and three teenage kids. I'll send him my "special Christmas letter," as follows.

November 15, 2002

Dear Mr. Andrews:

My, how time flies! Only six more weeks until Christmas. As you know, I've been sending monthly payments to you since I bought your property on Ugly Street nearly two years ago. Today, I just received word that I'll be getting a substantial cash distribution from my late Aunt Lucy's estate. It's not quite as much as the balance I owe you ($56,570 as of 11-02), but I'm writing to everyone I make mortgage payments to, in order to find out who might need the extra cash. According to the terms of our promissory note, I still have about 15 years of payments left until it's finally paid off.

In the past, several people I send mortgage payments to have asked me if I could pay them cash, instead of monthly payments. Naturally they are willing to reduce the amount I owe them in exchange for immediate cash! Because my income is mostly from rents, I seldom have enough cash to take advantage of their generous offers, but I do appreciate them offering, just the same. Naturally, I'm happy to pay cash when I have it.

The way things look, I should have my money a couple of weeks before Christmas, but certainly not later than January 1. If you have a need for extra Christmas cash or perhaps for Jimbo's college tuition this coming spring, now would be the time to let me know, before I spend the money on something foolish! Also, if you could let me know how much of a discount you'll give for cash, I'd appreciate it very much. The best way for you to determine the true value is to call several professional note buyers in the yellow pages or newspaper ads. They will give you a quick estimate of the value—free of charge. I'll assure you, I'm always willing to pay more than professional mortgage buyers because I don't have a fancy office or the overhead to pay—and, of course, there are no fees dealing with me!

Sincerely,

Fixer Jay

Value, Like Beauty, Is in the Eye of the Note Holder

There are many books written about buying notes at discount, but the business of buying and selling notes is not what we're discussing here.

We're discussing buying back debt on properties we purchase without much regard for the standard yield computations. I know I'm going to hear from a few note buyers, but let me just say this anyway: I am more than happy to buy back my own mortgage debt and pay a little more money than most professional discount mortgage buyers would pay—and you should be too!

Investors Need a Healthy Financial Diet

Once you get a taste of buying back your own notes or mortgages at whopping discounts, you might just decide to expand your note-buying business and leave fixing toilets to someone else.

Before you sell your toilet auger, however, let me remind you that income earned from buying notes is not the same as income from rentals. For one thing, you will get no depreciation or capital gain treatment. In short, you won't get any tax shelter—and tax shelter has been a big part of my fortune-building strategy. My suggestion is to do both. Operating real estate and buying notes make excellent bedfellows. Check out the tax treatment with your local advisor.

21

Landlording Skills Can Make You Very Wealthy

Why in heaven's name would anyone of sound mind and body, who is capable of doing regular work, choose to become a landlord? That's a tough question for many folks, because it seems like many people have had bad experiences with rental units and tenants.

We Do It for the Money

The short answer is quick and easy—we do it for the money. If you buy income properties correctly—that is, you don't overpay for them—you'll soon discover, as I have, that your tenants will be paying for everything. They pay all the expenses for operations and all the mortgage payments to finance them. To my way of thinking, you'll need to look long and hard for a better deal. Think about it: your renters are paying for everything and, when they finally pay off the mortgages, it's you who ends up owning the real estate.

I often refer to landlording and managing as the 10% job that earns the other 90% of every rent dollar I collect. I charge 10% to manage properties (although I now do property management only for myself). I know many do-it-yourself landlord-owners who consistently earn $100 per hour or more doing landlord work. Landlording is the key for do-it-yourself investors to make big money.

The Dream: Working for Yourself

Besides making money, being a successful landlord offers some major personal benefits. For example, you can provide an excellent quality of life for yourself and your family. You can live wherever you choose and set your own work schedule. You can spend more time on hobbies and doing the personal things that never get done when you work for someone else. Being your own boss is the envy of every wage earner, because almost everyone dreams of making lots more money working for themselves. The good news is that investor landlording is a profession that will allow almost anyone to achieve financial independence and the highest quality of life, if they really wish to participate.

A San Francisco investor friend of mine, Richard Epley, writes about our task. The following is a quote from his book about managing properties: "If you are comfortable with the role of owner and landlord and are not intimidated by the responsibility for setting out the rules by which people may live in your property, you will find a vehicle for self-employment and self-expression that is difficult to match in our society."

I am in total agreement with my landlord friend. Hopefully, the information I give you will help get you started and prepare you for your role as manager and owner. Real estate investing can be a highly profitable and rewarding experience for you, if you know what you're doing and learn how to do it right.

Total Control over Money Decisions Is Key

In my opinion, when investing, you cannot leave out any step; otherwise, it causes a weak link in your investment chain. Under the slightest strain, that link always breaks first. One weak link can wreck your whole plan very quickly.

When small owner-operator investors decide to hire property management companies to handle the dirty work—like interviewing rental applicants, collecting rents, carrying out evictions, and anything else they do for their monthly fee—they give up far too much control, in my opinion. One of the most important things you need to make money as an investor is total control. Never allow others to restrict your ability to make money or earn profits.

The owner is the one who sets the rents, works on the buildings as much as he or she thinks is necessary, and finally decides when it's time to sell. In short, the owner must be responsible for the success or failure of the property. No other investing is quite like owner-operator investing, where all the control is in the hands of one person. If you can learn to do these things well, great success will be yours.

Proprietorship—A Must

Proprietorship is the big deal, because no one has the same level of motivation as the owner. Remember: it's owners who borrow money against their homes, who invest their entire life savings in an effort to make a better life for themselves and their families. Owners have a much greater interest in their own success than anyone else. That's what proprietorship is about—and it's something that fees from the rents can't buy. Picture this scenario if you will. It's Sunday afternoon and a tenant calls in a repair to fix the handle on her toilet. It broke off and the lever fell down inside the tank. The flapper chain came loose, so she can't flush her toilet. Naturally, all the grandkids are there on Sundays. She needs help now. I'll give you 10-1 odds, if you have a hired property manager, that toilet won't flush once before Monday morning. But if it does, I'll bet the owner drove out to fix it.

My point is this: if you collect rent for Sundays, you must also arrange for toilets to flush on Sundays. It's just sound business practice and common sense. Proprietorship is what's most important, especially for new investors who are just starting out. Professional managers might be all right for later on, but seldom in the beginning.

Success Means Wearing Many Hats

It's important to understand that you will need to perform many different functions to be successful as an investor. Landlording, although extremely important, is only one of these functions. You must also learn how to determine the right price to pay for properties and the reasons why. You must learn how to structure the financing. If you choose to do fix-up, you'll also need to develop those particular skills. Learning market trends, negotiating techniques, judging locations, understanding true costs of operating rentals, hiring workers, and developing good and usable records and a bookkeeping system are also necessary parts of being a successful owner-investor.

The First Rule of Business Is to Define Your Customer

When you begin to think of rental houses as a business venture, rather than simply as investing in real estate, it will open your mind to a whole new world of opportunity. The rules of business will help you immensely as an investor-owner of rental properties. Here's an example of what I mean.

In my town, I've discovered there are two primary groups of people who need rental houses. The first group consists of young folks, 20 to 35 years old. The second group is seniors, ranging from 60 to 78 years of age. My town provides the younger group with mostly service-type jobs— restaurants, stores, and gas stations. There are also a large number of single mothers, with children, who receive public assistance. Many senior renters are living on Social Security and about half of them receive additional income from private pensions. Approximately 75% of both groups can afford to pay between $400 and $550 rent per month. About 10% can pay more. The others must pay less.

Once you find similar statistics for your buying area—which I recommend you do—your strategy as an owner of rental properties will take a definite direction. In my case, for example, if I intend to rent my houses to the largest number of potential renters in my town, I must develop an investment strategy that allows me to own houses that I can profitably rent out for $400 to $550 per month. Obviously, if you buy, fix, and sell, you should think along the same terms. Many investors try to figure this out after they buy the property. That's doing business backwards, in my opinion.

Reasons Behind My Renting Strategy

The main reasons for my decision to enter the lower-income rental market were based on the economics—and it offered the least possible risk of going broke.

The economic reality for me was that I had very little money to buy real estate. Buying older, rundown houses and small apartments fit my budget. I found that buying "ugly duckling" properties and turning them into "beautiful swans" allowed me to obtain much higher rent markups than my competitors. For example, I might pay $20,000 per unit, then spend $4,000 on fix-up, after which I would rent the unit out for $400 per month, or $4,800 per year. That's a 20% annual return per unit ($4,800 annual rent divided by $24,000 value). Contrast this return with a "pride of ownership" property that costs $50,000 and rents for $450. Never lose sight of the reason for being in business—*to make a profit*.

Increasing My Odds for Success

Most everyone knows that any new business venture is filled with many uncertainties. Perhaps the most important question is "Will there be enough customers to pay the bills?" Renting houses is not much different from selling widgets or running a restaurant. Both depend greatly on paying customers.

In order to increase my odds for success, I decided that my rental houses should be priced so that the largest number of renters could afford to rent them. Stated another way, I wanted my houses to be within the price range of 75% of all tenants in my town. To do this I would need to own houses that I could profitably rent out for $400 to $550 per month.

I think you can see the safety part of my strategy. By targeting 75% of the renters, where low-income rentals were already scarce, I felt quite confident that vacancies would never be a serious problem for me. Vacant houses, providing no means to pay the mortgage payments, could have easily shattered my investment plan. I had no extra cash in the bank for a rainy day. That's why the least amount of risk was very important to me.

The Value of Tenant Cycling

What I tell you here applies mostly to fix-up investors like me. It has to do with tenant cycling. Let's say you purchase six apartments that need fixing up. Rents are $350 each when you buy them. However, you've determined that two-bedroom units, once you've fixed them up, should rent for $550 each.

I'll assume you're short of fix-up money, like most investors. You figure it should take at least 12 months doing the work yourself. It's important to keep your cash flow as high as possible during the fix-up phase, to pay the expenses and mortgage payment. That's the situation. Here's how to keep the rents coming in.

Interim Tenants Pay Your Bills While You Fix Up the Property

First, understand you can't jump up from $350 renters to $550 renters in one giant leap, not unless you empty the building and do a "rehab blitz." That means doing all the work in all the units at one time. That costs a ton of money, plus you lose all rental income—$2,100 per month, in this case, for several months. You'll go broke doing fix-up projects that way.

Many low-end tenants can't stay put. They move from place to place like gypsies. You need them. "Gypsies" will be your rent-paying customers for the next 12 months or longer. They will pay your bills as you transition from $350 rents to $550. It will take at least 12 to 18 months to make the changeover when doing most of the fix-up work yourself. Meanwhile, keep the units filled up with "gypsies"—and keep those rents coming in.

You can't fix up one unit in a six-unit building and immediately begin charging $550. The other five units will hold you back. You can, however, move up to the $425 to $450 range on the first change of tenants. The reality is that your normal $550 tenant won't live next door to $350 renters, no matter how nice the apartment is. On the other hand, "gypsies" will. They see your apartment as a bargain. They plan to stay only a short time anyway and don't care who they live next to, as long as the price is right, for now.

Your Broker Will Likely Never Understand This Strategy

During the 12- to-18-month fix-up period, it's customary for some of the tenants to move out. Obviously, they can see that rents will soon be going up. Better-class tenants won't show up for a while because most of them cannot visualize how attractive the completed project will look. Your interim solution to cash flow can be the "gypsies." They come and they go, but they pay their rent and that's what you need most during the fix-up stage.

I've found it takes most do-it-yourself investors a little while to perfect this strategy. My good friend and real estate agent, Fred, still doesn't understand how I do it. Nevertheless, he still agrees that it works very well for me.

Keys to Good Management Are Action and Enforcement

Enforcement of the rules, whether the civil code (laws) or your own house rules, is the best way to develop a smooth-running management operation. Preventive techniques are as important to managing tenants as they are for the doctor who manages your personal health. One of my main criticisms of professional property managers is that they very rarely act—mostly they react. They're always ready and willing to fix a malfunctioning toilet—but only after it has overflowed and ruined the living room carpet.

You Must Always Get the Money First

Rent monies are the "lifeblood" of apartment owners. Yet, I know many property managers and owners alike who participate with their tenants each month in a silly little "rent collection ritual." The tenant starts the game by saying, "The check is in the mail." Then the landlord begins calling every day or driving out to the property to inform the tenant that he hasn't received the check yet. Sometimes this goes on for weeks.

Playing this game will only eliminate whatever respect one party might have for the other. It generally leads to more bickering about other matters, as well. Don't allow yourself to be part of this game. You'll fare much better if you simply use the rules already on the books. I'm referring to your state's landlord-tenant civil laws and, of course, your own rental contract terms, to which your tenant has agreed.

Rent collection is a landlord's most serious business. Quick enforcement of the rules, when needed, is the best method I know to keep your tenants paying as they promised.

Good Tenant Records Are Essential

Some property owners tell me that it's not necessary to have written rental contracts and agreements, if you choose the right tenants. I certainly can't argue with that. The problem for me—as for most other landlords—is that it's impossible to do that 100% of the time. Obviously, folks who tell me this have never been exposed to a courtroom eviction drama. If they had been, they would understand that, if it's not in writing, you don't have a case.

Don't Take Shortcuts with Formalities

The tenant interview and application process do not change because a tenant is renting economy-priced rental property or because he or she does not have a regular job. You should follow the same application procedure, no matter what the applicant's circumstances. You must have complete tenant files in order to operate a rental business successfully. Don't misunderstand what I'm saying about tenants without regular jobs. This doesn't mean you should rent houses to unqualified people. Let's be clear on that point. Obviously, there must be sufficient income from some source or you don't rent to them, period.

The Application Form—What You Need to Know

It's very important to learn everything you can about an applicant before you hand over the keys. This information should be required whether you're renting $300 apartments or a suite on top of the Trump Tower.

The first thing you need to find out is if the tenant can afford to pay the rent you're asking. Second, what can you do to collect the rent in the event your tenant fails to pay during his or her stay with you?

The more personal information you can obtain on your rental application, the better prepared you'll be if something goes wrong. You need names and addresses of parents, friends, and co-workers. You also need references, including his or her last two landlords. One question on my application asks, "Who will co-sign for you if your own credit information is not sufficient to qualify you?" The answer may lead you to financially sound backups who don't mind co-signing your rental contract with the tenant. Often parents or in-laws will do this if you ask. Always have them fill out your application, the same as tenants, when they agree to be a co-signer.

There's absolutely nothing in my contract that should make it necessary for much further discussion beyond the initial rent-up. Obviously, when a tenant rents my house, he or she has already inspected it and decided to live there. I need to know just one thing—Are they qualified? That's it! It's not really necessary to like your tenants. A landlord's obligation is to provide the best housing for the tenant's rent dollar.

Can Your Tenant Afford the Rent?

As a general rule, young tenants can pay about 35% of their net take-home money (after taxes or payroll deductions) for rent. Older tenants and seniors can often pay 50% of their income and have no problems. The reason for this difference is because they have learned to budget their resources and because they're wiser. Obviously there are exceptions.

As a rule of thumb, the rent-to-income ratio must be lower for tenants with young children, automobiles, and pets. These things cost extra money. Whatever rent-to-income ratio you use, don't rent to applicants who do not have adequate income to pay the rent you charge. If you violate this rule, you'll end up chasing rents and listening to "tearjerker" stories every month about why the rent is late or how the check got lost in the mail. Clearly the saddest part of the story is that you'll have brought this on yourself.

Renting to Low-Income Tenants

One major difference I've found when renting to low-income tenants, as opposed to those with more money is that, when a crisis develops, they have no cash reserves to keep them afloat. Many do not even have decent-paying jobs. Others depend on housing subsidies, Social Security, and welfare assistance. Another problem, quite common with the younger renters, is their inability to handle money. Many have difficulty living within their means.

People often ask me if it's better to rent houses to tenants with low-paying jobs than to others in low-income brackets, such as tenants with HUD assistance (Section 8) or AFDC (Aid to Families with Dependent Children). Frankly, I see very little difference.

Service jobs in my town pay very low wages and don't include any benefits. Take-home pay, net cash, is about the same for a full-time service job worker as it is for a single woman with two dependent children receiving federal assistance. Financially, the woman may be slightly better off because she also gets food stamps and free health care. It's better for me if she doesn't have a car to buy gas for. Try to be objective here. Remember: we're talking about the tenant's ability to pay.

Section 8 Tenants: Rent-Assisted Program

Federally funded Section 8 programs, administered through local city and county Housing Assistance Programs offices, provide extra protection and sometimes higher rents to landlords. It involves extra paperwork, but the agency will prepare most of the documents for you. You, as a landlord-owner, will still select the tenants. Often they are sent to you by the agency from their waiting lists. Regardless of the extra paperwork required by HUD rules, you should still have every tenant complete your rental application and, if approved, sign your rental agreement or contract.

The major difference with HUD Section 8 tenants is you need good cause to evict. The good causes are listed on the HUD lease documents. Obviously, nonpayment of rent and property destruction are good causes. The best feature about the Section 8 program is the guaranteed rent provision. If your tenant goes bonkers, you can receive up to two months' extra rent. Also, should damage to your property occur, the agency will inspect the property, determine fault, and reimburse you for all authorized repairs, minus the wear and tear, of course.

Rental Contracts Don't Need to Be Complicated

Always use an application form and a rental contract or agreement. Ask prospective tenants to fill out your application first. If you approve their application, then prepare your rental contract. My contract specifies the terms (rules) that tenants must agree to, if they wish to live in my property.

I have never discovered any need for a long-winded rental contract with page after page of monotonous terms. For one thing, no one will ever read it—and, second, I might be asked to explain it someday. Remember: five pages of regulations are not worth anything unless your tenant is willing to abide by the terms. Never forget this: a good landlord-tenant relationship is not better because you have a "killer contract;" it's better because you learn to select tenants who will pay you and abide by the rules. Therefore, learning how to qualify and screen your tenants is the area where you should strive to improve. The contract will be needed only if that effort fails.

Rental contracts should specify that tenants are to keep the property in good repair, live peacefully alongside their neighbors, pay rent in a timely manner, and allow the landlord to inspect with proper notice. They should also specify who pays attorney fees to enforce violation of rules, when a late fee is required and the amount, and who is responsible for tenants' personal property losses. Make it a point to have all adult tenants sign the agreement, as well as co-signers, if they guarantee the rents.

Other important terms should include the tenant's liability regarding his or her personal property, when late fees are due and the amount due, and who is responsible for repairs when things break while the tenant is in possession. My agreement is a legal-size (8½ x 14) sheet, printed on both sides. I have amended it several times over the years. It's very basic, but it covers about everything.

In the event you discover you've rented to a deadbeat, a simple, straightforward contract will serve you best as an attachment (exhibit) to your lawsuit (unlawful detainer—a suit by a landlord to evict tenants and receive back rent). Surprising as it may sound, judges want to find out very quickly who has done what to whom and why. A well-written contract helps them understand. If there is any confusion or doubt concerning the paperwork, nine times out of 10 the tenant is automatically given the benefit of the doubt. Therefore, my rule concerning a rental contract is this: "If it's simple, it's good." Keep it simple for them and you'll walk out of court a winner.

Large Deposits Provide Added Protection

I do not collect first and last months' rent from my tenants. However, I collect larger deposits than many other landlords. It's easy to justify a large deposit when you explain that it's still cheaper to move into your house because, unlike other landlords, you're not charging last month's rent in advance.

Typically, a landlord in my town will ask $450 rent for the first month, $450 for the last month, plus a $300 security deposit. So, the move-in will cost the tenant $1,200 total. I think it's much better to charge $450 rent with a $650 security deposit. My total move-in cost is $100 less than others and the $650 deposit is fully refundable if the tenants leave my place clean when they move. Obviously, I'm much better secured with the larger deposit.

This strategy avoids a "game" tenants often play with landlords. On the first of the month, they are short of money. So, they give a 30-day notice to move—"New job," they say. They request that the landlord apply their prepaid, last month's rent for the current rent due. The landlord must comply. Then, toward the end of the month, they proudly announce, "I won't be leaving after all. My new job fell through." Obviously, most landlords don't want vacancies so they feel somewhat relieved. The problem is that now the last month's rent is used up and it never gets put back in the landlord's account. This means the landlord is holding a very small deposit ($300, in this example). This is not enough money to adequately protect the landlord or to make a tenant think twice about skipping (not paying rent) and staying as long as possible before the marshal arrives to toss him or her out.

One final note: when something goes wrong, act immediately. Serve the proper notice to begin eviction. Action makes a believer out of your tenant quicker than any words you could ever find.

Tenant Urgency—Not My Urgency

It is your business to see that rents are collected and that tenants abide by the rules and regulations stated in your rental contract agreement. You must never allow a tenant to intimidate you. It will almost always lead you to make poor decisions. In my view, the most common mistake landlords make is to allow the tenants' urgency to become their urgency. Let me explain.

After many years of doing this job, I'm hard pressed to think of any situation so compelling that there wouldn't be enough time to think it through. For example, if there's a fire at my property, the community fire department will handle everything. As for me, I'm protected by insurance on the building. Should someone die in my house, I've yet to meet the landlord who'd be of much help. The county coroner is the person you need.

In short, leaky pipes, broken windows, and cockroaches are no more urgent to a landlord than dying patients are to a doctor or raging fires are to a firefighter. They are simply a part of doing business.

Pipes will always leak, people sometimes die, and buildings occasionally burn to the ground. That's just normal stuff when you own a lot of rental houses. Your job as a landlord is to be as responsive as possible to your tenants. But never, never allow yourself to be stampeded into making rushed decisions, simply because your tenants think you should.

Landlords Must Know the Law

Every landlord should know and understand the landlord-tenant laws in his or her area. Once you know the laws, your fear of renters or of being intimidated by them will vanish. An overwhelming number of owners incorrectly assume these laws favor deadbeat tenants. I can assure you this is not the case, although it appears that way sometimes. Laws are mostly about equity. It's well to remember that there are unscrupulous landlords just as there are bad tenants.

Owners Should Do Evictions

Landlords should do their own evictions, at least the first few times. This provides "combat training" and some valuable experience learning how the system works. Besides experience, there are two other important reasons. As always, the first has to do with money—yours. The second involves time, but since time is also money, you can see an obvious connection.

The simple truth is that knowledgeable landlords can save a sizable sum of money in attorney fees—and are in a much better position to move quickly and get rid of undesirable tenants. Quite often attorneys consider evictions as "fill-in" or "bottom-of-the-barrel" work. Unless you're a regular client, your eviction problem will not have a very high priority with most lawyers. They've got more important things to deal with. Tossing out deadbeat tenants is not the kind of work that will get an attorney's name painted on the front office door. Besides, most are far too slow, in my opinion.

Naturally, owners have the advantage with evictions because they know all the details about their tenants. Another plus is that owners can give immediate attention to a single problem, whereas attorneys, more often than not, are working on many cases at the same time. This immediate-attention issue is most important, because you don't want hostile tenants living on your property any longer than absolutely necessary.

Here's what happens—the longer an eviction gets delayed, the more angry and hostile most tenants become, and the more your property is at risk for a trash-out. Trash-outs happen when a tenant goes bonkers, kicks in the plasterboard, plugs the toilets, cuts wires inside walls, and spray-paints the interior black. You can greatly reduce the risk of a trash-out by conducting quick, efficient evictions. That means no name-calling and no threats, confrontations, or harassment. When you know the laws and understand what you can and must do, you are in the driver's seat.

Learning Eviction Paperwork Is Not Difficult

Filling out the proper forms and going to court, when required (90% of my evictions default before ever facing the judge), is as easy as changing locks, painting walls, or fixing a faucet drip. The key is you must learn the procedure. Although court clerks are generally forbidden to give you legal advice, they are quite helpful and will tell you what forms to use. After you've been through the routine a few times, you'll feel like Perry Mason. Who knows? You might even develop a brilliant law career to fall back on in case you flop as a landlord.

Repairs and Customer Service

If you rent houses, you should think of yourself as a businessperson. Businesspeople provide a product or service for money. You're providing houses for rent. It's basically the same. The point I wish to emphasize here is that, if you provide top-grade service to your customers, you'll stay in business a long time. You'll also come out far ahead of your competition, which improves your bottom line (cash flow).

Many part-time landlords get themselves into serious difficulties by stalling or putting off repair call-outs. Here's a typical "putting off" response: "Yes, Mr. Renter. I know it's only Wednesday, but if you'll just be patient and hold off using the toilet until Saturday, that's my husband's day off, you know." Ask yourself, if you were the renter, would you appreciate that response? I rather doubt it. So, then, neither will most of your tenants.

If you collect rents, you are obligated to keep the property in good working order. Pattern your repair visits after Sears or the telephone company. Both have been in the service business 100 years or so. It's interesting to note that neither company sees the necessity of doing routine repairs during nonbusiness hours. The key to good repair service is to determine the urgency, schedule the job realistically, and then get it done.

What will set you apart from other landlords is how well you handle repairs. Tenants will always complain about high rents. You can't change that; however, when they get top service for their money, they will accept rents better. As a result, they'll remain your customers much longer, which, of course, is what all owners want.

Be Snoopy, When You Can—but Be Tactful

A bonus benefit for hands-on owners is that call-out repair visits provide the opportunity to "snoop" around inside your property without the normal 24-hour notice formalities. The more things you know about your tenants—like if they're decent housekeepers, the number of beds (the count should match the authorized tenants), and the number of pets living on the property versus those listed on the rental agreement—the better control you will have as owner-manager.

Obey the Laws of Habitability

It doesn't matter whether you rent $100-a-month river-bottom shacks or $10,000-a-month hilltop mansions, the rules are the same. Pro-tenant states, like California, have nasty penalties for what they call "slum land-lording." Slumlords are owners who milk their properties, pocket the rents, and never contribute a nickel to their upkeep. This is a very short-sighted plan and a straight path to disaster.

California Civil Code, Section 1941.1, specifies the minimum habit-able living standards for California. Other states have similar statutes. However, even if there are no statutes, common sense would dictate adhering to these minimum living standards.

Here are the laws of habitability for rental properties in my town. You should use them too.

1. No leaky roofs, doors, or windows. Exterior of house must be weather-tight. Cardboard on windows won't qualify.
2. Plumbing and gas facilities must comply with building codes. They must be kept in good working order.
3. The building must have a properly approved water system, with hot and cold running water. Drains must be connected to an approved sewer or septic system. Hoses running out the back door from a washing machine are not approved, when anyone's looking.
4. Heating is required. It must be approved in accordance with local codes. Gas appliances must be properly vented and maintained in good working order.
5. Electrical wiring (lights) and other equipment must conform to building codes and must be kept in good repair. Be careful with electrical fixtures in bathrooms near water. Shocked tenants might forget the rent payment day, which could shock the landlords.
6. Apartments and houses must be clean when you rent them. There can be no junk piles or garbage lying around. Also, rats, mice, roaches, and other pests must be eliminated—or at least relocated. Always rent clean properties. It's good business.
7. Owners must provide garbage cans or city receptacles (bins). They must be routinely emptied and cleaned and they must be in place on the day you rent the unit.

8. Floors, stairs, and handrails must be kept in good repair. Also, make sure lighting is provided in stairways. If your tenant can't see the handrail at night, why bother having one? Watch for weak spots in flooring.

Don't forget these eight items. They are not optional. They are the law. If you rent with violations and if your renter turns you in, you'll have the kind of problems you don't need, believe me. Landlords have found themselves in serious trouble for noncompliance. Even worse, they may be sentenced to live in their own units with—guess who?

22

Tips for Dealing with Tenants

Managing people is a difficult job. Managing people who are also your tenants and have an obligation to pay you their hard-earned rent dollars, every month, can be particularly challenging to your sanity. Ask almost anyone who owns rental houses to name the worst thing, and they'll tell you, without even taking time to think, it's the tenants. It seems quite clear that property owners who wish to survive very long in the business and who expect to make any serious money in it are well-advised to learn early on the job how to manage tenants.

Like anything else in life, you must pay your dues up front. Managing tenants is the price of admission for investors who operate income properties. And everyone knows that dealing with people, especially one on one, can be nasty work. It's only natural in situations where one person always pays money and the other always receives it that disputes can surface quickly. Landlords with any experience at all understand it doesn't take very long on rent day for normal conversation to erupt into a shouting match. Still, there are methods you can use to avoid most problems.

Your Tenants Are Your Customers

The first rule of good landlording is to treat it exactly like you would any other well-run business. Managing your property is a business and the tenants are your customers. It's your job as a landlord to provide the best product (houses) and the best service you possibly can. If you do this better than your competition you'll obviously enjoy much greater success. Customers (tenants) will naturally beat a pathway to your doorstep when they feel that you offer the most value for their housing dollar.

To make sure you're ready for the kind of business you want and expect, you must try hard to offer your customer the best value in the rental business. That means a clean house or apartment, priced ideally at $10 or $20 below the competition. This may not seem like much, but for renters who compare houses and watch their expenses closely, it's enough to swing many deals your way. It will also keep your houses full of tenants, while the other guys worry about vacancies.

How can you tell if you're $10 or $20 below the competition? The best way I know of is to study your local classified ads—"Houses or Apartments for Rent." Then drive out and see what the competition is offering at comparable rents. Adjust yours up or down according to what you observe.

One of the most important questions all landlords should stop and ask themselves is "Would I rather be popular or profitable?" You don't have to be sinister or dishonest to be a wealthy landlord. What you must be is a good businessperson. "Good business" means that you collect accounts receivable (rents) in a timely manner and that your assets (houses) are maintained properly by tenants who lease them. See how simple this is.

Landlords will not be disliked or hated anymore than the supermarket cashiers when they demand the rent due. Everyone knows that cashiers will not allow groceries to leave the store until they collect the money for them. Customers expect that and don't hate cashiers for following the rules. Landlords who insist on collecting the rents on time are no different from supermarket cashiers.

Emotions Should Not Control Landlord Decisions

I've worked very hard to develop my low-profile landlording techniques, which minimizes personal contacts between landlords and tenants. I see no reason for landlords to hang around their tenants, except for maintenance visits and repair calls. Obviously, I don't chase my tenants down to get the rents. This practice lends itself to emotional confrontations, which is exactly what landlords need to avoid. I avoid personal conflicts over such matters as lifestyle, inside housekeeping, and moral issues. That's not my business. All matters relating to tenancy should be kept strictly business.

Obviously, it would be a poor business decision to keep an unruly or destructive tenant, because it would cost you money. Making money is top priority in the landlord business, the same as in any other business.

Landlords often find themselves in trouble with tenants because they try to inject too much logic and common sense into tenant management. Logic and common sense have their place, but seldom count for much where legal issues are concerned. For example, it is nearly impossible to effectively force your personal living standards and ideals on your tenants—a very common mistake for many new landlords. I would advise any rental owner to seriously think about what I'm saying here, because it has a lot to do with sanity, your sanity. What good would it do you to make a million dollars from your rental properties if your tenants drive you crazy?

Always Act–Don't React

Good landlords always act—they don't react. Don't fight and argue with tenants, anymore than your boss would fight and argue with you about work requirements on your job. Obviously, discussions are all right and fairness should always prevail. Landlords are the bosses of their houses and they make the rules for tenants who live there. Never compromise the issue of who's in charge. When tenants living in your rental property have the upper hand, you've got big problems.

Most beginners don't fully understand the true value of learning to be good landlords. You don't have to agree with me about any of this. You don't even have to like it. But please keep an open mind. Also, don't forget, I'm still in training myself. I have many teachers every single day of every month, living in my rental houses and apartments—my tenants. They've taught me many tricks of the landlording trade—and the experience has been priceless, believe me.

I continue to receive letters from subscribers and distraught landlords who can't control the people living in their properties. I must tell you now that if you cannot handle your tenants—that is, make them pay rents and follow a few basic rules—you can expect a very miserable existence owning real estate. Worse yet, you probably won't be around long enough to enjoy those big profits I promised you in earlier chapters.

Horror Stories Are Caused Mostly by Ignorance

Almost everyone has heard about "the tenant from hell" who trashes the house and leaves owing six months' rent and fix-up costs in the thousands. Movies have been made about the subject to further dramatize it. There is no question that this kind of thing does happen. However, it doesn't have to happen to you—nor should it if you pay attention to what I tell you.

Often, you will hear discussions to the effect that "deadbeat tenants know all the rules, which enables them to stay in your property month after month without paying any rent." Sometimes, the storyteller says this is so because the tenant has minor children and receives welfare or other public assistance.

The problem with this picture is that the storyteller is giving far too much credit to the tenant for being street-savvy and knowledgeable. The chances are the tenant's success is much more likely attributable to an ignorant landlord.

Seldom will a tenant stay long in my property if he or she doesn't pay rents. After you've done a few evictions yourself and learned what papers to file and how to do it in a timely manner, you'll have enough confidence so that horror stories won't happen at your properties. Again, I'll repeat, know-how is the difference between owners who operate their rental properties successfully and those who are simply hoping for the best.

Most Tenants Will Pay the Rent

Contrary to these landlord-tenant horror stories, most tenants who agree to rent your property, whether they work or not, will pay their rent. This fact eliminates about 95% of your collection worries. Trust me on this: I have enough tenants to prove it. The big problems are caused by the remaining 5% who can practically destroy your life. It's the old story about the rotten apple in a barrel, unfortunately. "Destroy your life" is not too strong a phrase for what can easily happen when innocent but ignorant landlords do battle with savvy, deadbeat tenants.

Fewer Rules Are Best—but Be Sure to Enforce Them

Two of the rules that I insist must be followed are that tenants must pay rent on time and pay a late fee when rents are more than five days past due. If you don't collect late fees, tenants will have no incentive to pay on time.

Another rule I follow is that no extra persons are allowed to move into my houses without prior authorization. I don't usually deny permission as long as an additional tenant doesn't exceed my occupancy limits and he or she fills out a rental application and is qualified to be added to the rental contract.

I do not permit parking unauthorized cars on my property (sometimes towed there). I do not allow working on cars (other than minor maintenance) for more than one day. Junky cars with their hoods up or sitting around on wood blocks give a property an unsightly image. It also sends the wrong signal about the type of tenants I want. If you allow trashy-looking cars to accumulate on your properties, they will soon look like junkyards. Enforcing this rule is a continuing effort, but it pays off at the cash register.

Limit Improvements to What the Rent Can Support

Several years after I became a full-fledged landlord, I found myself trying too hard to make my tenants extra happy. I didn't realize it at the time, but that will never happen again. It seemed like the more I tried to please them, the more my tenants wanted. For example, some of my inexpensive apartment units have only linoleum on the floors and several of my economy houses have carpets in the living rooms and hallways, only. The tenants were always asking for extra carpets after they rented the property. My houses are always clean and painted with my standard off-white color inside; however, tenants wanted me to furnish them paint of their choice to repaint because they didn't like my color.

Many of the requests I've received would have cost me a ton of money if I agreed. Often, they will ask me for rear yard fences, where there were none when they moved in, generally because they acquire a dog or decide to baby-sit small children in the backyard for extra income. Don't misunderstand me here: I'm very much in favor of rear yard fences, and front ones, too, for that matter. But there is something missing in all of these requests. It's called "consideration"—the contract term for the extra money. Who should pay for these special upgrades and add-on requests? Houses without carpets are like cheeseburgers without fries. However, you get the fries only when you pay extra for them.

Cut Down on Repair Visits—Get the Details over the Phone

One of my special techniques to help me cut down on extra repair visits is to ask tenants who phone to thoroughly explain their problems. This has two positive effects. First, I can get a good idea of what's wrong. I am better able to judge the seriousness of the situation and can quite often instruct the tenants on how to fix the problem themselves. Also, good explanations over the telephone help landlords decide what type of service is needed. My "how-to-help-yourself" instruction over the phone is especially helpful when problems involve things like resetting a fuse or breaker, what to do about noisy neighborhood kids, or how to flip the toilet handle so the water stops running.

Summer months bring on a rash of calls about evaporative coolers that don't seem to work. Often, it's merely a case of the control knob being switched to the wrong position. Most coolers can be set to "vent only" (only the fan operates) and tenants mistakenly think something is wrong. Many don't bother to read the knob setting; instead, they immediately call the landlord.

I have found about 30% of my tenants' repair calls are really unnecessary. Getting good information from the caller and providing self-help instructions by telephone can save landlords many trips—and obviously a great deal of money.

Playing 20 Questions Can Discourage Unnecessary Calls

The second reason for asking my tenants lots of questions is to discourage unnecessary calls. Tenants don't like to answer lots of questions. Don't ask me why; I'll probably never know. I do know, however, they won't call nearly so often if they know I'll quiz them. Perhaps some realize how silly the call is, so the next time they try to help themselves first, rather than calling right away.

If there's a leak, I always ask my tenants to describe what is leaking and if they can actually see where the water is coming out. By listening to their explanations and descriptions over the telephone, I can generally determine if a supply line or drainpipe is involved. Obviously, water supply lines, under pressure, are a far more serious concern to me than dripping drainpipes.

Collecting the Rents and Knowing Where to Draw the Line with Deadbeats

One of the most controversial issues in the landlording business has to do with collecting the rents and knowing where to draw the line on late payers. First, it should be perfectly clear that landlords do not contract with tenants for the purpose of extending credit or providing free shelter. In my own county, there are 19 agencies that already do that—and I see no reason to become number 20. On the other hand, I'm a businessperson, so I recognize the need to be somewhat flexible, particularly with long-term tenants who are valuable customers to me.

My policy regarding late payments or split payments is to be fairly strict about enforcing the terms of my rental contract during the first six months of every tenancy. After six months—a period that allows me to observe a tenant's paying habit—I will generally become a bit more flexible, assuming the tenant's pay record is OK. During the first six months, I routinely issue three-day pay-or-quit notices no later than five days after the rent is past due—sometimes sooner, depending on how the weekend falls. If the rent remains unpaid, I usually evict the tenant. If I receive at least half of the rent, I generally accept it and reissue the three-day notice, showing the balance due. Don't forget: rents are the wheels on your investment vehicle. If you don't collect them, you'll get left behind sitting on your axle.

Discrimination Laws Do Not Protect Deadbeats

If you decide to use a three-to-one ratio (income-to-rent), it means a renter with $900 per month income can pay you $300 per month rent.

Obviously, you must be able to verify the income. I always insist on seeing all occupants who will live in my houses—adults and children. If I don't like what I see, I don't rent to them. Disliking people is not discrimination. Discrimination is unfair treatment of renters based on race, color, religion, sex, ancestry, national origin, age, family status, and physical or mental handicap. You'll notice that deadbeats aren't protected by fair housing laws. If you don't want them as customers, you don't have to rent to them.

Should I Accept Partial Rent?

Quite often landlords ask me, "Should I accept partial payments for rent?" My answer is generally "Yes, if you feel that's all your tenant has. Of course, you should always give him a notice to pay-or-quit for the balance as soon as you get the money in your hands."

Let's face it: many low-end renters are lousy money managers. Most can't ever save a dime. Do you think you should ever tell this person not to come back until he or she has all the rent money? Can you imagine how lonely you'll be, waiting for that to happen?

Splitting Rent Payments Can Help Tenants Pay You

I rent to a number of welfare tenants who receive assistance checks twice monthly. It's nearly impossible for many of them to pay me the total rent from one check, unless they have other income or housing subsidies. It's my policy to try and work with tenants by splitting their rent payments. I ask for 60% on the 1st and 40% on the 15th. In exchange for this favor, I require a larger security deposit, just in case something goes wrong. With larger deposits on hand, I reduce the risk of rent losses. Obviously, this arrangement is a compromise, but it seems to work quite well for me.

Never Change Your Paperwork to Do a Favor

An important point here is to never modify or change your written rental agreement or contract to show anything other than month-to-month tenancy. You should rent by the month, period. Your decision to accept more than one payment is strictly a verbal agreement (nothing in writing) between you and your tenant. You should explain it to your tenant—"This is strictly a special favor to help you pay. In the event you don't do as you promise, this favor is immediately withdrawn and it's back to the terms of the written agreement."

Let me remind you what I said before—rents are the wheels on your investment wagon. Collect them any way you can or you could find yourself sitting on your axle with a broken bank account.

Don't Accept Excuses for Nonpayment of Rent

If you're intimidated by tenant threats or if you're hesitant to begin a nonpay eviction because your renter has had problems in the family or some other crisis, you'll have great difficulty operating your rental business. How many supermarkets would tell their customers to take groceries home without paying for them? How many banks would allow you to skip the mortgage payment this month because a tenant hasn't paid his or her rent yet?

No other business could operate very long by trying to accommodate the never-ending hard-luck stories—and neither can you. Fair business dealings are the key to a landlord's success. No jury would ever render a judgment for tenants who make up ridiculous excuses for not paying their rents. Therefore, your decision to quickly evict nonpaying renters is based on simple fairness and should never be based on personal emotions.

One rule that has served me well for many years, in terms of fairness—which is generally thought to be a 50-50 proposition—is to try my very best to give my tenants a full 60% worth of fairness in exchange for them giving me just 40% in return. 40% is all you'll ever need to become very successful and very rich.

Noncontact Management Works Quite Well

As my business has grown in size, my employees deal directly with my tenants. I'm mostly involved in the background. Naturally, I make most important decisions. However, in the background, I can stay neutral and objective about my business—and it works very well for me.

Additionally, years ago I discovered I could manage tenants more effectively without making house calls. I do it with written memos and a telephone answering machine. The answering machine allows me to take repair calls and conduct regular landlord business—and to monitor all incoming calls. As a general rule, most tenants don't like talking to a recorded message and tend to hang up a lot, unless, of course, they actually have an important reason to call. Tenants don't like this arrangement as much as I do, but it works very nicely as long as I handle repair calls promptly and provide good service. Eventually, they get used to the recording.

There are two major benefits of using these memos to help collect rents and enforce rules. First, you can avoid getting personally involved in the emotional discussions about late rents, extra cars, or too many visitors that always develop whenever you make personal house calls. The second benefit is having a written record of everything you tell your tenants. Written memos eliminate all the confusion about who said what to whom and when. If you end up in court with your tenants, copies of memos advising them about what to expect if they don't pay the rent will go a long way toward winning an eviction judgment.

If there are any problems with my rent or rules, I simply write a memo to my tenant advising him or her what needs to be done to fix whatever's wrong.

23

The Big Picture and Long-Term Wealth

Remember: planning is necessary for success. According to Robert Schuller, "Yard by yard, life is too hard; but inch by inch, it's a cinch." And baseball great Yogi Berra seconds the idea: "If you don't know where you're going, you could end up somewhere else."

Seldom do I begin a chapter with poetry. However, I think it's particularly appropriate here, since we'll be discussing a treetop view of investing and landlording. It's good to step back and add up the score every now and then, for the purpose of self-examination. Are we investing according to our plan? Do we even have a plan? If so, are we working the plan on schedule?

Don't Get Bogged Down with Routine Stuff

It's very easy to inadvertently allow yourself to get bogged down with the daily routine and completely lose sight of your investment goals. I've said this many times: you'll never get to where you'd like to be without a good plan or without the means and skills necessary to make your plan work. Making lots of money in real estate is deliberate. It's not an accident and it certainly has very little to do with luck.

Most folks in the real estate business, including me, have no trouble whatsoever with visions and dreams. It's easy to picture myself with an overflowing bank account, driving a high-priced sports car and living in a million-dollar mansion. But there's an awfully long stretch between my dreams and reality.

The Home Field Advantage

It is not realistic for start-out or part-time investors to waste their time, thoughts, and energies figuring out how to buy properties in some distant location, far from where they live. I could offer you at least 10 convincing arguments why you shouldn't do this, but we're talking about the "big picture" here, so I'll sum them up by saying one thing—you lose the home field advantage.

That's far too much to give away, in my judgment. People who determine the gambling odds in football know from experience that the home team has a three-point advantage because they're playing on their own turf. The advantage comes from the local fans and familiarity with the playing field. There's really not much difference in the real estate investment game. Why in the world would you ever want to bet against the odds?

The Wall Street Journal Dream

Reading newspaper ads can be fun and enlightening. We all do it and it's likely we'll all end up with about the same results. I must confess that I enjoy reading Friday's *Wall Street Journal* special real estate section. I love ads that say, "5 times gross in the Ozarks, $7,000 per unit in Houston, Far below the replacement cost in San Francisco." These are exciting ads to us real estate junkies. Reading national papers makes it easy to stay "high." Why? Because it's like reading about Fantasy Island—faraway places always make for sweeter dreams.

Over the years, I've made some hefty profits with my real estate projects. However, looking back, I can't think of a single time when reading national real estate articles has helped me financially.

Join the Real World of Investing: Find a Mentor

Most folks who follow my teachings and investment strategies see me as a very practical person; I think I've learned to separate my dreams from the real world stuff that earns money. I also learned a valuable lesson years ago, that it pays big dividends to find a good mentor early on in your investment career. You can save yourself a lot of time and effort—especially efforts that are taking you in the wrong direction.

Obviously, you should thoroughly check out a potential mentor before settling on him or her. Find someone who is successful at doing what you want to do and then learn everything you can from that person. You'll end up light years ahead if you copy successful people. Don't worry: there's still plenty of wide-open territory for individuality and creativity. In fact, there's no end to learning, when it comes to real estate investing. That's the reason it's so exciting.

There are basically two ways to learn landlording—and neither one is fun. You can learn it from your tenants or learn it from people like me. I always recommend a combination of on-the-job training (with real live tenants) and formal, classroom-type education (schooling) from an experienced landlord-teacher (like me).

People often ask, "Why should I pay for a seminar to hear about renting my own property out?" Every person who asks that question I can introduce to a "beat-up" landlord who will tell them exactly why—very convincingly and very quickly.

Landlording is not a question of having good luck or picking all the right tenants. Certainly, that's a part of it. However, during any reasonable investment career (over several years) you'll need all the expertise you can get. Forking out money for a seminar from an expert will seem like peanuts compared with what tenants will cost you for the lessons you'll learn the hard way.

Landlording is a business. You must accept it as such and treat it very seriously. Remember: some of my best real estate purchases (discount prices and liberal owner financing terms) have been from sellers who had been driven completely over the edge by their tenants. They simply couldn't handle them. They were forced to give up their properties for a pittance. I'll assure you—when it comes to the business of landlording, education is far cheaper than the results of inexperience.

The Dream Alone Is Not Enough

Your investment plan must be workable and realistic. Those characteristics are essential, not optional. Earlier, I said investing away from home is not a good idea. I mean this seriously. It's also not a good idea to invest your money in a property when you have very limited knowledge about it.

A friend of mine bought an old hotel 60 miles away from where he lives. I advised him not to do it, unless he moved there and operated it himself. He showed me some impressive income figures and, I must admit, they looked great—if he could keep all the rooms rented. The problem was that he couldn't or didn't. He frequently changed managers and completely wore out his new Toyota truck driving back and forth on evenings and weekends.

His original plan was to convert the small sleeping rooms to regular monthly rentals. The plan was to remodel the hotel, combining two sleeping rooms to create larger more desirable efficiency apartments. (Efficiency apartments are always in short supply.) Each new unit would have cooking and plumbing facilities, so it would be much easier to rent to permanent tenants.

My friend's plan was very workable, but not realistic for him. His regular 40-hour weekday job was naturally his main priority. Although he had purchased the hotel for an excellent price and terms, he was tapped out after the down payment. He had no other funds available for remodeling the way he wanted to. It's quite obvious, in hindsight, that even if he had the money to remodel, he still didn't have the time to do the job. Almost every manager he hired was a drunk. Obviously, he needed a bit more practice interviewing perspective employees.

Eventually, the inevitable happened, and he lost the hotel. What had seemed like a genuine cash flow bargain at the beginning turned out to be a $46,000 loss. The saddest part of the story is the building had all the potential for making $100,000 net profit in the hands of an experienced operator. My friend had owned only one single rental house before leaping into a management-intense, 33-unit hotel 60 miles from home. Simply put, the property was much more than he was capable of handling at the time.

Looking for Gold Buried in Mud

Not long ago, a young man came to me with a problem. He had an opportunity to buy six dumpy houses extremely cheap. Just when he was set to close the deal, a local real estate agent advised him that he would lose his shirt. "The reason," he said, "is the location. The houses were located directly behind a soap factory. They'll never appreciate in value. Plus there's a better than average chance you'll be stuck with them forever."

That's typical salesman advice and—who knows?—he might be absolutely right. But he's got blinders on. He's already thinking about future sales and appreciation. Those things might not be too important. Many folks, including real estate professionals, are quite good when it comes to finding shiny gold nuggets that sparkle brightly in plain view. However, their detection abilities quickly diminish when the golden nuggets get slightly tarnished or buried beneath the mud.

Remember this: it's not the location or how they look that makes gold mines valuable. Most of them are smelly holes in the ground. Most are rather ugly. The point I'm making is that value isn't always apparent when you first look at something.

High Rent-to-Value Ratio Indicates Profits

The six houses behind the soap factory are really hidden gold. They had a 2.0% rent-to-value ratio at the close of escrow. As you remember from Chapter 9, rent-to-value is a number that expresses the monthly rent in relation to the value of the property. It's calculated by dividing the monthly rent by the total value of the house.

Old-timers used to talk about the 1% rule for renting. It means a $70,000 house should rent for $700 per month. With a 2.0% rent factor, the same house would rent for $1,400 per month.

The young man bought the entire property (all six houses) for $135,000. Let's look at the big money picture here. The six houses are earning $450 each, or a total of $2,700 per month. Four out of the six are rented to HUD tenants with guaranteed rents; the other two could easily be the same if the owner wants to go that way. Here's a good way to analyze profitability. Each house is earning 24% of its total value annually.

The value or purchase price of each house is $22,500. Rent equals $450 per month or $5,400 annually. Divide that $5,400 annual rent by the $22,500 value and you get a rent-to-value ratio of 24%. A 24% rent return means that each house will earn its entire cost ($22,500) back in just slightly over four years time—4.16 years to be exact.

If you have a nose for making money, you should at least start sniffing about now. Many folks get cold feet when they think about the soap factory—they suddenly develop blinders. They fail to scratch the surface to find the shiny gold. Anytime an asset generates enough income to completely pay itself off in just four years, you should be very interested. They're not all that easy to find. When you do, don't pass it up without a thorough investigation.

Selling for What You Paid—and Still Making a Profit

When I was telling this story to an investor group, a woman asked how you can tell if a deal is good or not. She said, "You haven't told us what the down payment was or what the monthly expenses and the mortgage payment cost." My answer: it doesn't matter much, unless, of course, something is terribly out of whack. In this particular case, I happen to know the cash down payment was $18,500 (13%), which means the mortgage balance was $116,500.

Even with high-leverage deals like this, it's quite easy to structure the seller financing (quite often interest only) in a way that will allow the owner to enjoy a very respectable cash flow, starting with the first day of ownership. It's also very common, with these types of rental units, to earn handsome profits, even if the property doesn't appreciate at all. That's because the property is a cash flow machine. You've actually acquired a gold mine: every month you'll be able to mine out fresh green cash.

Let's suppose you're able to net out $500 each month from the "soap factory houses." That adds up to $6,000 the first year, so your return on cash invested is 32%. You have also acquired approximately $100,000 worth of depreciable property (income shelter).

Forget about the future of the houses for a moment and consider only the income stream. For the next 10 years, even with very modest cost-of-living rent increases, it's a very good bet you'll be netting out $10,000 annually, by the end of the term. It's not the least bit difficult to visualize this one small property generating $100,000 worth of cash and tax benefits in just 10 years. Even if you sell the houses 10 years from now at the same price as you paid, that's not all bad. I will assure you, much worse things can happen to real estate investors.

Here's an important thing to remember. When you're lucky enough to locate income properties that have a rent-to-value factor of 1.5 or above, it's like the gold miners say—"You're beginning to see some very good colors." Stick with the deal and figure it out. There's a very good chance you're standing real close to a cash flow spigot.

I Didn't Grow Up to Be a Landlord

Remembering back (it seems like 100 years now.) to when I traded my traditional corporate job for my current career as investor, horse trader, and landlord, I had lofty dreams and visions of sugarplums. The bottom line was that I wanted to make a lot of money, instead of being stuck in a job where my future earnings would always be limited to those meager cost-of-living increases. Of course, back then, I didn't even think about the possibility of my corporate job disappearing; however, several years later that's what happened.

I felt real estate investing offered the best opportunity for me to earn more money without restrictions, based on how hard I was willing to work. I must tell you—I don't mind working long hours, weekends, nights, or whatever else it takes if the rewards are in line with my extra efforts. What I've always been opposed to is working at some fixed-pay job regardless of my initiative or the extra efforts I contributed. Naturally, that's one of the big differences with my real estate career—being my own boss has been a very rewarding experience. Besides, there's absolutely no limit to my paydays anymore.

I'm in the housing business to make money, not to simply own a bunch of rental properties. In fact, as much as I like owning houses, my underlying motive sounds almost selfish. Houses are the best vehicles I've found to take me where I wish to go. But my houses are certainly not the end—they are the means to the end. If you understand this, it's much easier to make sound investment decisions. My goals and personal dreams are probably quite similar to those of every other investor I know—my main goal is making money.

I've discovered that all properties are not the same when it comes to making money. For example, I own several properties that just sit there and cost me money. They are not active vehicles taking me toward my investment goals. In fact, one property is pulling me backwards, away from my money-making goals. The problem is, I paid too much for looks. Every month it costs me $335 for the privilege of being the owner.

When you understand that goals are the objective and not the vehicle, it helps you zero in on an investment plan that makes the best use of your time and resources (money). In my case, for example, I needed to quickly develop monthly cash flow without paying out a ton of cash (which I didn't have) for my properties. Only certain types of properties will provide cash flow, so that's where I directed my energies. Also, another one of my personal goals was to quit my regular, salaried job. That put some tight restrictions on my time limits because I had to start earning a living on the income from my houses within three years from the day I started buying properties.

A Diverse Investment Portfolio Is Best

It's my feeling that all investment portfolios should be diversified. You need some properties that provide good cash flow and some that just occupy the lot waiting for appreciation or higher and better usage. By setting goals, schedules, time limits, and minimum cash return requirements, you'll quickly determine what kind of properties you need and how many of each it will take to get you where you're going.

Avoid Doom and Gloom like the Plague

> The days of opportunity are over. There's no longer any use trying to save for investment. The best you can hope for is to keep a steady job and stay off welfare. Nobody will ever again be able to build an estate large enough to produce an independent income.

Those are words from a speech given by an economics professor at Fresno State College to more than 300 graduating students.

Folks familiar with California's economy would have little quarrel with the professor's bleak assessment. With the huge layoffs at IBM and the telephone company, thousands of jobs lost in the defense industry, and downsizing by the state's largest corporations nearly everywhere, it would be hard to find fault with the professor's reasoning. However, he wasn't talking about the economy today. He was making his speech to the graduating class of 1931, in the middle of the Great Depression.

William Nickerson was in that class. Fortunately for him, he didn't pay much attention to the professor's advice. Bill recalls the speech in his best-selling book, *How I Turned $1,000 into Five Million in Real Estate in My Spare Time* (New York: Simon and Schuster, 1980). According to Nickerson, the professor really didn't mean any harm; he simply didn't know any better. And obviously, it's a good thing for self-made millionaire investors like Bill that most doom-and-gloom predictions are merely opinions of the misinformed. It's unfortunate that many who are charged with teaching others have great difficulty seeing beyond the ends of their noses.

History has clearly proven that economic opportunity for enterprising students didn't end with the class of 1931—and there's certainly no end in sight today. Unfortunately, most teachers don't encourage students to develop their entrepreneurial skills and rely on themselves to earn a living. Hopefully, these 23 chapters have convinced you there are numerous possibilities.

Roadblocks—Your Momentum Will Carry You Around Them

The single, most dangerous roadblock facing every new investor or career changer is *procrastination*. There is no doubt that many folks, with the best intentions and even a good workable plan, will procrastinate forever. Look around you. How many people are financially independent compared with all of those who just talk about it? The answer: "Very few."

However, don't let the numbers discourage you. Remember: financial success is not some wild stroke of luck. It's a solid workable plan—and it's you working the plan. Your success will come almost automatically when you do the things I've suggested.

Positive Cash Flow Makes It All Worthwhile

Over the years I've discovered that investing in cash-flow-producing real estate is even better than I dreamed it would be when I started out—financially speaking, that is. People often ask me, "Isn't it hard work renting your houses to Section 8 (HUD) tenants?" and "Don't you have a lot of trouble with people who don't pay on time?" and "Don't you ever get fed up cleaning filthy properties when trashy tenants move out?" The answers are "YES," "YES," and "YES." But just remember: those are very "narrow vision" items. They're simply part of the vehicle that takes me where I'm going.

The big picture is that my rewards are very generous compared with the tasks I perform. That's exactly what I wanted when I started investing.

I once had 218 houses that produced average rents of $388 per month. Even though rents are relatively low in my area, the math shows how quickly they add up to substantial annual income. As my mortgages are paid off, obviously, I get to keep a bigger share of the rent money each month. And who pays off the mortgages? The same folks who pay all my other expenses. Is this a great program or am I still just dreaming?

Appendix A

Income Property Analysis Form

On the next page, you will find the blank form I introduced in Chapter 9. Use this to determine the viability of properties you are considering.

Income Property Analysis Form

Line No.	Income Data (Monthly)	Per Month
1	Total Gross Income (Present)	$_____
2	Vacancy Allowance Min. 5% Line 1. Attach copy of 1040 Schedule E or provide past 12 months income statement for verification.	$_____
3	Uncollectable or Credit Losses (rents due but not collected)	$_____
4	Net Rental Income	$_____

Expense Data (Monthly)

Line No.		Per Month
5	Taxes, Real Property	$_____
6	Insurance	$_____
7	Management (Allow Min. 5%)	$_____
8	Maintenance	$_____
9	Repairs	$_____
10	Utilities Paid by Owner (Monthly)	$_____

Electricity	$_____
Water	$_____
Sewer	$_____
Gas	$_____
Garbage	$_____
Cable TV	$_____
Totals =	$_____

Line No.		Per Month
11	Total Expenses	$_____
12	Operating Income (Line 4 – Line 11)	$_____

Existing Mortgage Debt

			Monthly	Due Mo/Yr
1st Bal Due	_____	Payments	$_____	_____
2nd Bal Due	_____	Payments	$_____	_____
3rd Bal Due	_____	Payments	$_____	_____
4th Bal Due	_____	Payments	$_____	_____
5th Bal Due	_____	Payments	$_____	_____
13	Totals	13A	$_____	
14	Monthly Cash Flow Available		$_____	
	(Line 12 – Line 13A)	(Pos or Neg)		_____

Appendix B

Typical Property Sketch

When you're looking at a property, putting together a sketch like the one on the next page can help you have a concrete sense of exactly what it is you're buying.

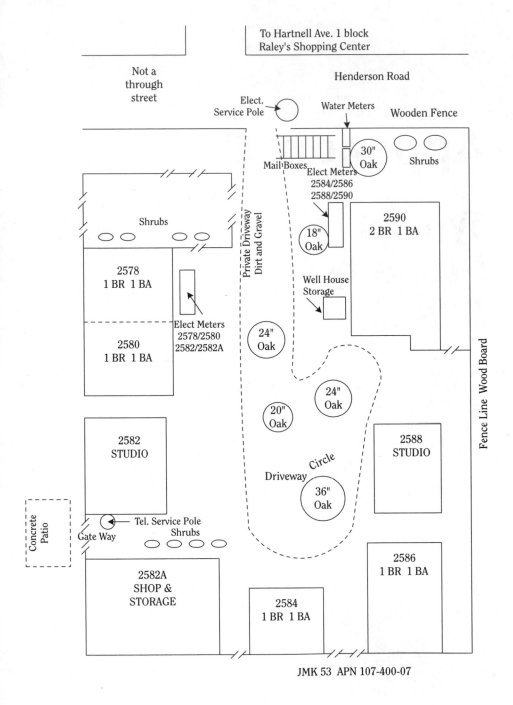

To Hartnell Ave. 1 block
Raley's Shopping Center

Not a
through
street

Henderson Road

Elect.
Service Pole

Water Meters

Wooden Fence

Mail Boxes

30"
Oak

Shrubs

Elect Meters
2584/2586
2588/2590

Shrubs

2590
2 BR 1 BA

Private Driveway
Dirt and Gravel

18"
Oak

2578
1 BR 1 BA

Well House
Storage

Elect Meters
2578/2580
2582/2582A

24"
Oak

2580
1 BR 1 BA

24"
Oak

Fence Line Wood Board

2582
STUDIO

20"
Oak

2588
STUDIO

Concrete
Patio

Circle

Driveway

36"
Oak

Tel. Service Pole
Shrubs

Gate Way

2586
1 BR 1 BA

2582A
SHOP &
STORAGE

2584
1 BR 1 BA

JMK 53 APN 107-400-07

298

Appendix C

Sample Co-Ownership Agreement

1234 Easy Street, Golden City, California

THIS AGREEMENT is made effective as of the first day of April, 2002, between Fixer Jay and Sam Moneybags.

1. Transaction: Fixer Jay (Jay) and Sam Moneybags (Sam) will join together as co-owners for the purpose of owning and operating that certain real estate located at 1234 Easy Street, Golden City, California (the Property), for the mutual benefit and profit of each. Each party agrees to perform fully under this Agreement for the success of both parties herein.

2. Acquisition of Property: Sam and Jay have purchased the Property for a purchase price of Seventy-Five Thousand Dollars ($75,000). The cash down payment of Twenty Thousand, Five Hundred Dollars ($20,500) was paid by Sam. Both parties will take title subject to the existing mortgage lien in the amount of Thirty-One Thousand, Five Hundred Dollars and 00/100 ($31,500). The seller of the Property has agreed to finance the balance of the purchase price, approximately

Twenty-Three Thousand Dollars and 00/100 ($23,000), with install-ment payments of Two Hundred Dollars and 00/100 ($200) or more per month, including seven percent (7%) interest until the entire princi-pal is paid in full.

3. Cash Distributions from Rental: All excess cash derived from rental of the Property, after payment of all expenses and debt service, shall be divided eighty percent (80%) to Sam and twenty percent (20%) to Jay.

4. Cash Proceeds from Sale or Refinancing of the Property: Net cash proceeds derived from the sale or refinancing of the Property shall be shared as follows:

> First, Sam shall receive back all of his capital invested in the Property by way of the initial down payment, fix-up expenditures, and operating expenses made pursuant to Paragraphs 2, 11, and 12 hereof. Thereafter, all remaining proceeds derived from the sale or refinancing shall be shared eighty percent (80%) to Sam and twenty percent (20%) to Jay.

5. Management: All decisions regarding the management of the Property shall be made upon the joint approval of both Sam and Jay provided, however, it is agreed that Jay will have primary responsibility for the day-to-day management operations, such as rent-up, property maintenance, repairs, cleaning and the like, in order to conduct an effi-cient rental business. (Rent-up is the time it takes for newly construct-ed or renovated rental properties to be fully occupied.) Jay shall receive a 6% management fee per month (fee based on income) for managing the property. In addition, Jay shall be reimbursed for his actual out-of-pocket costs and expenses incurred in connection with such manage-ment.

6. Books and Records: All books and records will be kept at the office of Jay. A statement of operations will be provided to Sam on a monthly basis. This statement will be prepared by Jay as part of his manage-ment duties.

7. Bank Accounts: Jay shall maintain a commercial checking account at Gold Street Bank, 2930 Silver Lane, Golden City, California, or at such other banking institution that shall be approved by Sam, for the purpose of operating the Property.

8. Indemnification: Each party shall indemnify and hold harmless the other party and the Property from and against all separate debts, claims, actions, and demands of said party.

9. Termination: This Agreement shall terminate upon the sale of the Property or by mutual consent of Sam and Jay. Sam shall have the sole right to determine when the Property is to be sold, provided, however, that Sam shall first offer Jay the right to purchase the Property for the same amount and upon the same terms and conditions as Sam is willing to sell the Property pursuant to a bona fide offer received from any third party. Jay shall exercise said right of first refusal within ten (10) days after the receipt of notification from Sam of his intention to accept said third party offer. Jay shall consummate the transaction within sixty (60) days after the exercise of his right of first refusal.

10. Death of Parties: Upon the death of Sam, Jay shall have the right to either purchase Sam's interest in the Property in the manner described in Paragraph 9 hereof, based upon a bona fide offer received by Sam's estate or, in absence of such an offer, Jay shall have the right to cause the Property to be sold and the proceeds divided in accordance with Paragraph 4 of this Agreement. In the event liquidation is elected, Jay shall proceed with reasonable diligence to liquidate the Property within twelve (12) months after Sam's death.

11. Initial Fix-Up Expenditures: Initial fix-up funds for rehabilitation of the Property will be contributed by Sam. All work will be performed by employees of Jay. Employee time sheets and material invoices shall be part of Jay's record keeping.

12. Operating Funds: All expenses for repairs, improvements, taxes, insurance, maintenance, and other operating expenses deemed necessary for the operation of the Property shall be paid first from rental income derived from the Property and, thereafter, from additional funds to be contributed by Sam.

13. Business Address: The official management office for the Property will be Jay's One-Stop Rental Company, located at 2020 End of the Trail Drive, Golden City, CA 96001. The mailing address is c/o Fixer Jay, P.O. Box 492029, Redding, CA 96049-3039.

14. No Partnership or Joint Venture: The relationship between Jay and Sam under this Agreement shall be solely that of co-owners of real estate and under no circumstances shall said relationship constitute a partnership or joint venture.

IN WITNESS WHEREOF, the Parties have executed this Agreement as of the day and year first above written.

_____

Sam Moneybags

_____

Fixer Jay

Appendix D

Resources for Real Estate Investors

Books

Gene Autry with Mickey Herskowitz, *Back in the Saddle Again*, Doubleday.

Suzanne Brangham, *Housewise*, Harper & Row.

Robert J. Bruss, *Effective Real Estate Investing*, Regency Books, Inc.

Richard Jorgensen, *The New No-Nonsense Landlord*, McGraw-Hill, Inc.

A. D. Kessler, *A Fortune at Your Feet*, Probus Publishing Co. (Irwin)

Ray Kroc with Robert Anderson, *Grinding It Out–The Making of McDonald's*, Berkley Medallion Publishing.

Albert J. Lowry, *How You Can Become Financially Independent by Investing in Real Estate*, Simon & Schuster.

John T. Reed, *Aggressive Tax Avoidance for Real Estate Investors*, Reed Publishing.

Leigh Robinson, *Landlording*, Express Publishing.

Newsletters for Do-It-Yourself Investors (Free copy for asking)

Common Wealth Letters (Monthly)
Jack Miller
Common Wealth Press, Inc.
P.O. Box 21172
Tampa, FL 33622
813-286-8478

Creative Real Estate Magazine (Monthly)
A. D. Kessler
Drawer L
Rancho Santa Fe, CA 92067
858-756-1441

The Money Maker Report (Monthly)
Jim Napier, Inc.
P.O. Box 858
Chipley, FL 32428
800-354-2072

Mr. Landlord (Monthly)
Jeffrey Taylor
Mr. Landlord, Inc.
Box 64442
Virginia Beach, VA 23467
800-950-2250

Real Estate Newsletter (Monthly)
Robert J. Bruss
251 Park Road
Burlingame, CA 94010
650-348-6916

Strategies and Solutions (6 issues annually)
John Schaub
Pro Serve
2677 South Tamiami Trail, Ste 4

Sarasota, FL 34239
800-237-9222

Trade Secrets Newsletter (Monthly)
Jay P. DeCima
KJay Publishing
P.O. Box 491779
Redding, CA 96049
800-722-2550

Real Estate Training Seminars & Workshops

Fixer Jay, call 800-722-2550
Peter Fortonato, call 727-397-1906
Jack Miller, call 813-286-8478
Jim Napier, call 800-354-2072
John Schaub, call 800-237-9222
Jeffrey Taylor, call 800-950-2250

Index

# Index

A

Abatement committees, 67, 164
Action, importance of, 41–42
Adair, Paul (Red), 124–125
"Adding value" strategy
    advantages to small investors, 27–29
    basic approaches, 29–30
    potential, 10–11, 14
Advertising for partners, 179
Air conditioning, 137
Answering machines, 282–283
Antidiscrimination laws, 280–281
Appearance
    fixing up for, 130–135
    importance to lenders, 217–218
Applications
    for government funding, 239–240
    for tenants, 264–265
Appreciation
    cash flow versus, 10–11, 42
    forced, 103
    as major benefit of investments,
        154–155
    recommended approach to,
        148–151
Assessor maps, 61

B

Bad areas, avoiding, 95–96, 99

Banks. *See also* Lenders
    disadvantages of loans from, 22–23,
        171–172
    motivation to sell REOs, 77–78
Bargains, 51, 68
Beneficiaries, buying back debt from,
    247–249, 251
Brain compounding, 156–157
Business financial statements, 226
Buying back debt
    conditions favoring, 244–249
    finding right notes for, 253–254
    negotiation, 247–251
    profitability of, 158–159, 175,
        243–244
    seller motivations, 251–253

C

Cabinets, 142
Cap rate valuation method, 73
Carpets, 136
Carryback notes
    desirability of, 55–56, 172–173
    flexibility with, 20–22
    with 30-30 plan, 214–220
    variable rates on, 221
    when prohibited, 23
Cash flow
    estimating before purchase, 114

Cash flow (*Continued*)
  as major benefit of investments, 7, 28, 153
  rental income importance, 8, 104–105
  selling half of property to increase, 195–201
Ceiling fans, 137
Charm, accentuating, 132
Chattel lenders, 213
Christmas cards, 252, 255
Christopher Columbus technique, 47, 67
City loans, 237–238
Classified ads
  comparing rents in, 275
  finding properties in, 16–17, 56–57
  seeking partners with, 179
Cleanup work, importance of, 11
Clinics, fix-up, 143
Closing costs, 74
Cold calls, 60–64
Colors, best for painting, 134
"Columbo technique," 118–119
Commissions, 86, 89, 90
Community development block grants. *See* Low-income rental-housing rehabilitation
Competition, 12, 87–88
Compound earnings
  basic benefits, 6, 42–43
  maximizing, 151–155
Computer programs, 92
Concessions from sellers, 124–125
Conduit, 141
Contracts, 264, 266–267
Conventional loans, disadvantages, 22–23, 171–172
Co-owner agreements
  details of, 188–194
  90/10 plan, 203
  to reduce partner risk, 184
Co-signers, for rental contracts, 265
Cost estimates, 81, 143–146

Countertops, 137, 140–141
Creative financing, 173–174. *See also* Seller financing
Credit losses, calculating, 111, 123
Credit ratings, 221–223
Curtains, 135
Customers, tenants as, 271, 275–277

D

Deadbeat tenants. *See* Tenant problems
Death of parties
  in partnerships, 193
  private mortgage holders, 247–249, 251
Deferred payments, 125
Dense slums, 99
Deposits, 268
Depreciation
  as major benefit of investments, 153–154
  money partner benefits, 205–206
Discounted notes, buying, 160–161. *See also* Buying back debt
Discrimination laws, 280–281
Diversification, 49–50, 291
Divorce, 252
Documentary transfer tax, 55
Documentation
  financial record keeping, 223–226
  of partnership terms, 188–194, 203, 209
  rental agreements, 264, 266–267
Do-it-yourself tasks, 139–143
Dollar limits for matching grants, 234
"Don't wanters," 66–67
Doors, 136–137, 141
Down payments
  creating notes for, 159–160
  minimizing, 13, 48, 156–157
  in 90/10 plan, 202–205
  selling property without, 167–168
Downtown commercial areas, 98
Drapes, 135

Dual-glaze windows, 144–146
Due-on-sale clauses, 246, 253

E

Earnings from self-employment, 3–6, 258, 290
Electrical systems, 272
Electrical work, 141–142
Emotions, 120
Energy efficiency, 144–146
Equity
  looking for sellers with, 69–70
  as major benefit of investments, 154
Evaporative coolers, 137, 279
Evictions, 15, 269–270
Expenses
  estimating, 111–114
  examples, 197
  verifying with seller, 123–124
Experienced real estate agents, 87
Exterior doors, 136–137
Exterior painting, 136. *See also* Painting
External improvements, 24

F

Feasibility meetings, 239–240
Fences, 4, 138
FHA foreclosures, 70
Financial records, 223–226
Financial statements, business, 226
Financing. *See also* Lenders; Seller financing
  evaluating personal status, 43–45
  flexibility in negotiating, 20–22
  government loans, 233–234, 236–239, 241
  HUD grants, 228–231, 234–237
  mistakes to avoid, 22–23
  thrifts versus banks, 213–214
  typical examples, 73–74
  Yellow Court example, 80–81, 83–84

Finding properties
  basic methods, 56–64
  information profiles, 54–56, 89
  making offers, 73–75, 79–82
  overview of house detective approach, 53–54
  snooping around, 70–73
Fire insurance, 112
First Main Street Apartments, 206–210
Fixer clinics, 143
Fixer-uppers
  advantages of investing in, 10, 12–15, 27–29
  value versus quality, 101
Fix-up guidelines
  basic strategy, 131–132
  cost estimating, 79, 143–146
  do-it-yourself tasks, 139–143
  importance of appearance, 130–135
  importance of payback, 129–130
  specific recommendations, 135–139
Fix-up skills
  applying for highest profits, 31–34
  assessing, 34–35
  minimal requirements, 11, 23–24, 30–31
Flexibility
  of government loans, 237, 238
  of loan terms, 213–214
Floor coverings, 136
Foo-foo strategy, 132–133
Forced appreciation, 103, 155
Friendships, partnerships and, 178

G

Game-playing in negotiation, 118, 121
Garages
  appeal, 139, 146
  fix-up recommendations, 138–139
  investing in, 144, 146
Goals
  for fixing up properties, 131–132

Goals (*Continued*)
    for negotiation, 121–122
    required for successful investing,
        40–41, 284–285
Godfather loans, 213
Golden Rule of investing, 173, 206
Government funding. *See* Low-income
    rental-housing rehabilitation
Government-owned foreclosures, 70
Grant deeds, 55
Grant funding. *See* Low-income
    rental-housing rehabilitation
Gross income, 110–111
Gross rent multipliers (GRMs)
    improving, 102–103, 198
    overview, 30, 93–94
    purchase terms and conditions
        based on, 149–151
    using to calculate offers, 100
Gypsies, 262–263

H

Habitability laws, 67, 272–273
Half sales, 159
Handyperson skills. *See* Fix-up skills
Haywood houses
    discovery, 16–17
    fixing up, 23–24
    sale of, 25–26
    seller financing, 20–21
    symptoms of neglect, 17–18
    tenant problems, 18–20
Heating and air conditioning, 137, 272
Help Wanted ads, for partners, 179
Hidden costs, with matching rehabili-
    tation grants, 235–236
High rent-to-value, 288–291
Hillcrest properties, 5–6, 162–168
Home field advantage, 285
House detective approach, 53–54
Houses, rundown. *See* Fixer-uppers
Housing authorities
    approaching, 231–233
    HUD grants from, 228–231

loans from, 233–234, 236–239
pressure creating motivation to
    sell, 67
*How I Turned $1,000 into Five Million
in Real Estate in My Spare Time*,
50, 292
HUD foreclosures, 70
HUD funding. *See* Low-income rental-
    housing rehabilitation

I

Improvement potential, 10–11
Improvements. *See also* Fix-up guide-
    lines
    limiting, 278–279
    payback value, 129–130
Income
    calculating before purchase,
        108–116
    goals for, 40–41, 106–107
    major sources, 6–9
    selling half of property to increase,
        195–201
    tax-free and tax-sheltered, 51
    traditional jobs versus self-employ-
        ment, 3–4, 5–6, 258, 290
    verifying in property for sale,
        71–72, 93, 123
Income property analysis form. *See
    also* Information profiles
    details of, 110–116
    examples, 115–116, 127–128
    importance, 48
    use in negotiation, 110, 116, 122,
        126
Income tax records, 111, 116, 123
Inflation of investment value, 154–155
Information profiles. *See also* Income
    property analysis form
    elements of, 54–56
    obtaining from real estate agents,
        58, 89
Inheritance, as motivation for debt
    buyback, 247–249, 251, 253

Initial investments, 9
Installment payments, lump-sum versus, 8–9
Insurance costs, 112
Interior painting, 136
Interviewing tenants, 264
Investing
    approaching as business, 37–38
    basic elements, 39–43
    evaluating personal finances, 43–45
    getting started, 36–37
    lack of cash and, 47
    lifestyle benefits, 155–156
    partnerships. *See* Partnerships
    selecting properties, 45–46
    spreading risk over more units, 48–49
    tips for success, 50–52, 284–293

J
Junk cars, prohibiting, 278

K
Key location maps, 55
Knowledge, desire to improve, 44–45
Kroc, Ray, 221

L
Labor costs, 31–32, 143, 151
Landlording
    defining customers, 260–261
    evictions, 269–270
    fielding improvement requests, 278–279
    habitability laws, 272–273
    learning, 51
    major benefits, 257–259
    mentors for, 286
    noncontact management, 282–283
    paperwork, deposits, and rent collection, 263–268, 280–282
    tenant cycling, 24, 138, 262–263
    tenant relations principles, 275–278
    tenant service, 268–269, 271

Late fees, 278
Lawns
    fix-up recommendations, 136, 138
    value of rejuvenating, 4, 24, 134–135
Lawsuits with tenants, 267
Leads from telephone calls, 57
Leaning owners, 64
Leasing with option to purchase, 160
Lemonade down payments, 13, 156–157
Lenders. *See also* Financing
    appeal of attractive properties to, 217–218
    bank loan disadvantages, 22–23, 171–172
    government financing, 233–234, 236–239, 241
    importance of credit rating to, 222–223
    motivation to sell REOs (real estate owned), 77–78
    personal property lenders, 213–214
    real estate agents' help with, 89–90
Letters, cold calls with, 60–64
Leveraging
    basic benefits, 6
    profits from, 155, 210
Liability insurance expenses, 112
Light fixtures, 136
Likeability of real estate agents, 87
Linoleum, 136
Listening, importance to negotiation, 119–120
Local trade accounts, 51
Location
    assessing, 94–96
    basic types, 97–99
    cash flow versus, 100
    effect on GRMs (gross rent mulitples), 93
    profits and, 101–102
Locks, 136–137

Long-term seller carryback mortgages. *See* Carryback notes
Lots, seller subordination in sales,
220–221
Low-down-payment deals, 195–196
Lower-income units, demand for, 39
Low-income rental-housing rehabilitation
approaching housing authorities,
231–233, 239–242
government loans for, 233–234,
236–239, 241
overview, 228–231
selecting properties, 234–236
Low-income tenants, 229–230,
265–266
Low purchase price, 12
Lump-sum payments, installments
versus, 8–9

M

Maintenance
debating with seller, 116
do-it-yourself tasks, 139–143
Maintenance expenses
debating with seller, 123–124
estimating expenses, 113
keeping rents low to avoid, 72
Management fees
debating with seller, 116, 123–124
estimating, 112–113
with 50/50 ownership, 201
including in partnership agreements, 182, 192
Management improvements, 29–30
Market, real estate, cycles, 104
Markets, learning, 51, 71, 79
Matching grants. *See* Low-income
rental-housing rehabilitation
Materials and supplies cost, 143, 151
McDonald's restaurants, 221
Memorandums
to record co-ownership agreements, 189–190
to tenants, 282–283

Mental exercise, 156
Mentors, 286
Money left over (MLO) formula, 196
Money partners
finding, 179–181, 190–191
90/10 plan, 202–211
Mortgages
buying back. *See* Buying back debt
buying discounted, 160–161
equity buildup, 154
estimating expenses, 114
on low-down-payment deals,
195–196
property information from, 54–55
in 30-30 plan, 214–220
as typical percentage of rental
income, 72
variable rate, 221
Motivated sellers
for buying back debt, 251–253
classified ad jargon, 57
finding, 46, 64–68
understanding, 163–165
Multiple-listing book, 59
Multiple-unit properties
advantages of, 75
fix-up recommendations, 138
matching rehab grants, 235
Murphy's Law of Estimating, 80

N

Neglect, symptoms of, 17–18
Negotiation
to buy back debt, 247–251
calculating profits before, 108–116
concessions to seek, 124–125
as game-playing, 118, 121
income analyses for, 48
of partnership terms, 187–188
sound approach to, 118–120
top buyer objectives, 121–122
typical scenarios, 125–127
using property analysis forms in,
110, 116, 122, 126
winning over sellers, 120

Net operating income, 225–226
Net rental income, 111. *See also*
  Rental income
Nickerson, William, 50, 292
90/10 investor plan, 202–211
No-money-down deals
  additional collateral for, 167–168
  high mortgage costs, 47, 195–196
  for HUD-funded projects, 233–234,
    236
  for partial ownership in fixed-up
    properties, 198–199
  30-30 plan, 214–220
Noncontact management, 282–283
Nontraditional properties, 75
Notes
  buying discounted, 160–161
  creating for down payments,
    159–160
  keeping, 81
  purchase money, 245, 246, 253

O
Offers
  calculating, 100
  calculating profits before making,
    108–116
  making, 73–75, 79–82
Older residential areas, 98–99
Operating expenses, reducing, 14–15
Operating income, 114
Options to purchase, 160, 185–186, 193
Out-of-town owners
  cold call letters to, 60–64
  discouraging, 285
  motivations to sell, 65
Overdue rent, 278, 280–282
Over-financed properties, 69
Overpayment, avoiding, 48, 105–106
Owner financing. *See* Seller financing
Owners
  discovering, 54–55
  selling by, 57
  written cold calls to, 60–64
Ownership, selling 50%, 196–201

P
Painting
  added value of, 4, 134
  exterior recommendations, 136
  improved materials and equipment,
    142
Parcel maps, 54
Partial rent payments, 281
Partnerships
  basic considerations, 176–177
  creating to increase cash flow,
    195–201
  documenting terms of, 188–194
  keys to success, 182, 187, 210–211
  negotiability of, 187–188
  sample structures for, 181–187
  selection process, 178–180
  splitting proceeds, 180–181,
    202–206
Payback value of improvements,
  129–130
People problems. *See* Tenant problems
Personal financial statements, 225
Personal property lenders, 213
Pessimism, 291–292
Picket fences, 4, 138
Piper Alpha Platform explosion, 125
Planning
  importance to success, 51
  keeping focus on, 284–285
  for profits, 25, 38, 42
  required for successful investing,
    40–41
Plumbing
  do-it-yourself tasks, 140
  fix-up recommendations, 136
  habitability laws, 272
  repair calls about, 280
Pocket listings, 56
Pre-hung doors, 141
Price
  avoiding complex formulas, 92–93
  as benefit of fixer-uppers, 12
  calculating, 100

Pricing strategies for rents, 260–261
Problem properties. *See* Fixer-uppers
Problem tenants. *See* Tenant problems
Procrastination, 292
Professional property managers,
    258–259
Profit and loss statements, 225–226
Profit bulbs, 157–158
Profits
    appreciation and, 148–151
    calculating before purchase,
        108–116
    with city loans, 237
    compounding and, 151–155
    dividing in partnerships, 182–183,
        203–204
    favorite techniques to enhance,
        158–161
    financing on sale of property,
        216–217
    learning new ways to create,
        156–158
    from leverage, 155
    location and, 101–102
    major sources from fixer-uppers,
        12–15
    planning for, 25, 38, 42
    rent-to-value ratio and, 288–291
Promissory notes. *See* Notes
Properties
    finding. *See* Finding properties
    fix-up recommendations, 135–139
    information profiles, 54–56
    over-financed, 69
    selecting, 45–46
    selling, 158
Property managers, 258–259
Property profiles. *See also* Income
        property analysis form
    elements of, 54–56
    obtaining from real estate agents,
        58, 89
Property taxes, 111–112
Proposition 13, 112

Proprietorship, 259
Purchase money notes, 245, 246, 253
Purchase price
    as benefit of fixer-uppers, 12
    calculating profits before offering,
        108–116
    varying GRMs and, 149–151
Pyracanthas, 136

Q
Qualifying property, 58
Quality properties, value versus fixer-
    uppers, 101

R
Real estate agents
    advantages of working with, 58,
        85–86, 88–90, 91
    finding properties via, 57–59
    preserving loyalty of, 90
    selecting to work with, 58–59,
        86–88
Real estate market cycles, 104
Real estate owned (REO), 77–82
Recording co-ownership agreements,
    189–190
Recordkeeping, 81
Redding, California, GRMs, 93
Red Mustang strategy, 247–249
Refinancing, 22–23
Regular employment
    importance to lenders, 222–223
    self-employment versus, 3–6, 258,
        290
Relationship building, with real estate
    agents, 58–59, 87
Remodeling, fixing up versus, 130
Rental agreements, 264, 266–267
Rental income
    benefits to cash flow, 8, 104–105
    calculating before purchase,
        108–116
    covering fix-up costs from, 144
    effect on price of property, 29–30
    location and, 102

Rental income (*Continued*)
post-improvement increases, 102–103
verifying in property for sale, 71–72, 93, 123
Rents
collecting, 263–264, 280–282
how to raise, 262–263
pricing strategies, 260–261
Rent-to-income ratios, 265
Rent-to-value ratio, 110, 288–291
Rent-up, 192
Repair expenses
debating with seller, 116, 123–124
estimating before purchase, 113
Repairs
do-it-yourself tasks, 139–143
expensive jobs in stages, 137–138
in fix-up strategy, 131
getting information on the phone, 279–280
government funding. *See* Low-income rental-housing rehabilitation)
making promptly, 271
recommendations, 136–137
Repair skills. *See* Fix-up skills
Reputation, attracting investors with, 181, 190–191
Risk
in partnerships, 183–185
spreading over more units, 48–49
Roofs, 137–138
Rough areas, avoiding, 95–96, 99
Rundown houses. *See* Fixer-uppers

S

Sales, 7–8, 167
San Francisco GRMs, 93
Schedule of real estate and notes owned (form setup), 224–225
Schedule of real estate owned (form setup), 224
Second opinions, 117

Section 8 subsidies, 229–230, 266
Section 1031 exchanges, 186
Security deposits, 268
Self-employment, 3–6, 258, 290
Self-evaluation, 34–35
Seller financing. *See also* Buying back debt; Carryback notes; Financing
benefits, 13–14, 171–175
flexibility in negotiating, 20–22
profits from, 158
typical examples, 73–74
Sellers. *See also* Motivated sellers
gathering and verifying information from, 122–124
trustworthiness, 71, 93
understanding motivations of, 163–165
winning over, 120
Seller's equity, 114
Seller's market, 7–8
Seller subordination, 212, 214–220
Seminars, 286
Showers, 142
Shrubs, 136
Shutters, 138
Siding improvements, 132–133
Simple partnership plan, 181–185
60/40 rule for partnerships, 180–181
"Sizzle" fix-ups, 32–33, 133–135
Skills. *See* Fix-up skills
Slum areas, 99
Small house advantages, 106
Snob Hill, 97–98, 101
Snooping around, 70–73
"Soggy notes," 127
Sonneborn, Harry, 221
Southside property, 214–215, 219–220
Specialization, 37–38, 49–50
Speculation, investment versus, 8, 38, 51
Split rent payments, 281
Spouses, second opinions from, 117
Subordination, 212, 214–220

Subsidized rents, 229–230
Suburbs, 99
Supply costs, 31–32

T

Target areas for HUD-funded projects, 228, 234, 237
Tax bills, 54
Taxes
    estimating expenses, 111–112
    on formal partnerships, 186
    on tenants in common, 187
Tax-free income, 51
Tax shelters
    as major benefit of investments, 51, 153–154
    for money partners, 182–183, 205–206
    not available when buying notes, 256
Telephone answering machines, 282–283
Telephone calls
    leads from, 57
    for repairs, 279–280, 282–283
Tenant cycling, 24, 138, 262–263
Tenant problems
    abatement in lieu of down payments, 67–68
    advantages to buyers, 18–20
    benefits of addressing, 15
    due to landlord ignorance, 277
    predictability of, 24, 274
    uncollectable rents with, 111
Tenants
    collecting overdue rent from, 278, 280–282
    contracts and deposits, 264, 266–268
    evicting, 15, 269–270
    improvement requests from, 278–279
    intimidation by, 268–269
    noncontact management, 282–283

qualifying, 264–266
    repair calls from, 269, 271, 279–280
    targeting, 260–261
    treating as customers, 271, 275–277
Tenants-in-common partnerships, 183–184, 186–187, 208
Termination of partnerships, 188, 192–193
Termite reports, 240
30-30 seller subordination plan, 214–220
Thrifts, banks versus, 213–214
Tighten-uppers, 125
Timing
    as advantage of working with real estate agents, 88
    of buy-back negotiations, 250–251
    importance to purchasing, 78–79
    importance to sales, 7–8, 103–104
Title companies, 54–55
Total gross income, 110–111
Trade accounts, 51
Trades in lieu of cash, 13, 45, 165
Traditional jobs
    importance to lenders, 222–223
    self-employment versus, 3–6, 258, 290
Trash-outs, 270
Trust deeds, 54–55
Trustworthiness of sellers, 71, 93
Tubs, 142
Two-for-one contracts, 168

U

Uncollectible or credit losses, 111, 123
Under-market rents, 72
Under-performing properties, 10–11
Unemployed borrowers, 223
Unit cost, 109
Up cycles, 7–8
Utilities
    estimating expenses, 113–114
    lowering costs, 145–146

V

Vacancy allowance, 111, 123
VA foreclosures, 70
Variable-rate mortgages, 221
Viola Cottages, 236
Volume, quality versus, 84

W

White picket fences, 4, 138
Window coverings, 135, 137

Window frames, 137
Windows, 141, 144–146
Women, advantages for, 31
Written memos to tenants, 282–283

Y

Yards
    fix-up recommendations, 136, 138
    value of rejuvenating, 4, 24,
        134–135
Yellow Court houses, 77–84

About the Author

"Fixer Jay" DeCima is widely regarded as the king of fixer-upper houses on the national teaching circuit. His monthly newsletter, Trade Secrets, is the only newsletter written specifically for do-it-yourself investors and career changers. Write for a free copy to: Fixer Jay, KJay Co., Box 491779A, Redding, CA 96049-1779. For bimonthly investor tips, visit www.fixerjay.com.